The Complete Lawrence Golan Violin Scale System

Lawrence
Golan

MEL BAY

WWW.MELBAY.COM

Contents

Major Scales

Minor Scales

Preface

Various approaches to the practice of scales have been passed on from generation to generation, stemming back to our musical forefathers—the great violinists of the 19th-Century. The *Lawrence Golan Violin Scale System* is a compilation of the techniques and philosophies that have been passed on to me by my private teachers throughout several years of musical training. This system has evolved from a pedagogical lineage which is both authoritative and eclectic. The three most influential characters in its development were 1) my father, Joseph Golan, Principal Second Violinist of the Chicago Symphony Orchestra, 2) my professor at Indiana University, Yuval Yaron, and 3) another teacher of both Mr. Yaron and myself, Josef Gingold. My father learned his scale routine from his mentor of twenty years, George Perlman (with whom I studied as well); Mr. Yaron was taught not only the art, but also the utmost importance of scale practice by Jascha Heifetz; and Josef Gingold's discipline and approach to bow control were instilled in him by his teacher Eugène Ysaÿe. (Mr. Gingold was very proud of, and often demonstrated his ability to sustain a single bow stroke for over five minutes. His all-time record—witnessed only by his wife—was thirteen minutes).

Because many of the principles contained hereinafter were transmitted orally, I have assumed the responsibility of clarifying, codifying, and most importantly, inscribing them—for myself, my students, and anyone else who cares to embody them into their studies.

Pedagogical Suggestions. The exercises in this book represent the most advanced forms of scale techniques and are not intended to be executed in their entirety at the onset of study. Rather, a graduated approach is recommended, adding the more advanced exercises only after the basic ones have been learned in every key. The following is the suggested manner in which to progress:

1) Start with the monophonic form only of the scales and arpeggios. Spiccato should first be applied to the entire allegro section in each key before it is applied only at the end, as indicated.

2) Add thirds and octaves without slurs.

3) Add sixths without slurs.

4) Add fingered octaves and tenths without slurs.

5) Gradually add the slurs to each double-stop exercise.

6) The four-octave scales and arpeggios in G, A-flat, and A Major, as well as the three-octave version of thirds in G Major should be added only after comfort is attained in performing the basic exercises.

7) The tempo of each exercise should be quite moderate until the intonation is under control, and then gradually be increased. This principle, however, does not apply to the whole-note exercise at the beginning of each key. Here, conversely, the tempo should be *decreased* as bow control is improved.

8) Eventually, every exercise should be performed in a different key each day, alternating between the major and minor modes.

9) Standard chromatic fingerings have been included as a reference and should be incorporated into scale practice as needed.

The utilization of this scale system will not only promote dexterity, facility, and a solid command of the fingerboard, but will also provide a forum for concentrated attention to several of the basic bow strokes. Thoughtful daily practice of these exercises is highly recommended inasmuch as the techniques involved form the absolute foundation for violinistic development.

L. G.

Lawrence Golan

Vibrant, inspired performances, imaginative programming and an evocative command of different styles and composers are the hallmarks of American conductor Lawrence Golan. He currently serves as Music Director/Conductor of the Yakima Symphony Orchestra (Washington), the York Symphony Orchestra (Pennsylvania), and the Lamont Symphony Orchestra & Opera Theatre at the University of Denver (Colorado). In addition, he is the Music Director Laureate of the Denver Philharmonic Orchestra.

Having conducted throughout the United States and in Bulgaria, Canada, China, Colombia, Czech Republic, El Salvador, England, Georgia, Germany, Hungary, Italy, Kazakhstan, Mexico, Poland, Portugal, Romania, Russia, South Africa, South Korea, Spain, Taiwan, Ukraine and Uzbekistan, Maestro Golan continues to develop relationships with orchestras nationally and abroad.

An accomplished violinist, Golan served as Principal Second Violinist of the Honolulu Symphony Orchestra (1989-1990) and then Concertmaster of the Portland Symphony Orchestra for eleven years (1990-2001) before focusing his career on the podium. He has appeared as soloist with numerous orchestras, including the Chicago Symphony Orchestra, and continues to perform, primarily to benefit the orchestras of which he is Music Director.

As a composer/arranger, Golan's edition and reduced orchestration of Tchaikovsky's *The Nutcracker* is published by Spurwink River Publishing. His scholarly-performing edition of the solo violin works of J. S. Bach, which includes a handbook on Baroque Performance Practice, and *The Lawrence Golan Violin Scale System* are both published by Mel Bay Publications. Golan's *Fantasia for Solo Violin* is published by LudwigMasters. His original orchestral compositions, *Fantasia for Orchestra* and *Giovanna d'Arco* (Joan of Arc), are both available through Notation Central.

Lawrence Golan was the Grand Prize Winner of the 2024 St. Cecilia International Music Competition in the UK and was also awarded First Prize in four different categories, both as conductor and composer. In addition, he is a 10-time winner of ASCAP Awards for the Innovative Programming of Contemporary Music, 5-time Global Music Award winner, 3-time American Prize winner, 3-time Downbeat Magazine Award winner, and 2-time Prestige Music Award winner. He was the Grand Prize Winner of the American Prize in Orchestral Programming and the First Place winner of the Ictus International Music Competition. Golan has made numerous commercial recordings, both as conductor and violinist, many of which have garnered international awards.

A native of Chicago, Golan has been Director of Orchestral Studies and head of the graduate conducting program at the University of Denver since 2001. Previous positions include Principal Guest Conductor, Bayerische Philharmonie in Munich, Germany (2022-2024), Music Director, Denver Philharmonic Orchestra (2013-2024), Resident Conductor, Phoenix Symphony (2006-2010), founder and Artistic Director, Atlantic Chamber Orchestra (1998-2003), Music Director, Portland Ballet Company (1997-2013), and Music Director, Southern Maine Symphony Orchestra (1990-2001).

www.lawrencegolan.com

Photo by Gary Miller

C Major

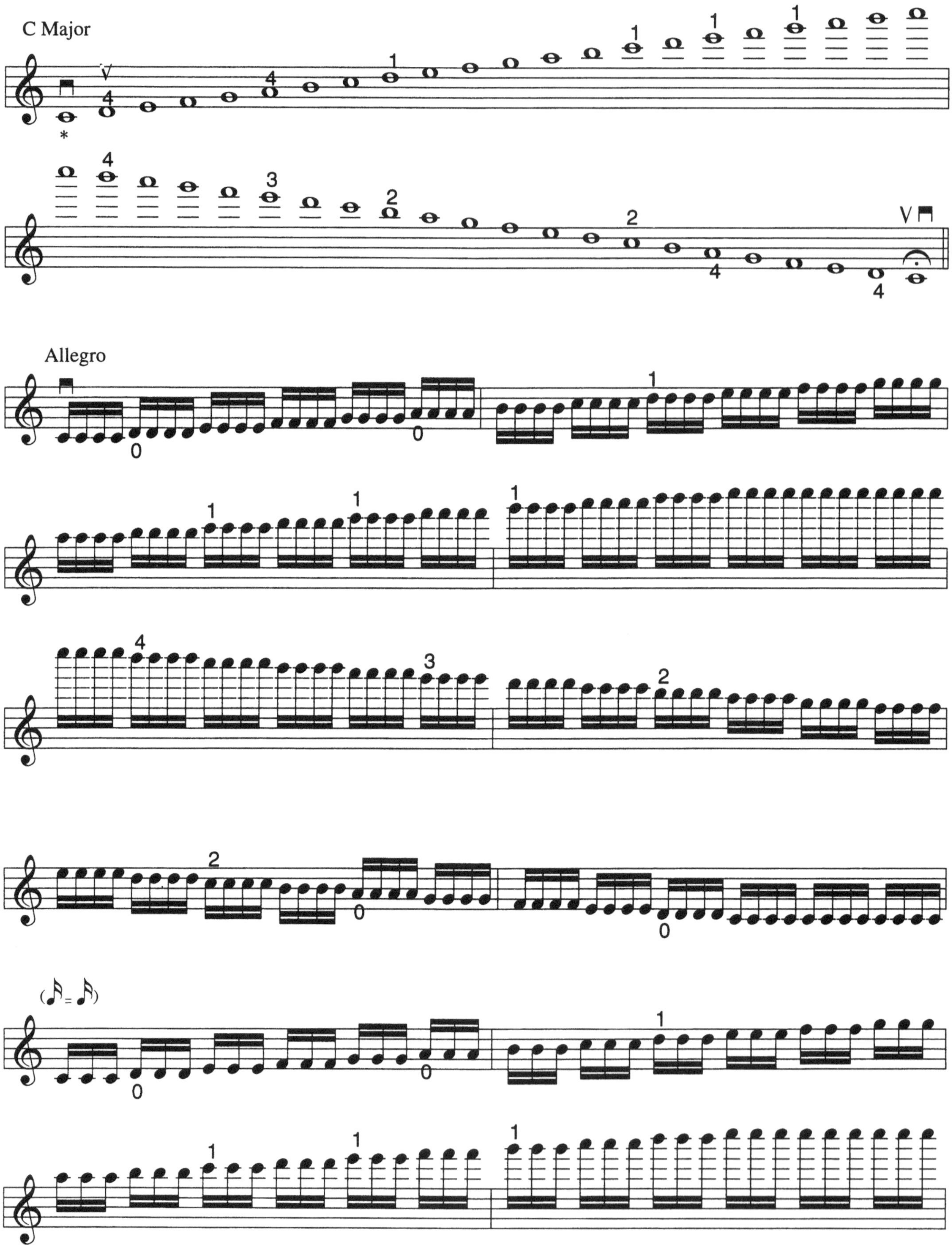

*each note as long as possible (10-20 seconds)

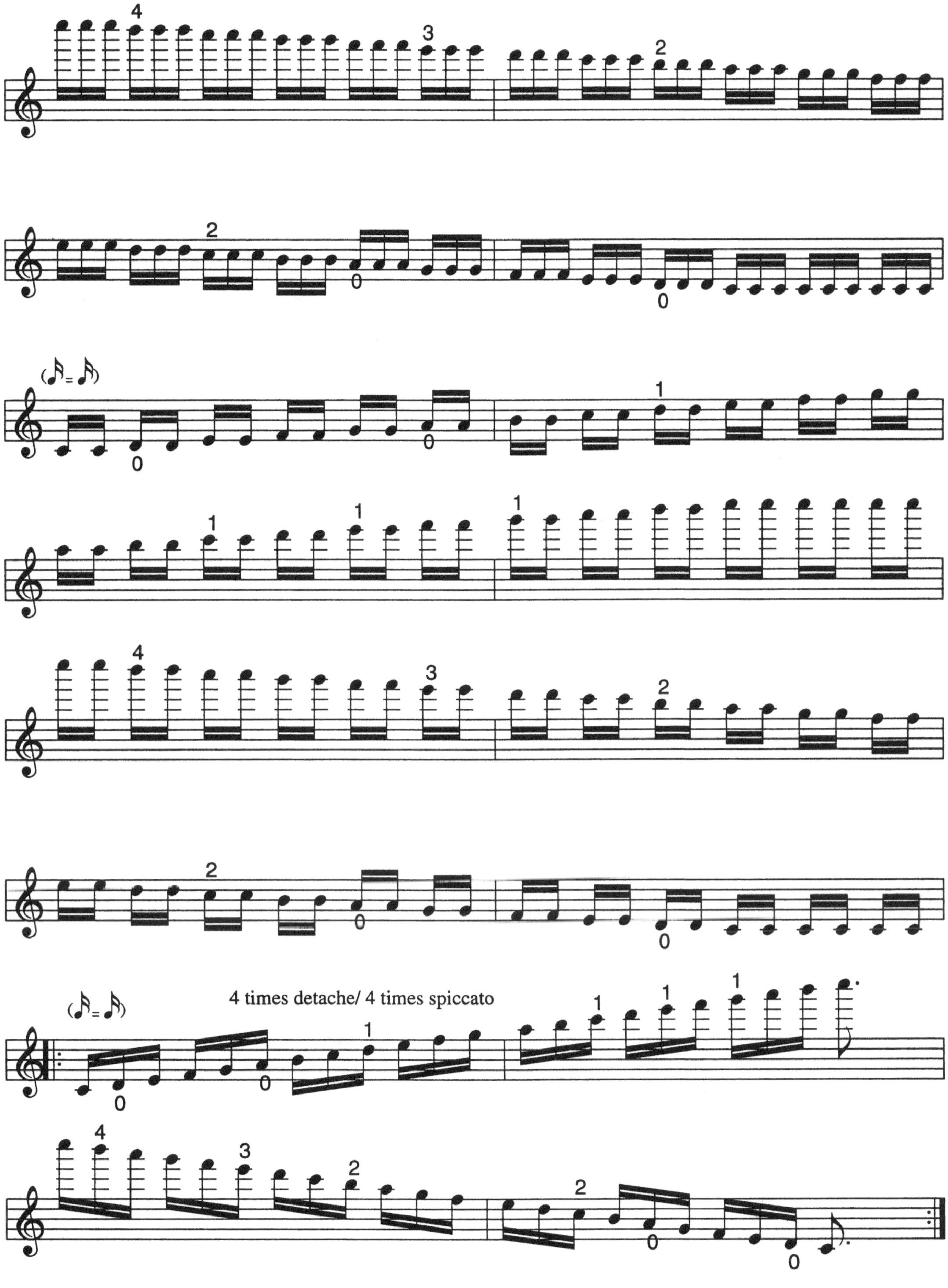
4 times detache/ 4 times spiccato

*tempo increases with each successive exercise

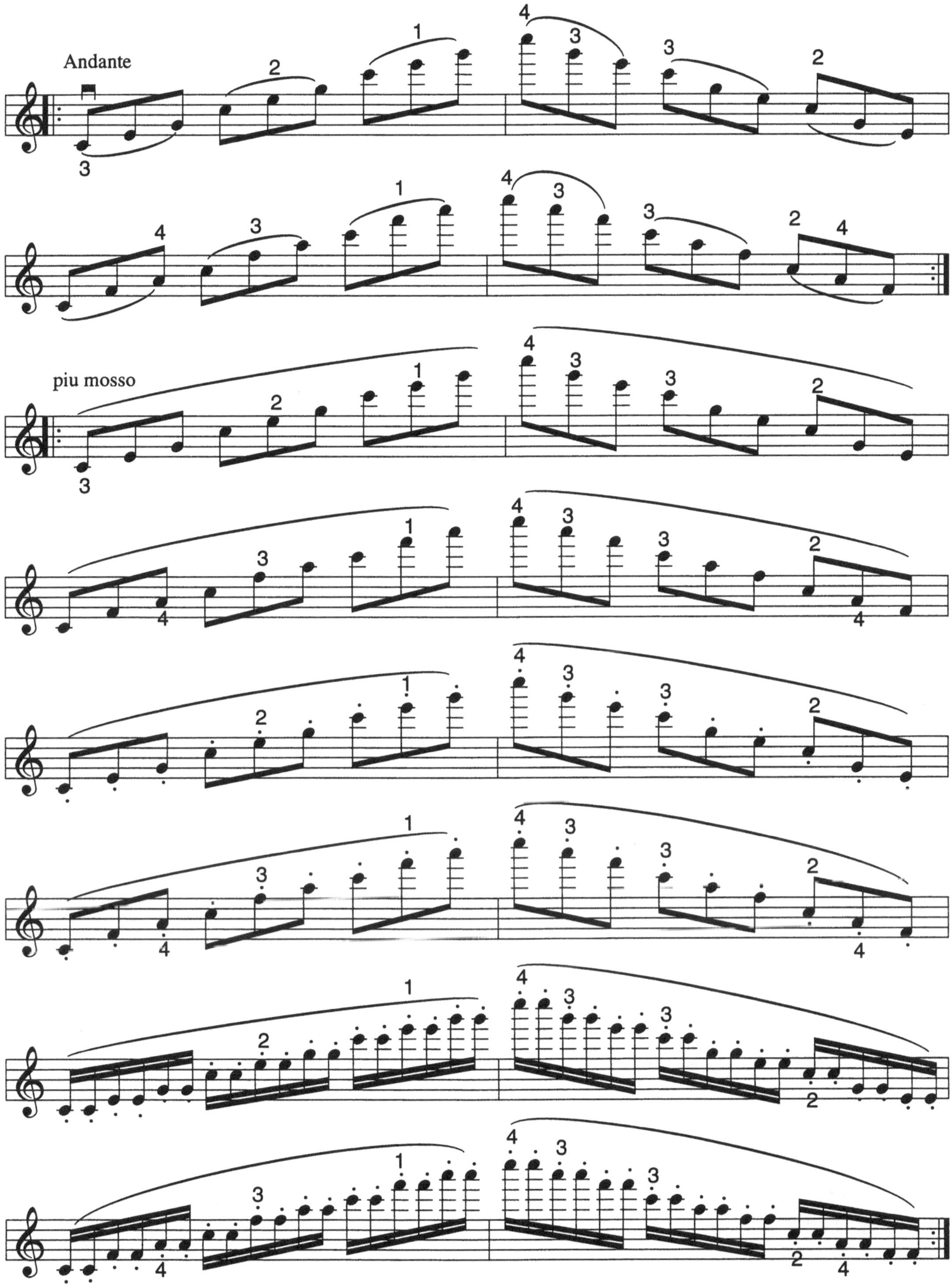
Andante
piu mosso

Andante

Adagio

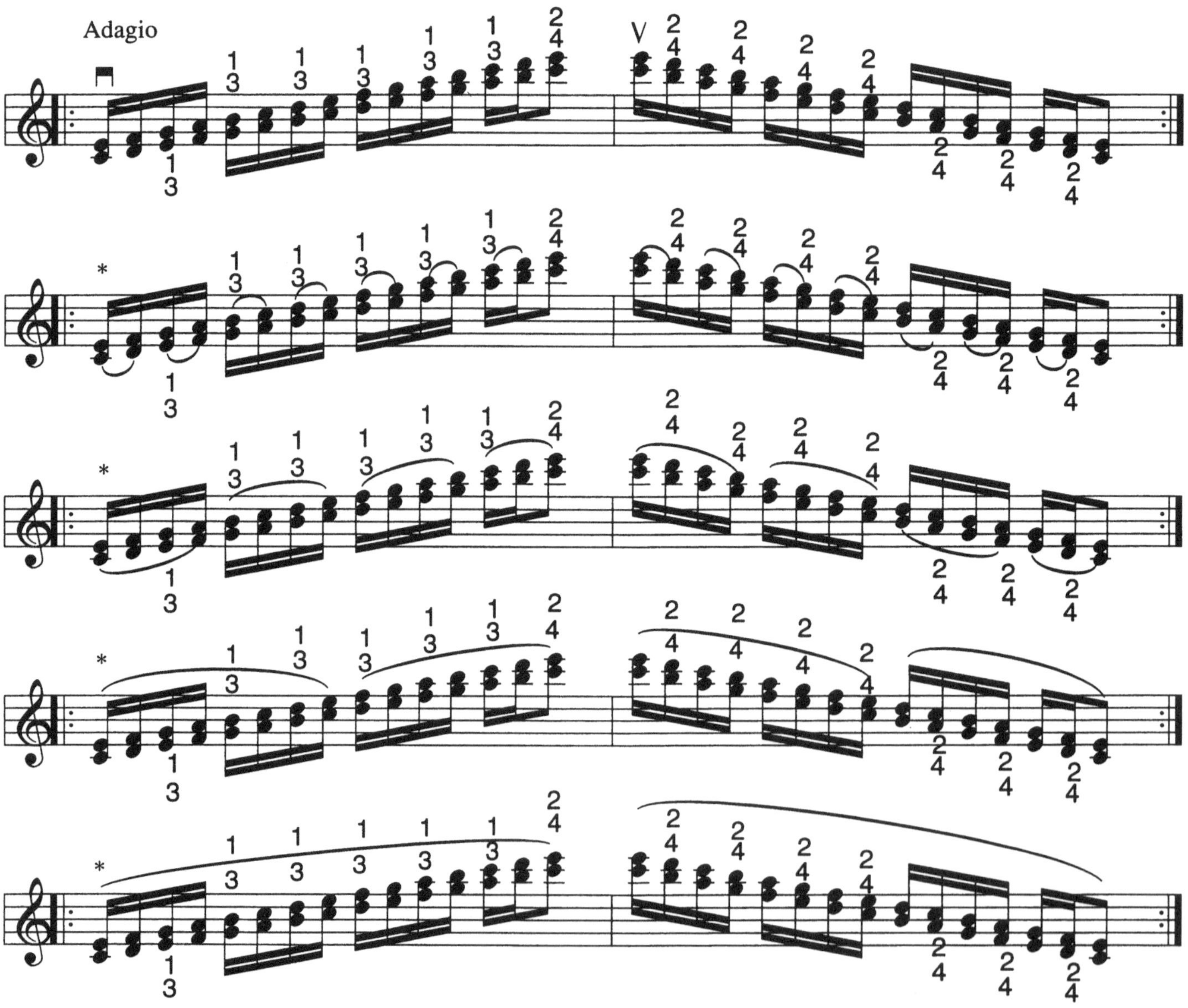

*tempo increases with each successive exercise

*tempo increases with each successive exercise

*tempo increases with each successive exercise

*tempo increases with each successive exercise

*tempo increases with each successive exercise

G Major

G Major

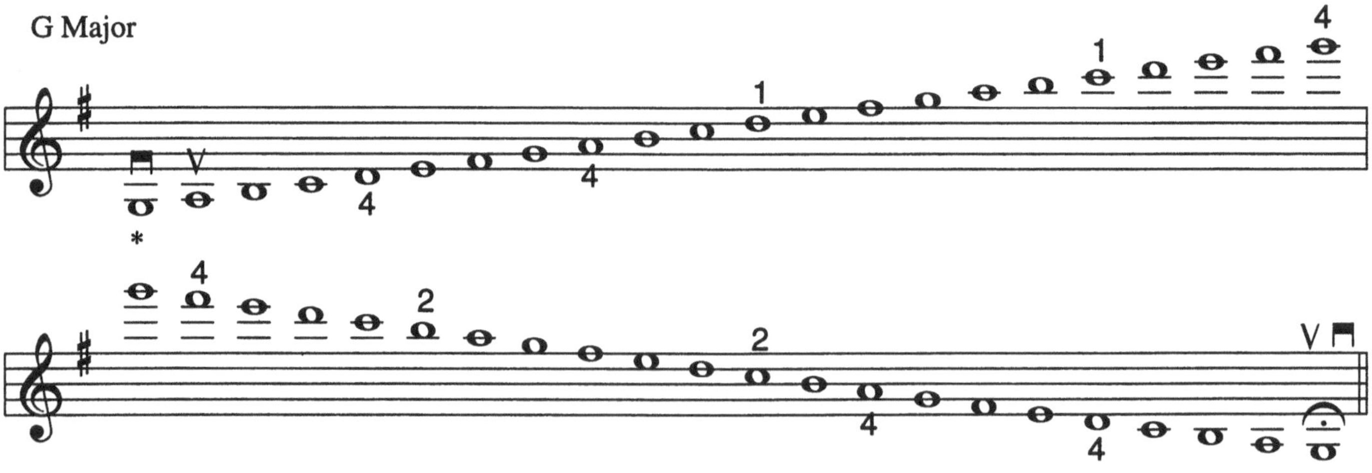

Allegro

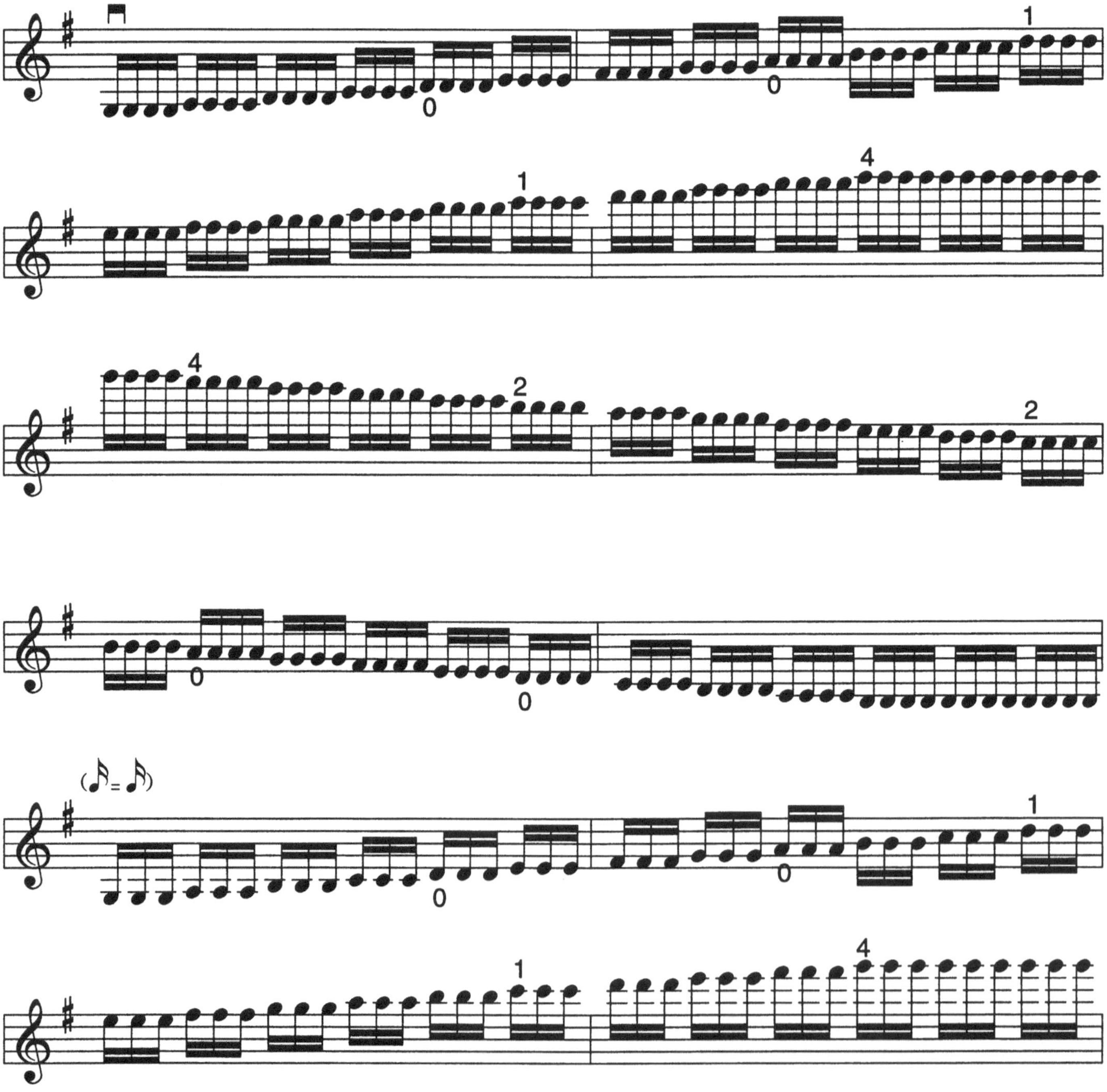

*each note as long as possible (10-20 seconds)

4 times detache/ 4 times spiccato

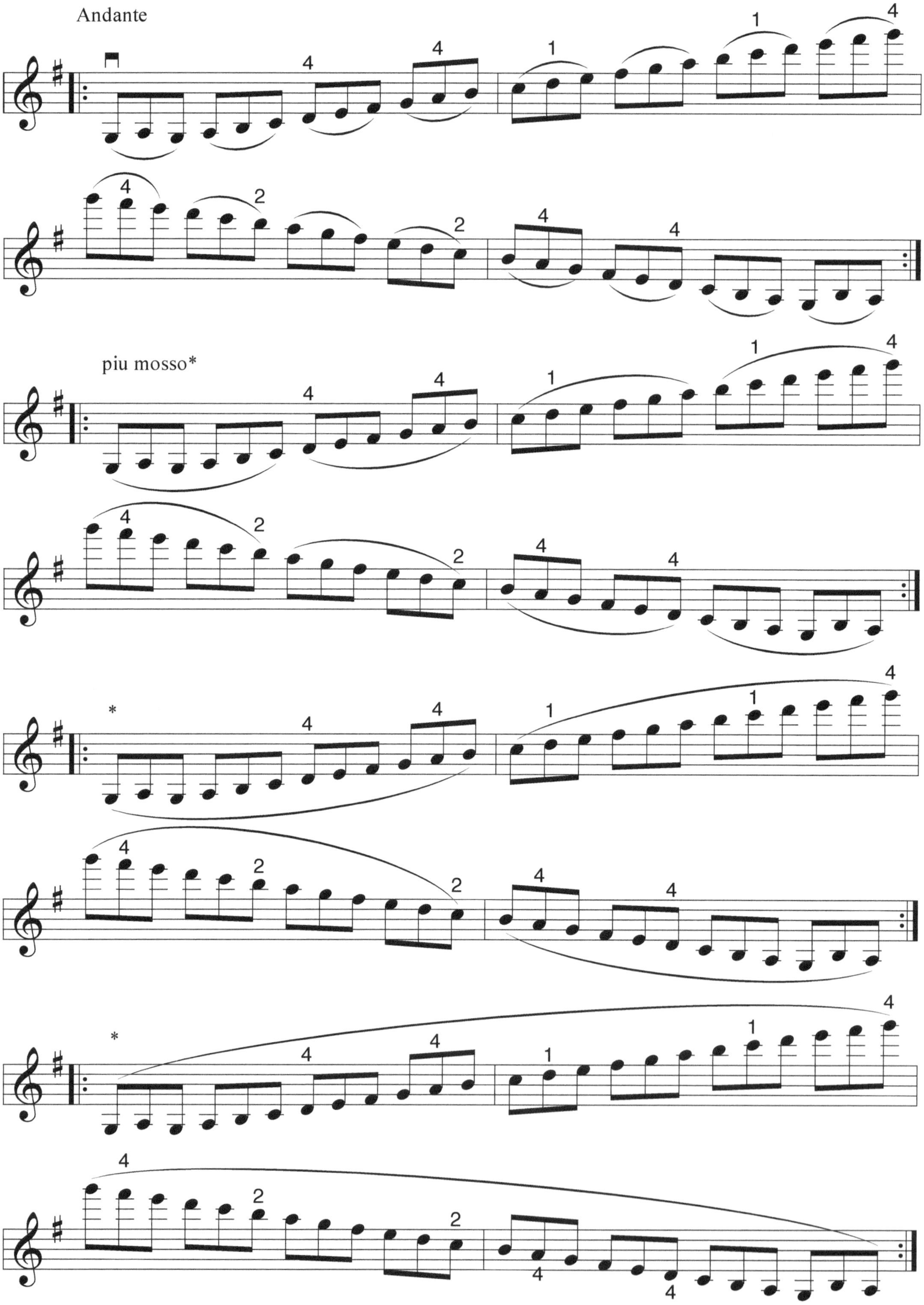

*tempo increases with each successive exercise

Four-octave scales

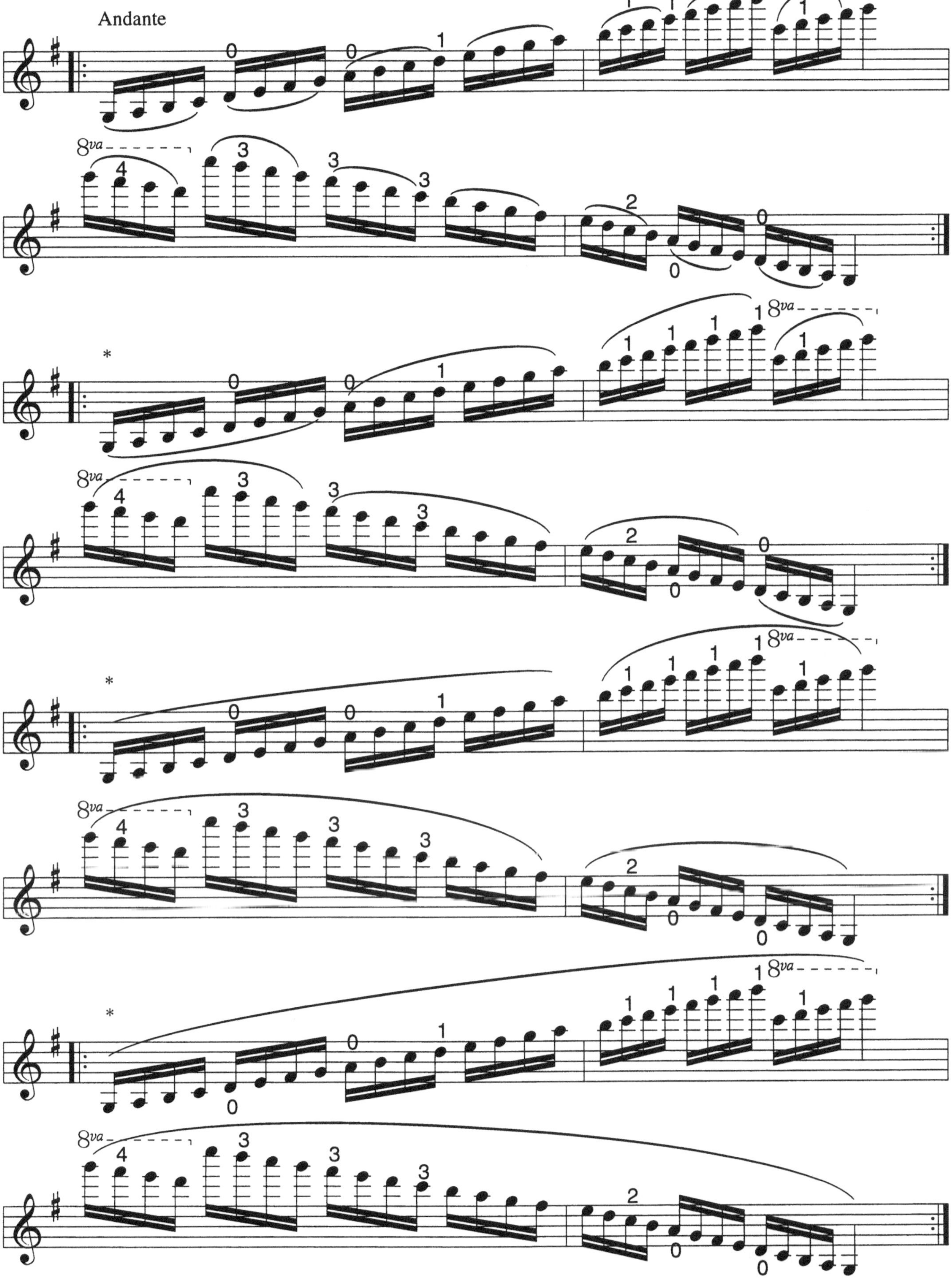

*tempo increases with each successive exercise

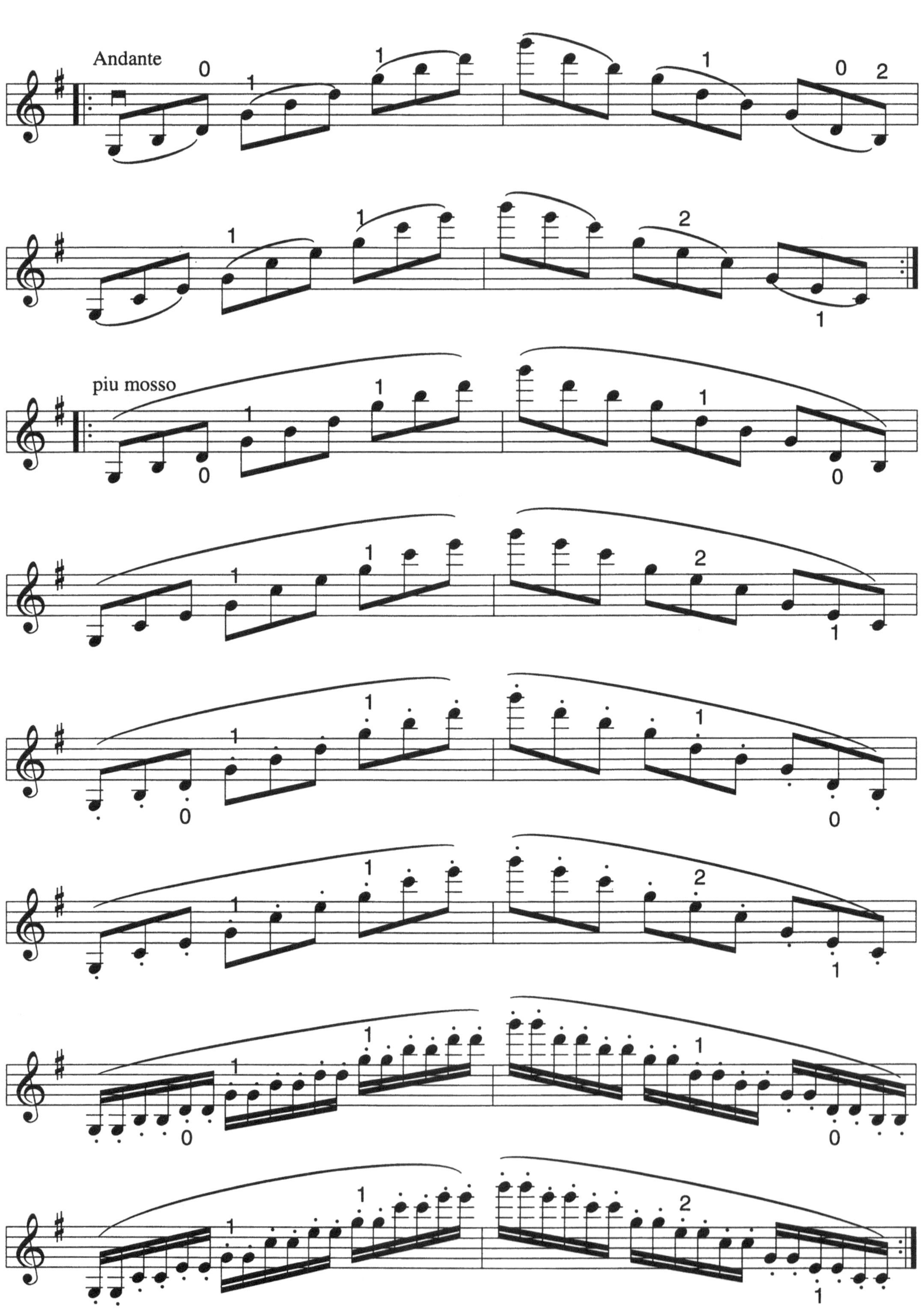
Andante
piu mosso

Four-octave arpeggios

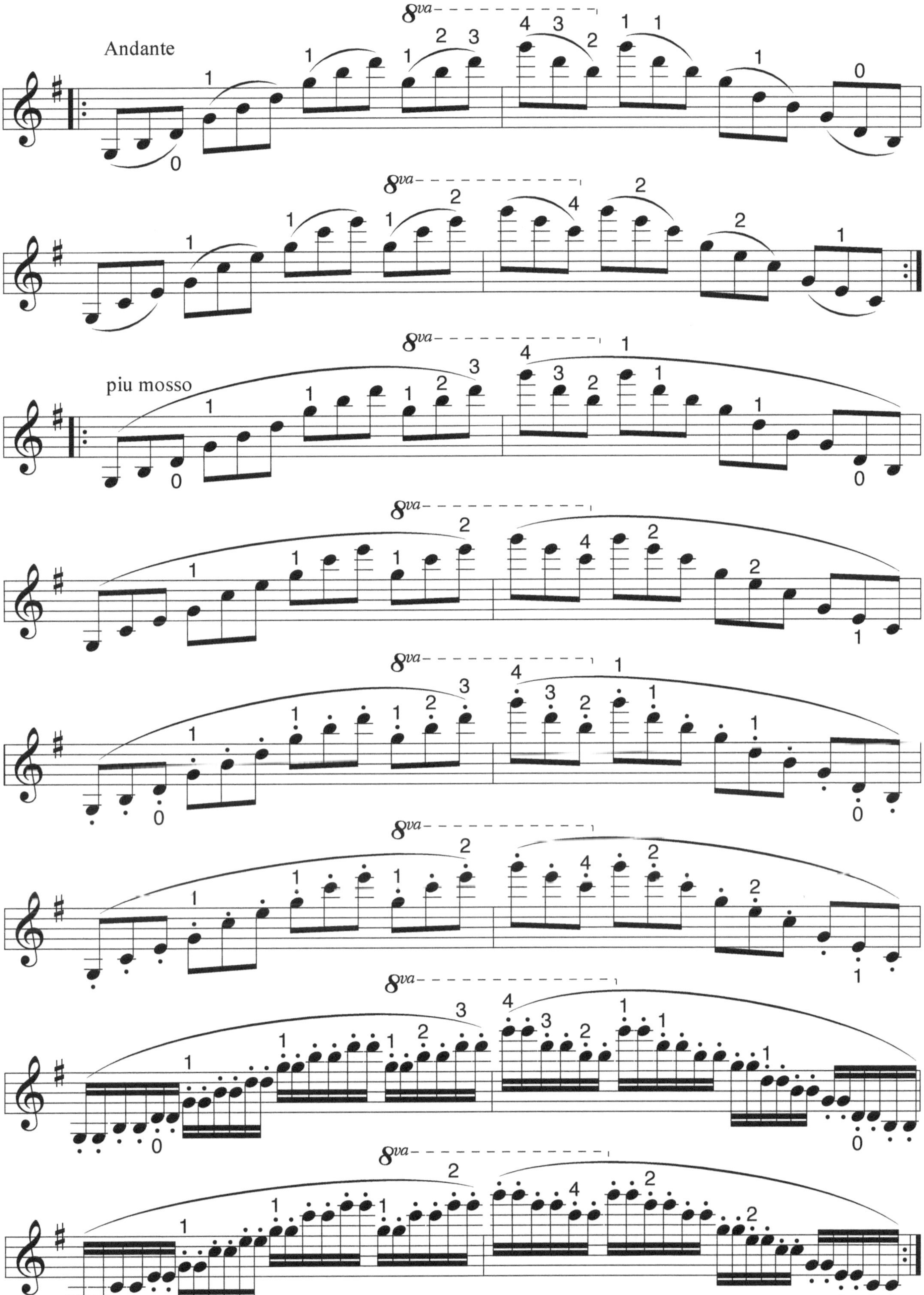

*tempo increases with each successive exercise

Three-octave scales in thirds

Andante

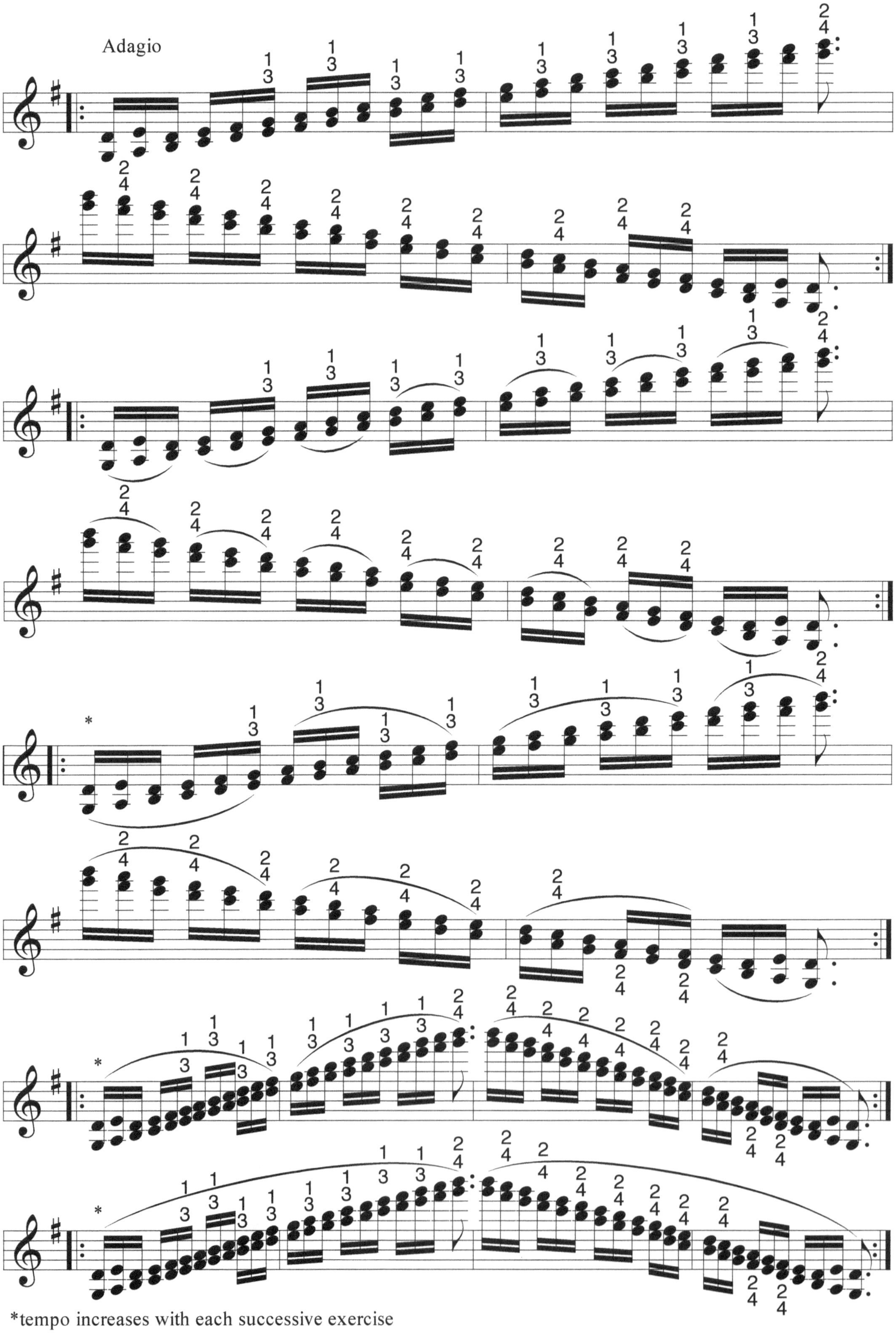

*tempo increases with each successive exercise

Andante

Adagio

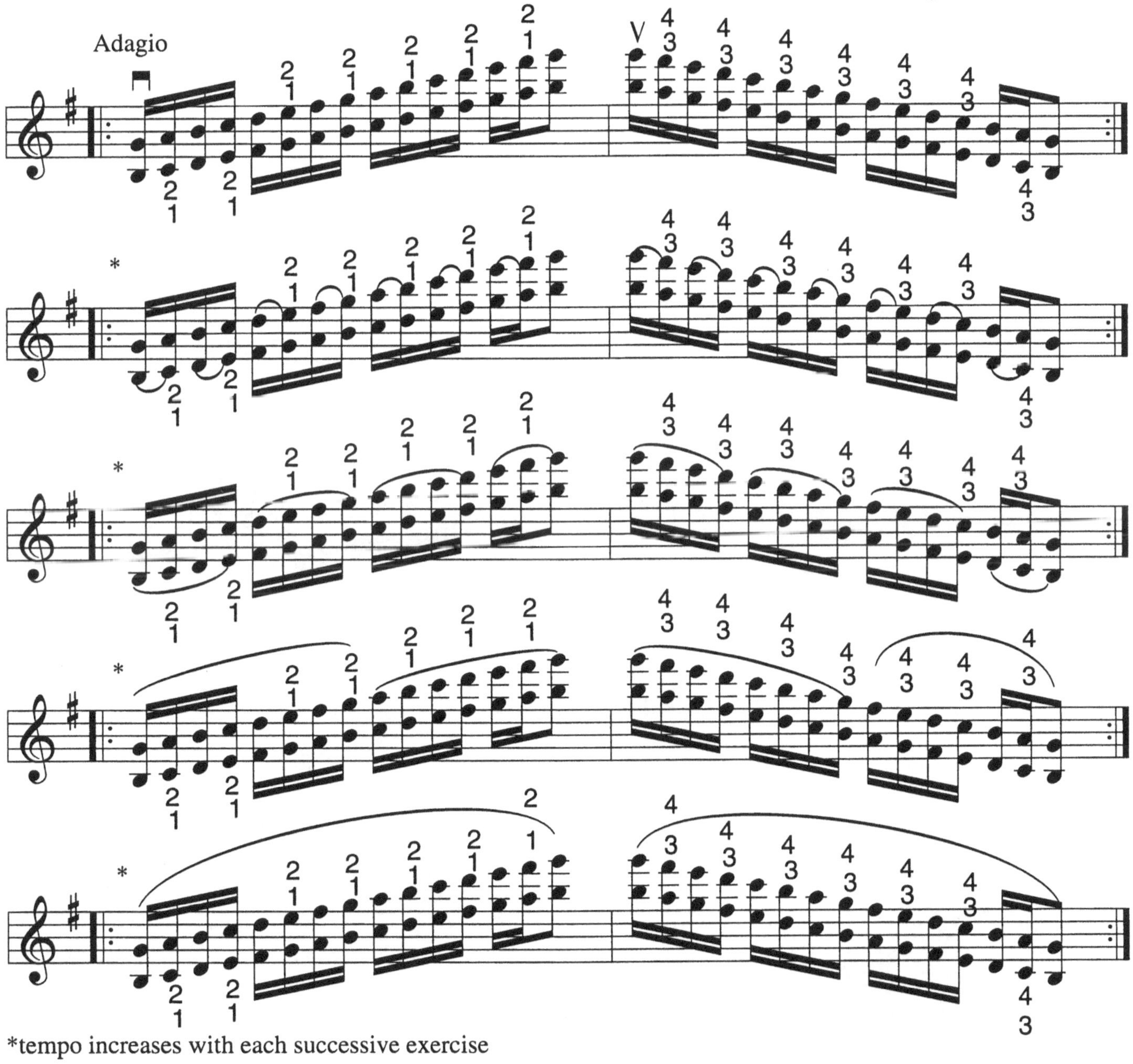

*tempo increases with each successive exercise

*tempo increases with each successive exercise

*tempo increases with each successive exercise

*tempo increases with each successive exercise

F Major

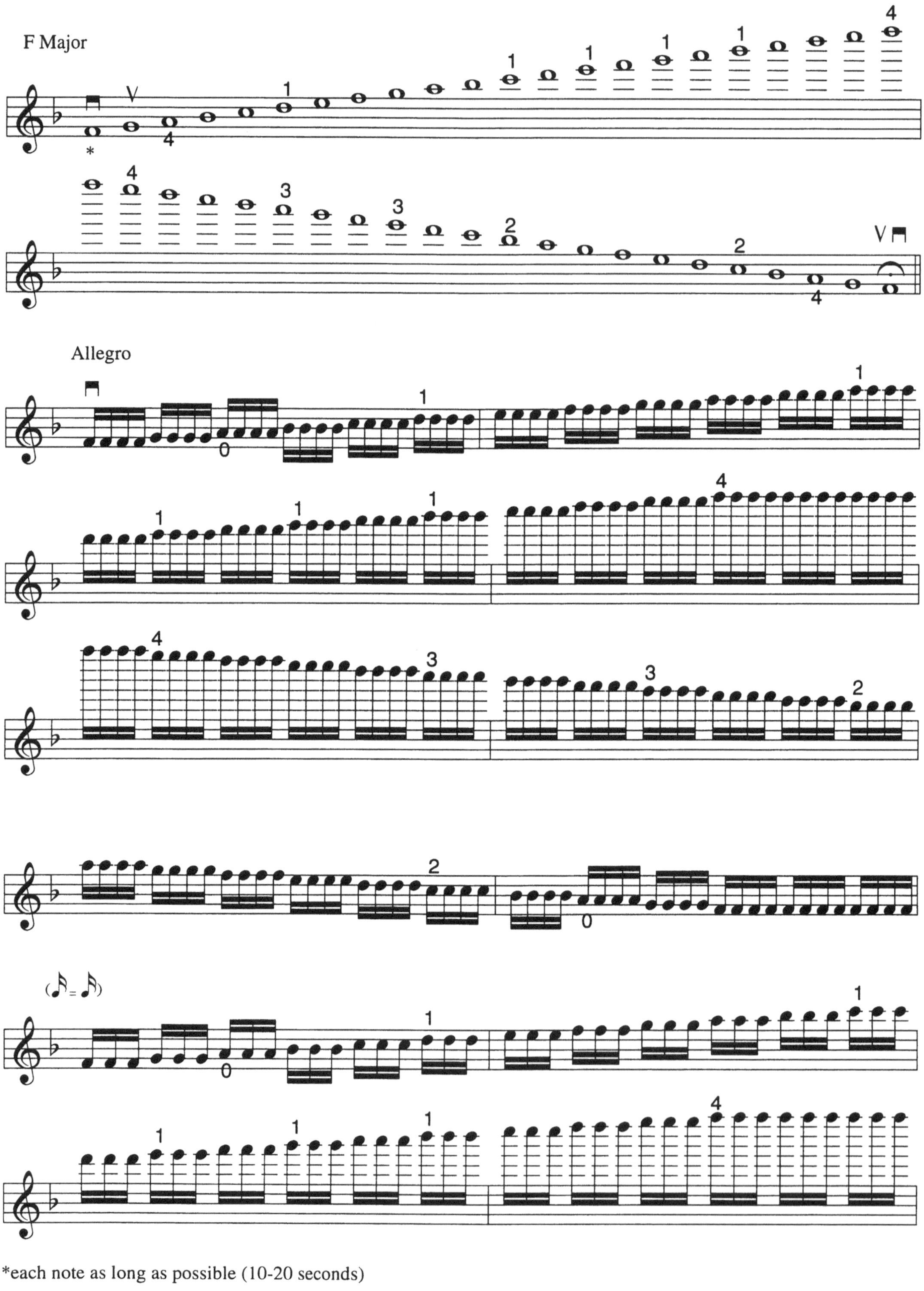

*each note as long as possible (10-20 seconds)

4 times detache/ 4 times spiccato

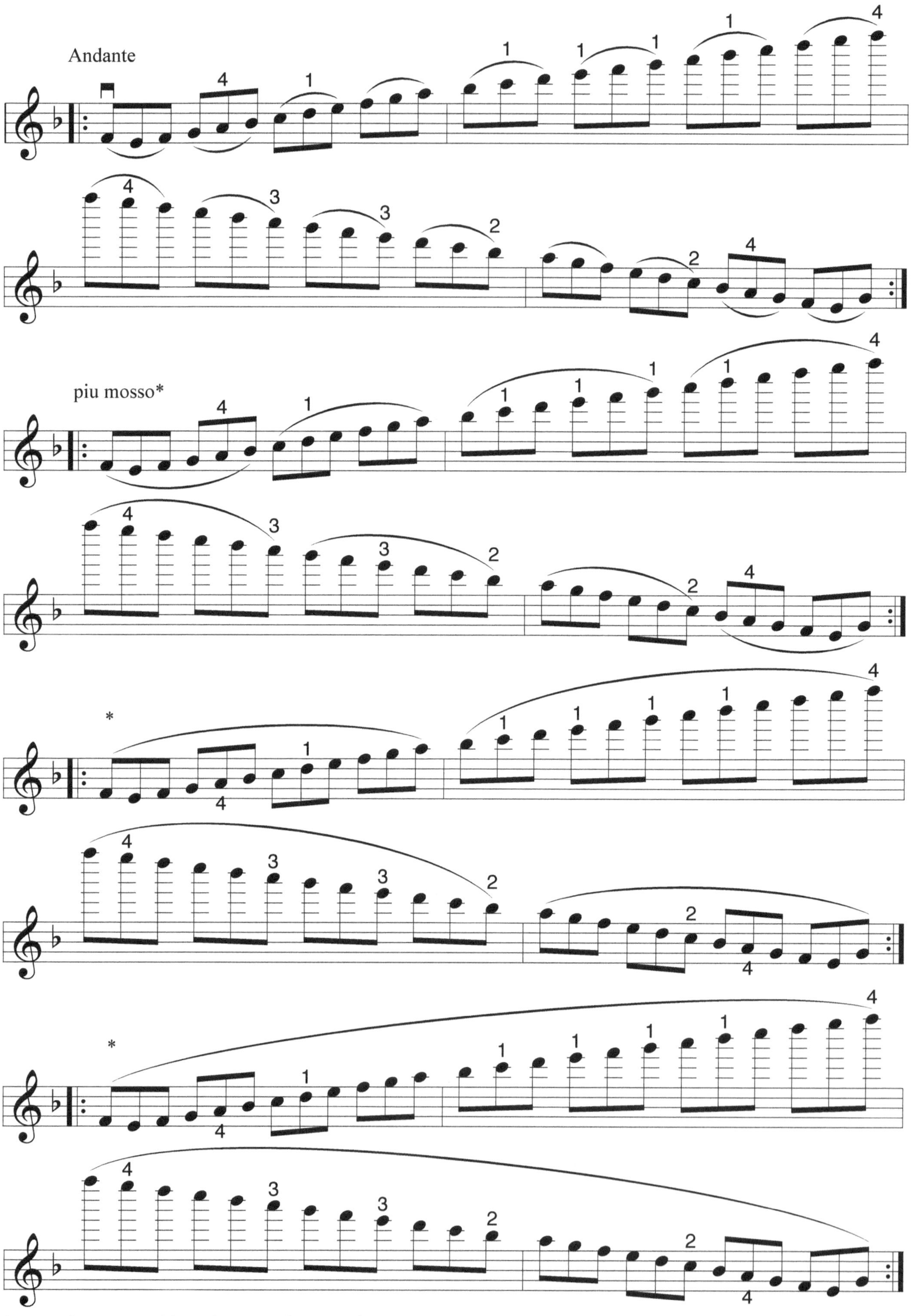

*tempo increases with each successive exercise

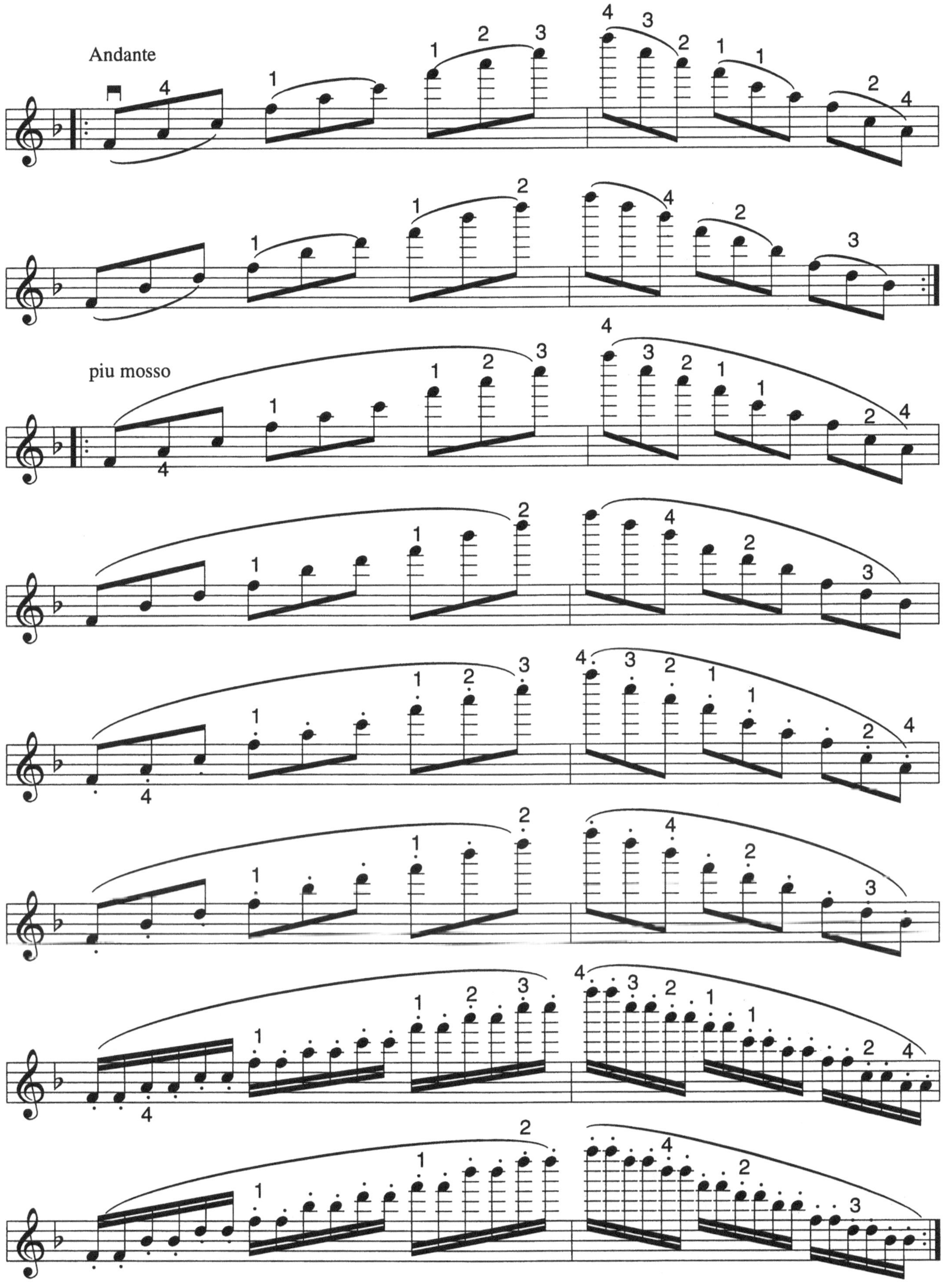
Andante
piu mosso

Andante

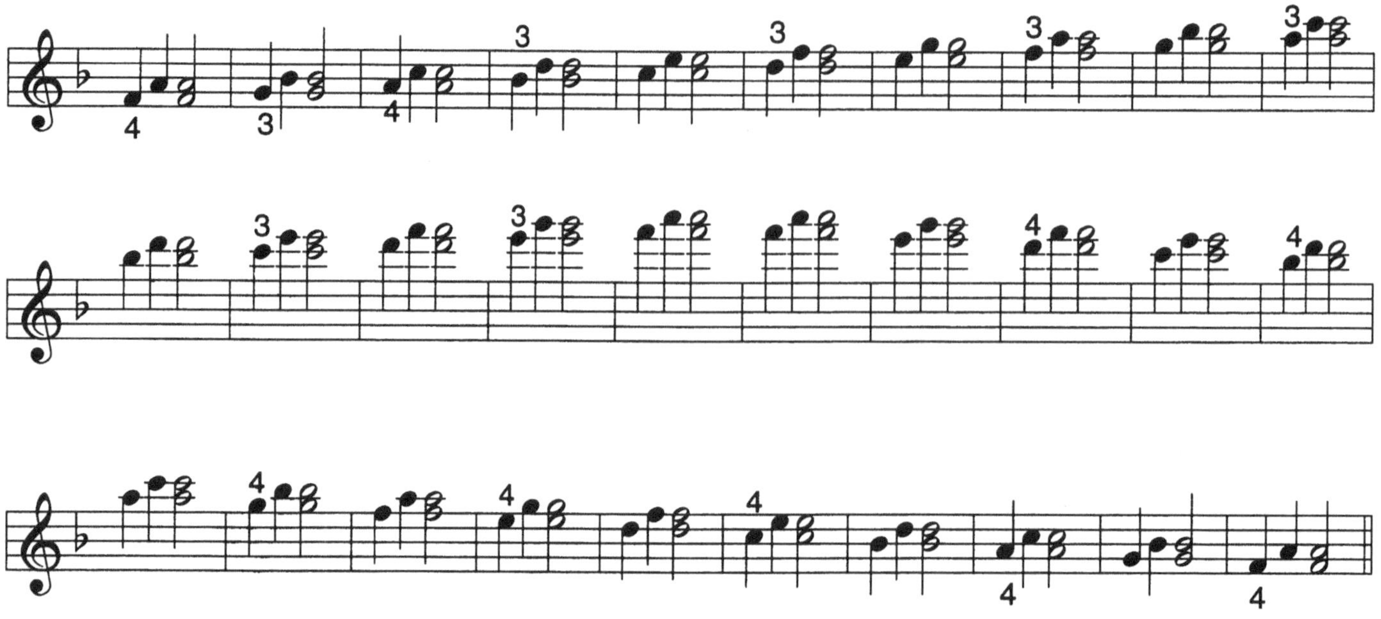

Adagio

*tempo increases with each successive exercise

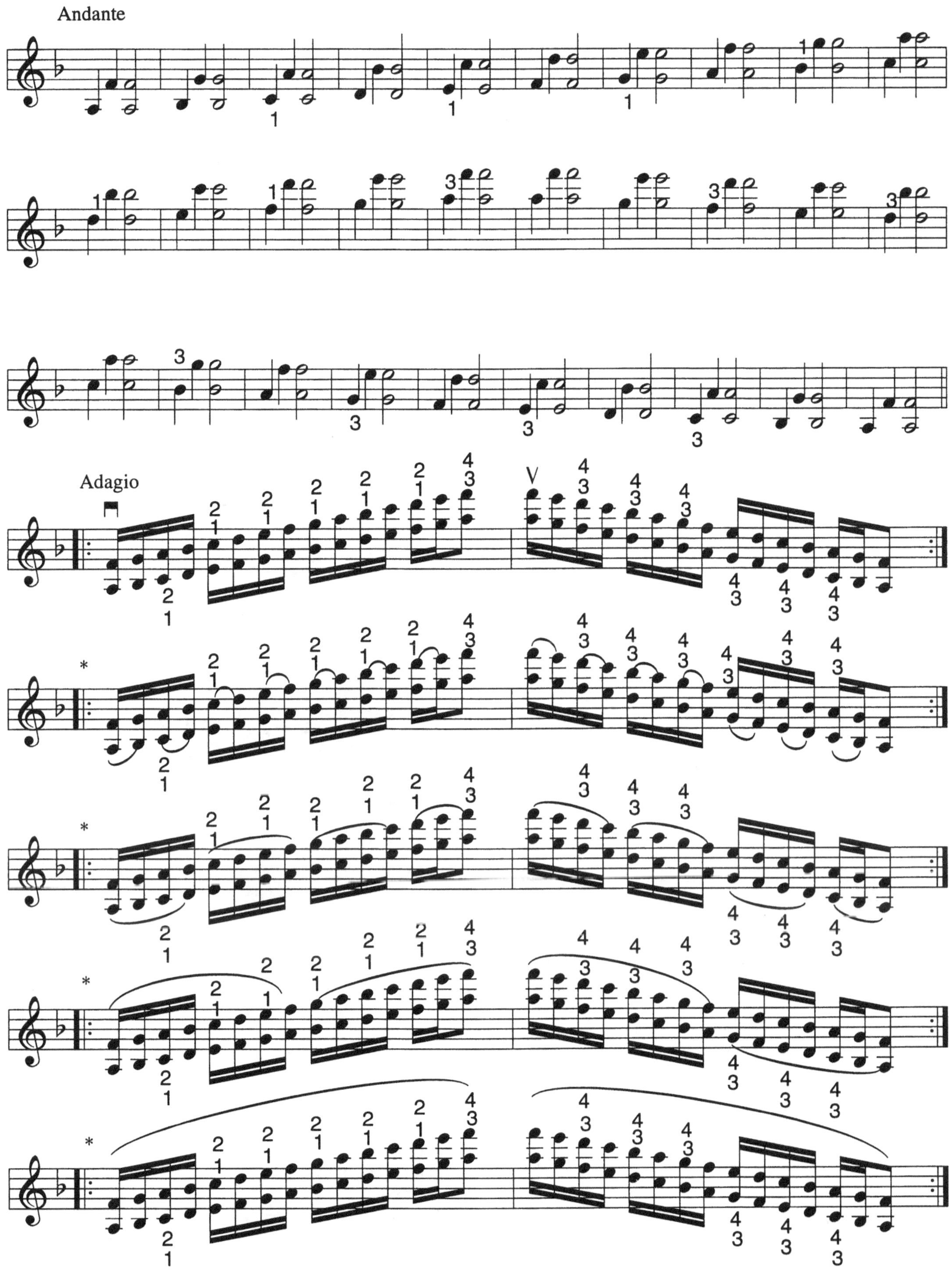

*tempo increases with each successive exercise

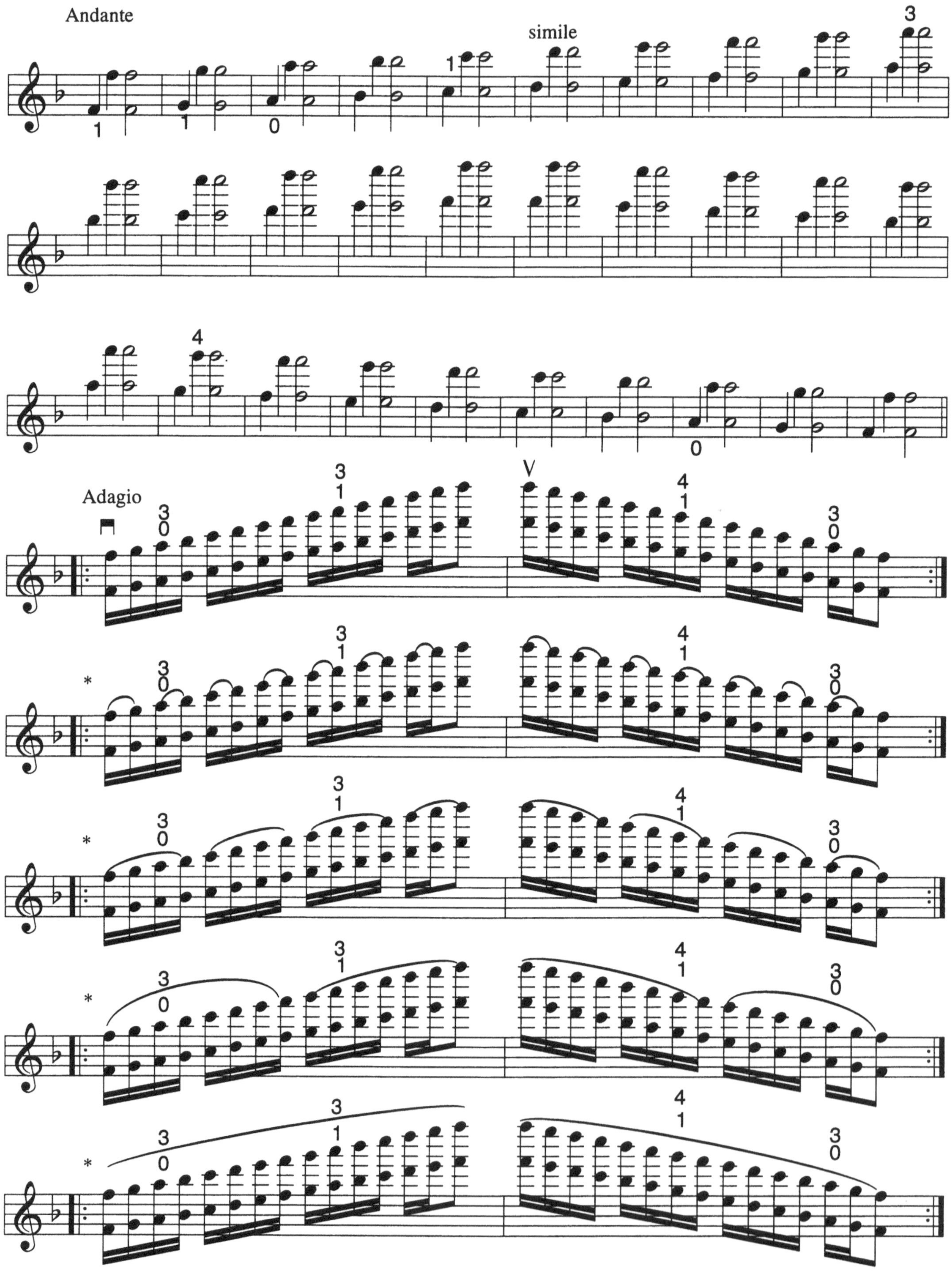

*tempo increases with each successive exercise

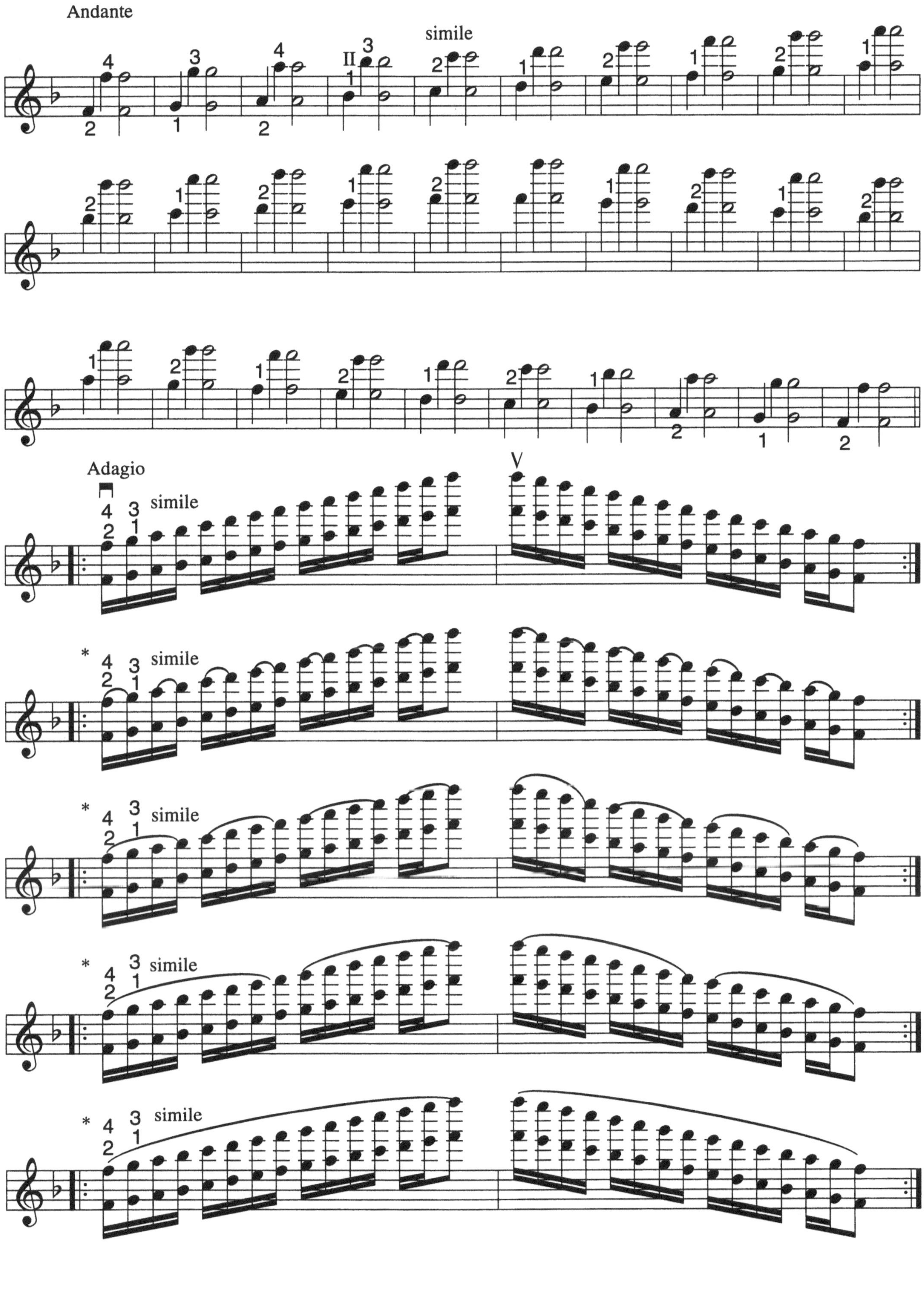

*tempo increases with each successive exercise

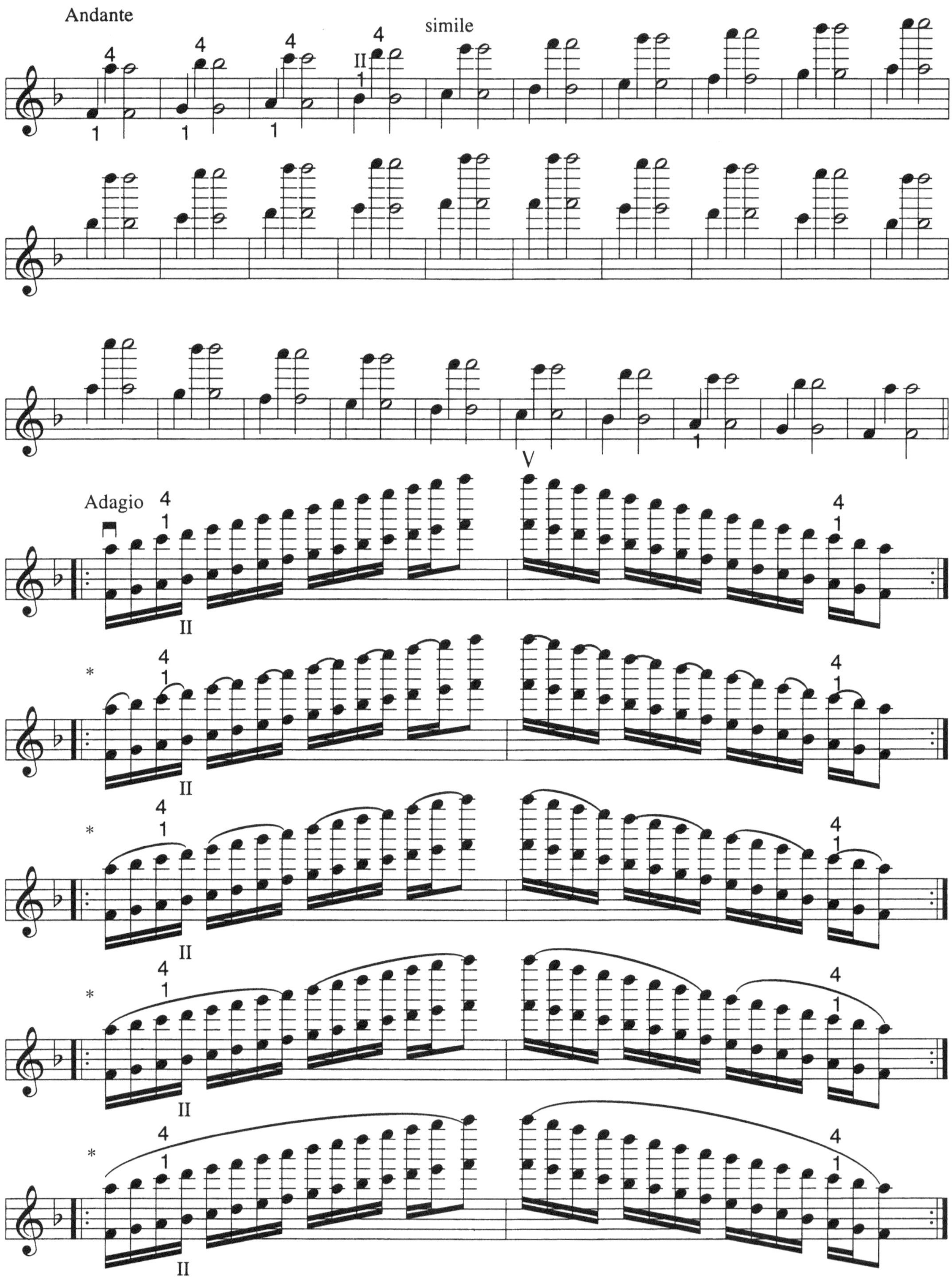

*tempo increases with each successive exercise

D Major

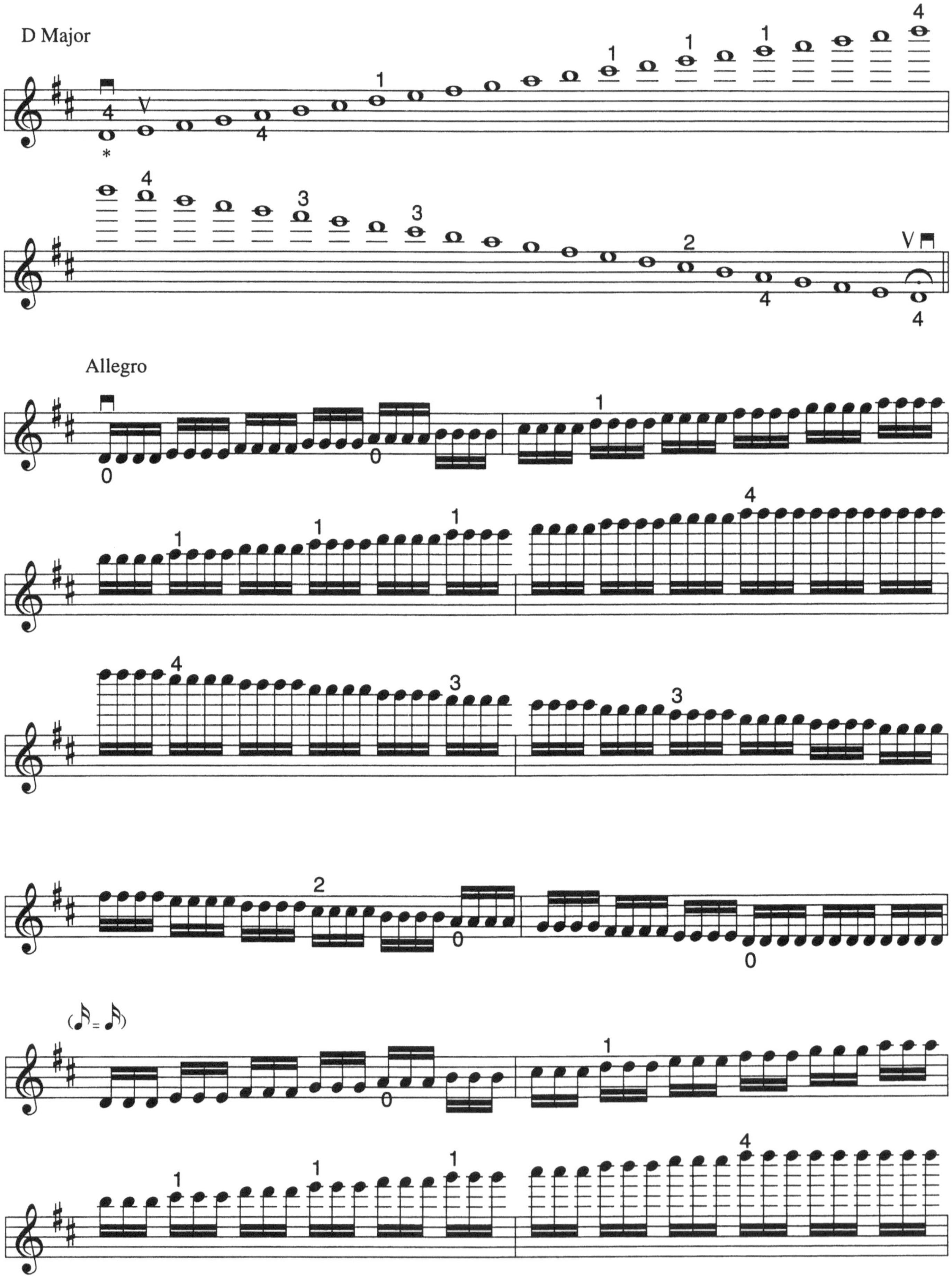

*each note as long as possible (10-20 seconds)

4 times detache/ 4 times spiccato

*tempo increases with each successive exercise

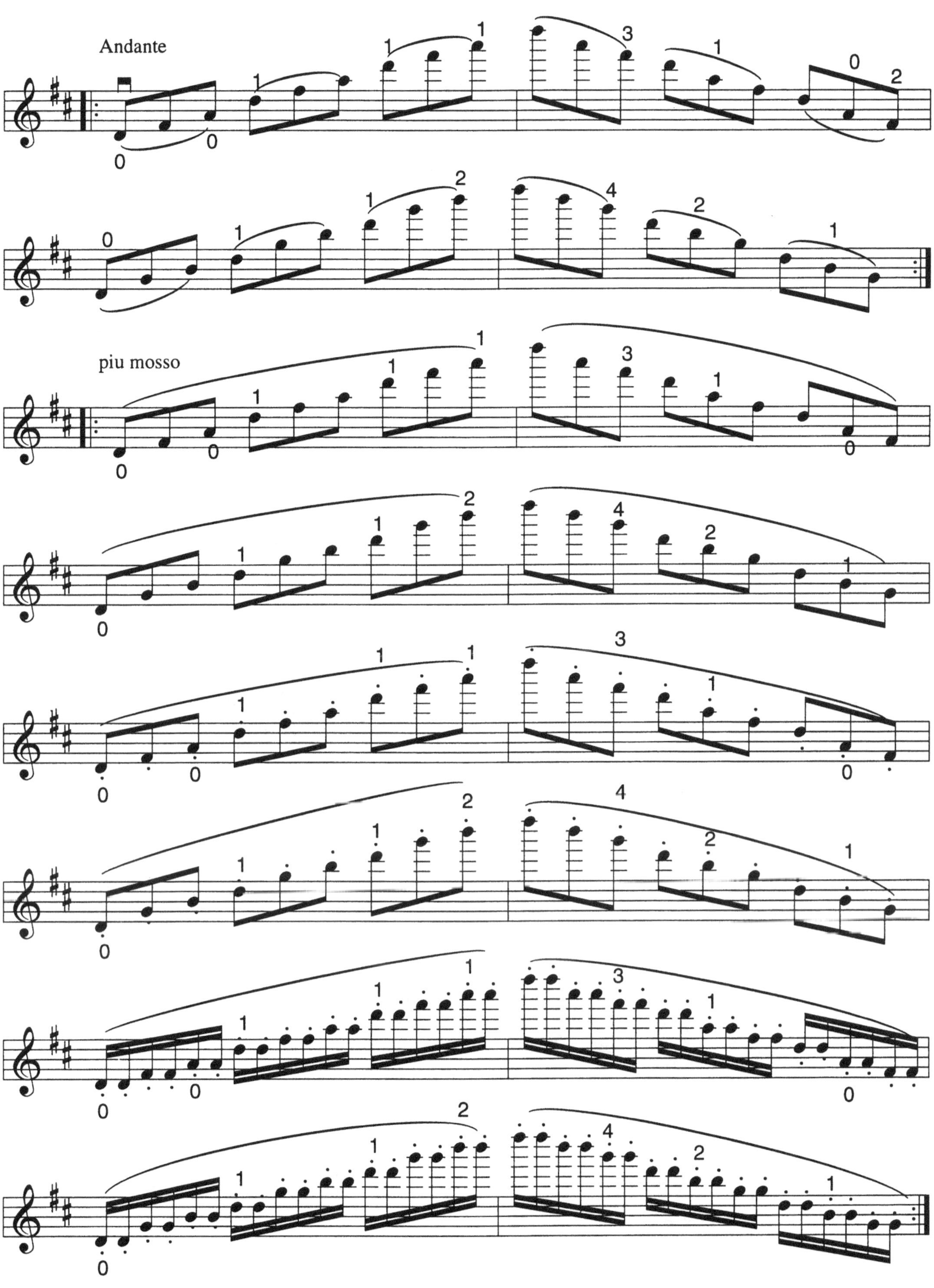
Andante
piu mosso

*tempo increases with each successive exercise

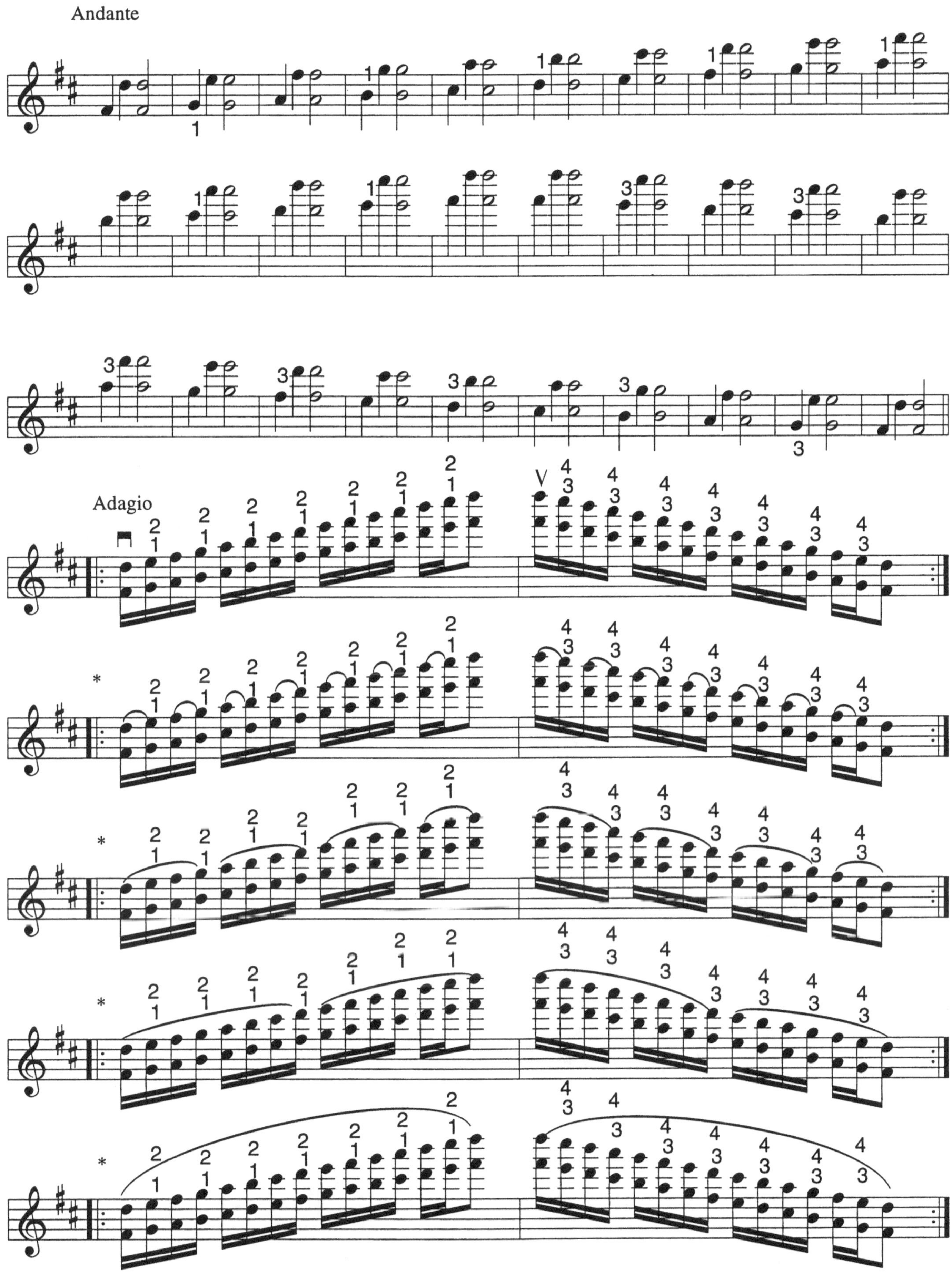

*tempo increases with each successive exercise

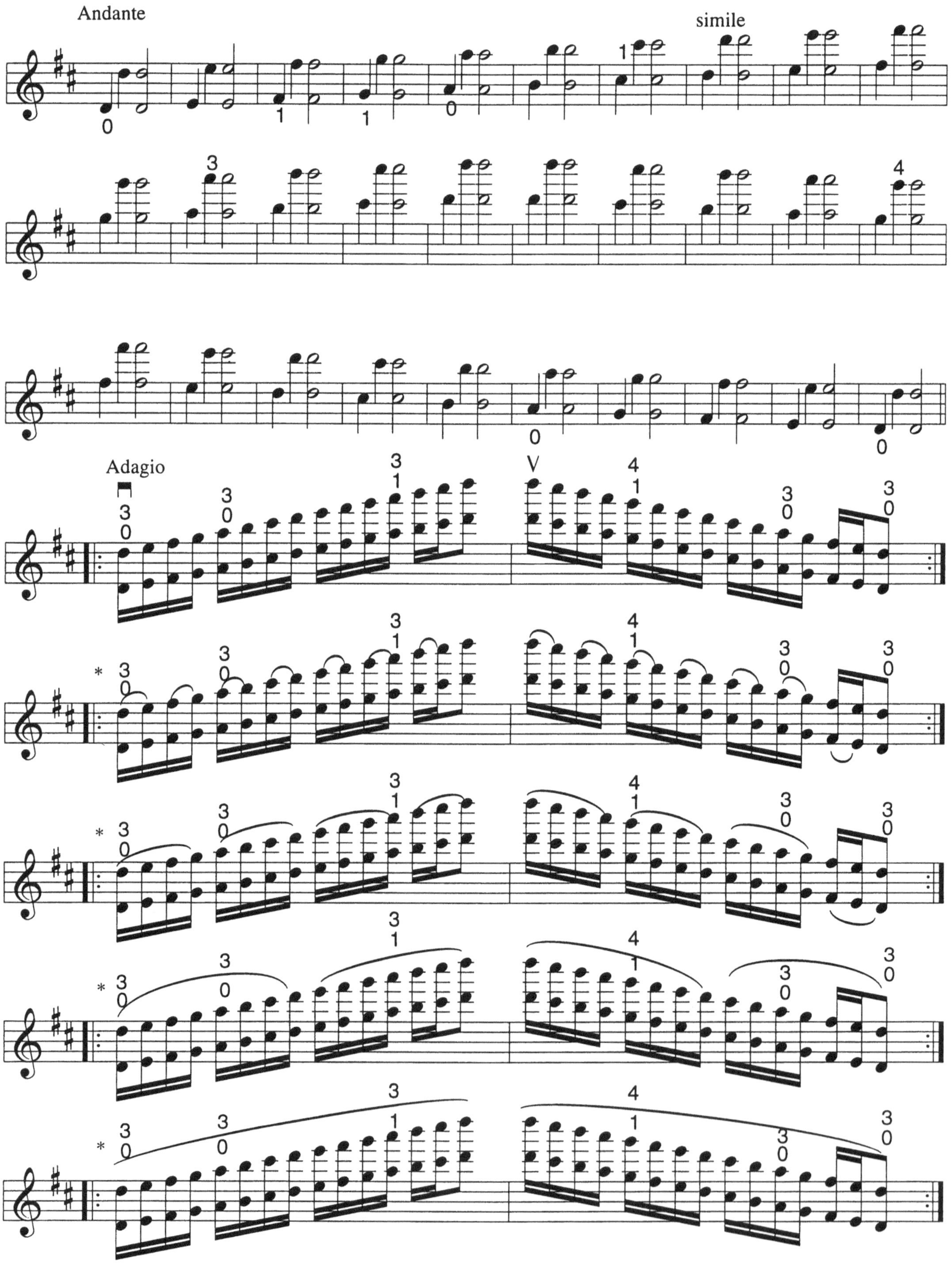

*tempo increases with each successive exercise

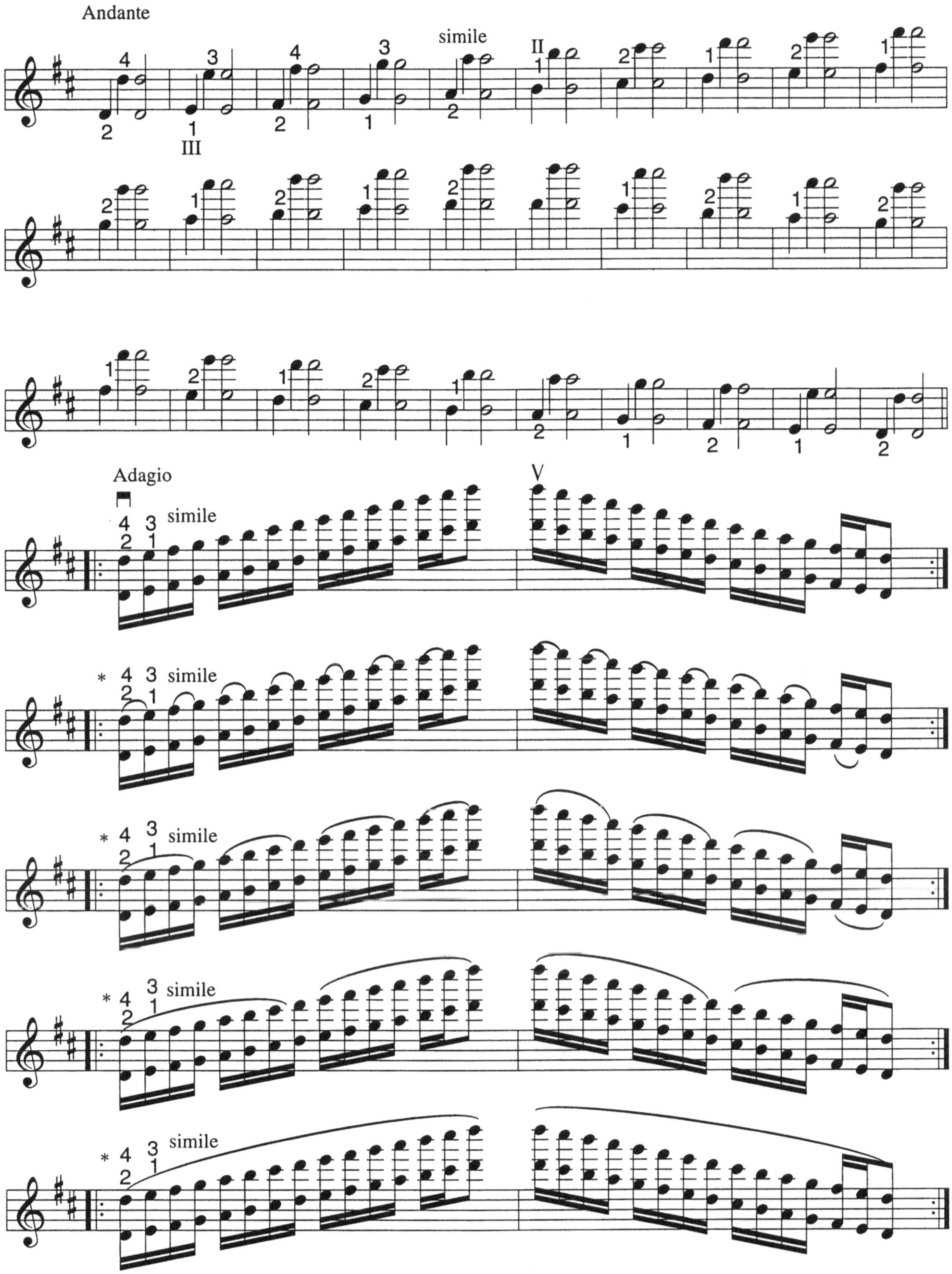

*tempo increases with each successive exercise

*tempo increases with each successive exercise

B-Flat Major

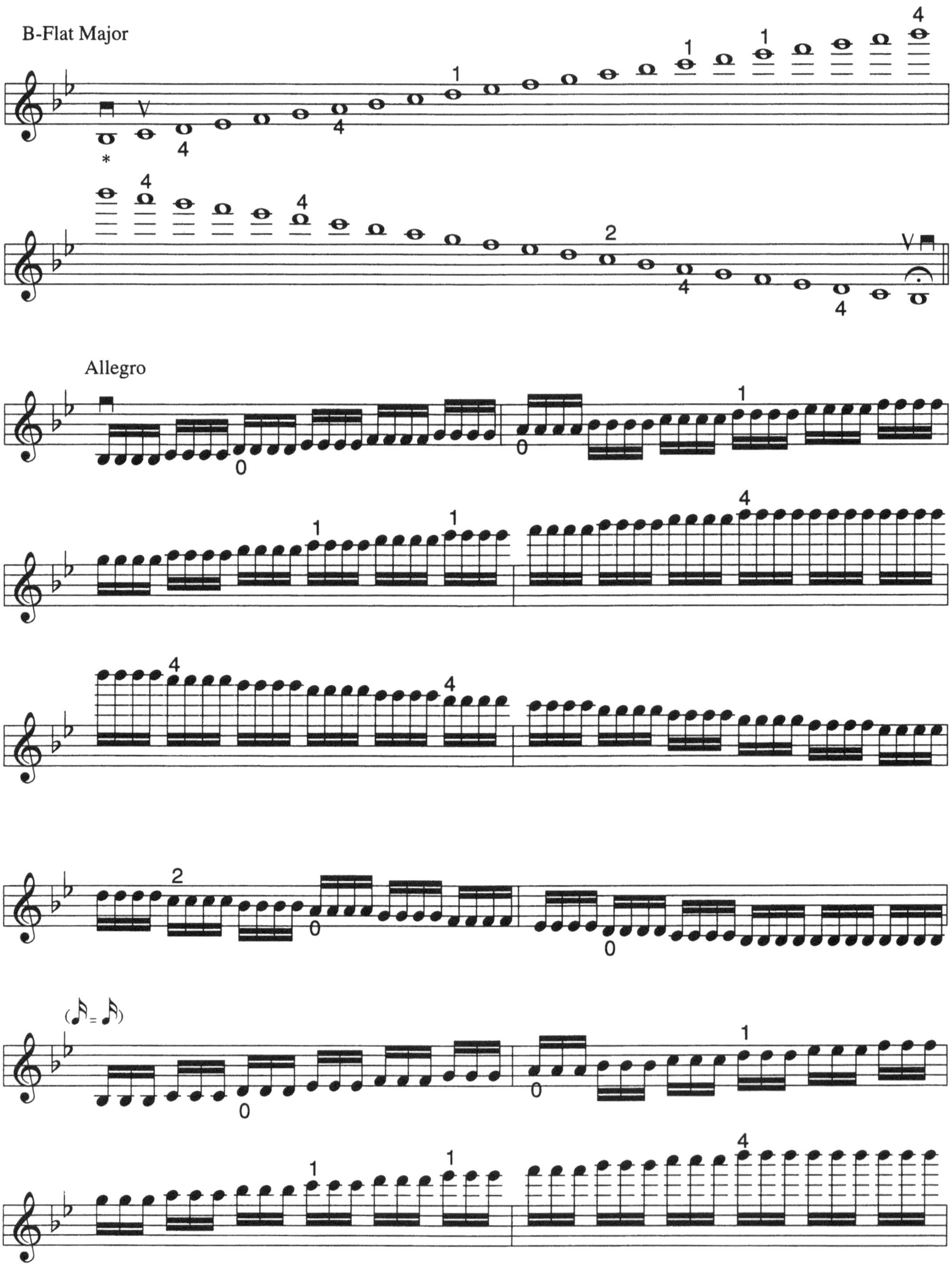

*each note as long as possible (10-20 seconds)

4 times detache/ 4 times spiccato

*tempo increases with each successive exercise

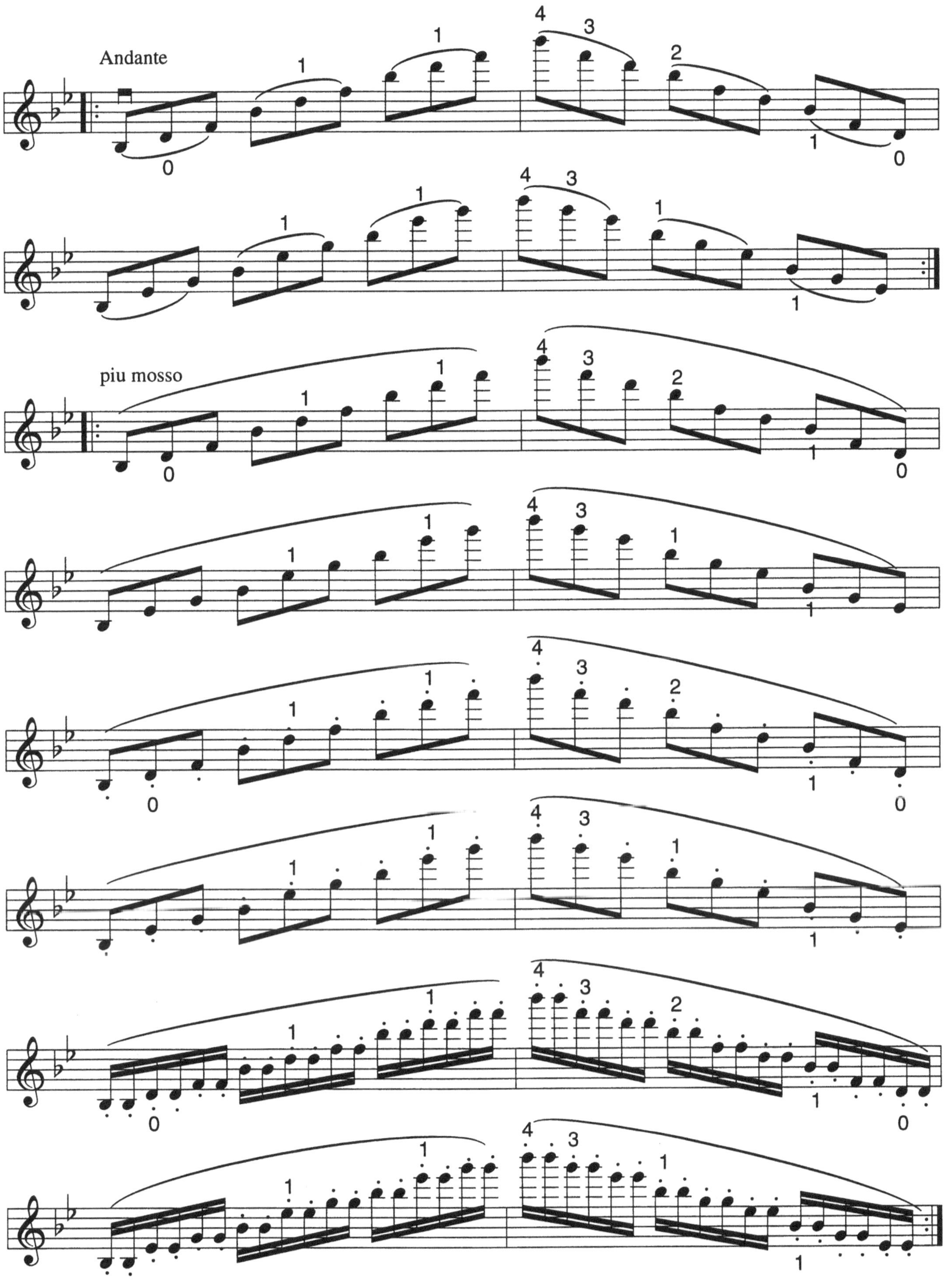
Andante
piu mosso

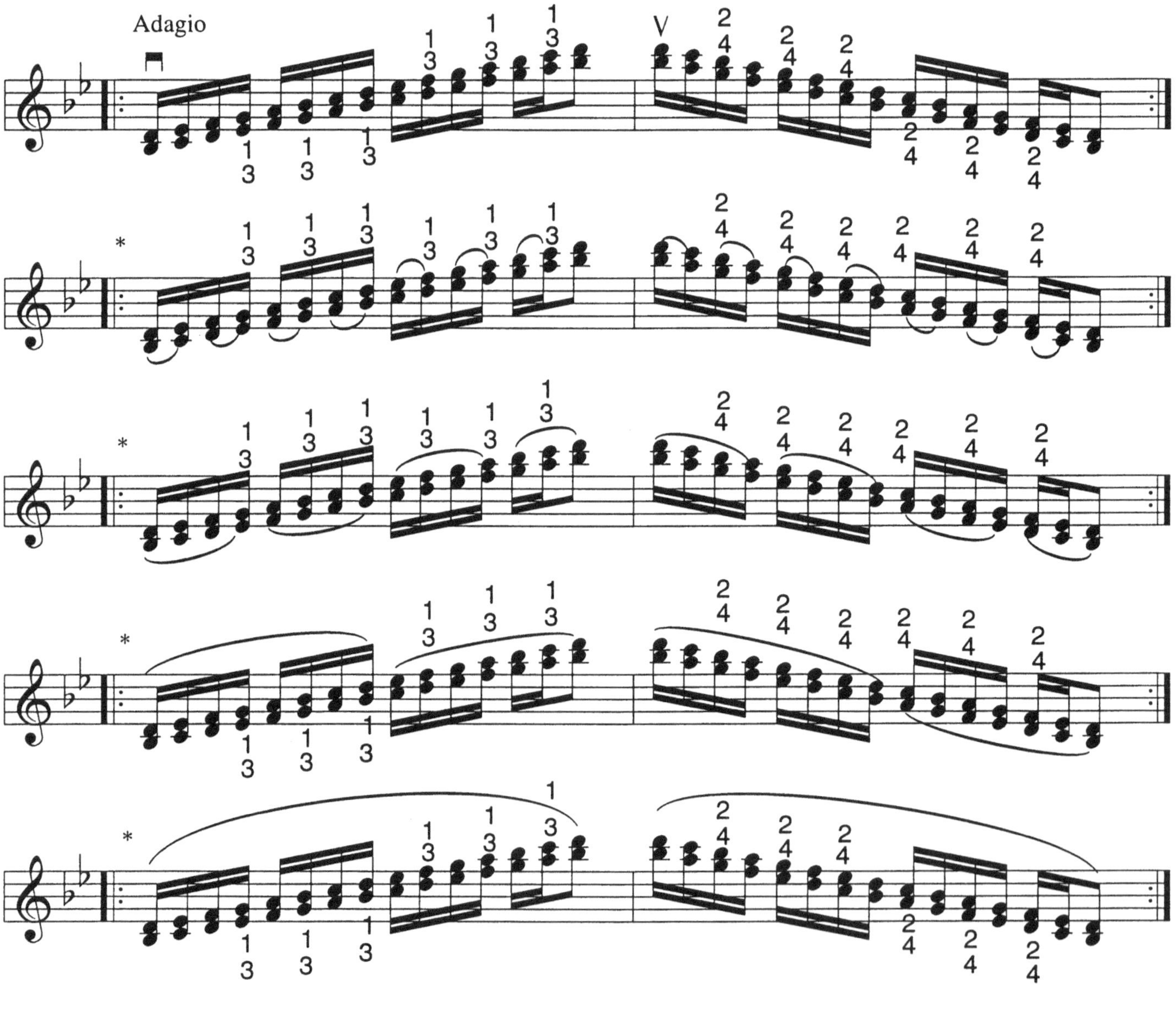

*tempo increases with each successive exercise

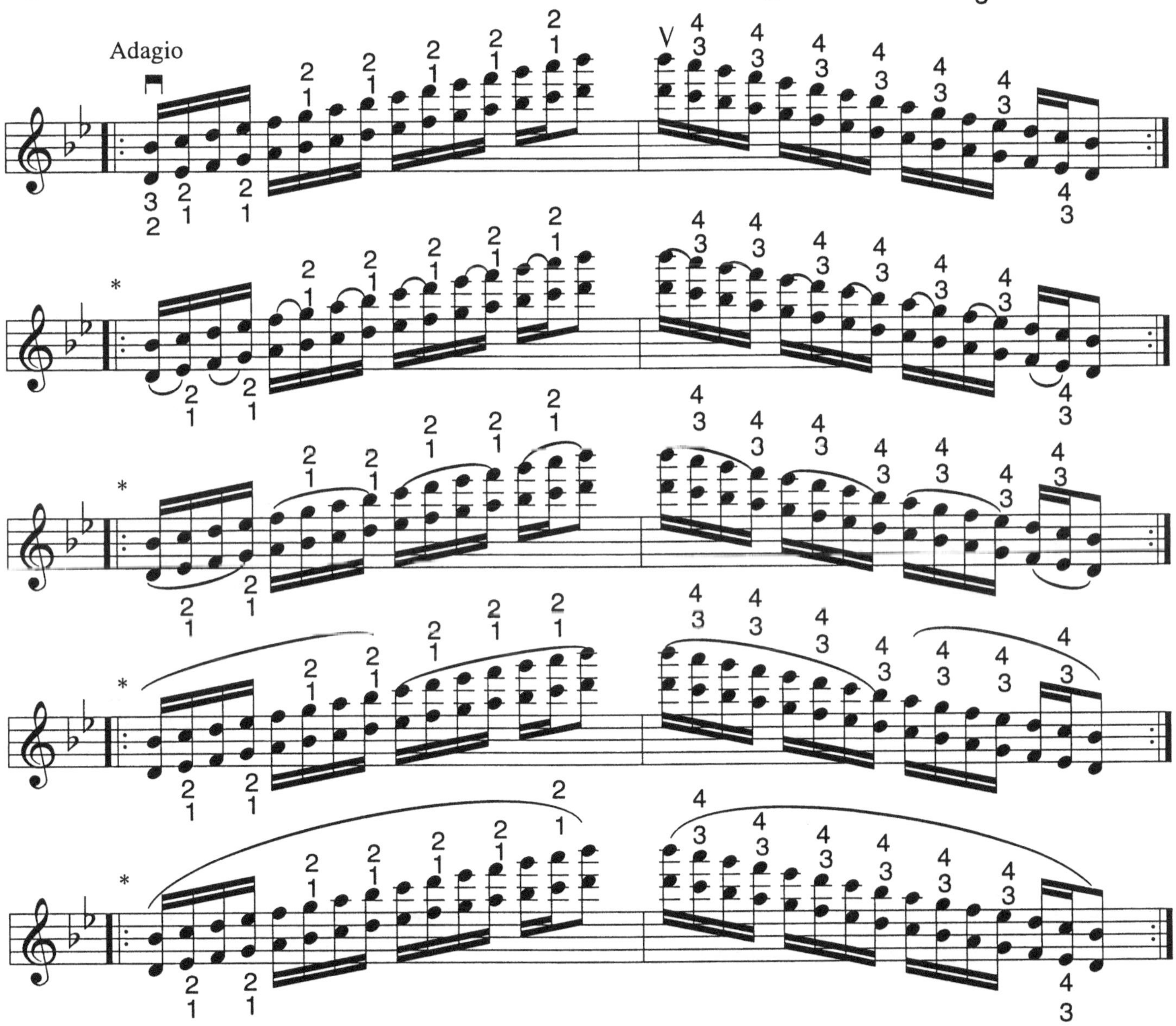

*tempo increases with each successive exercise

*tempo increases with each successive exercise

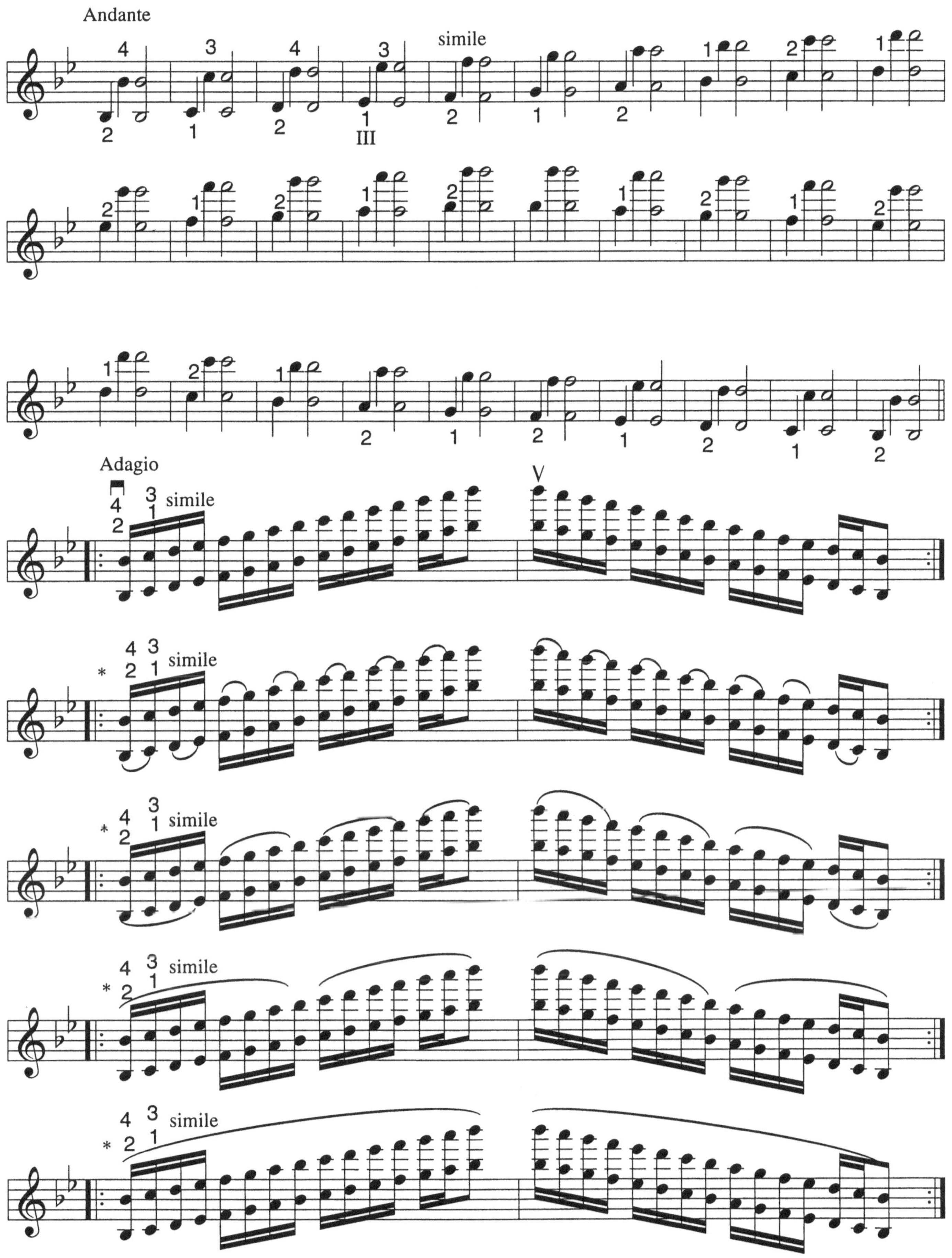

*tempo increases with each successive exercise

*tempo increases with each successive exercise

A Major

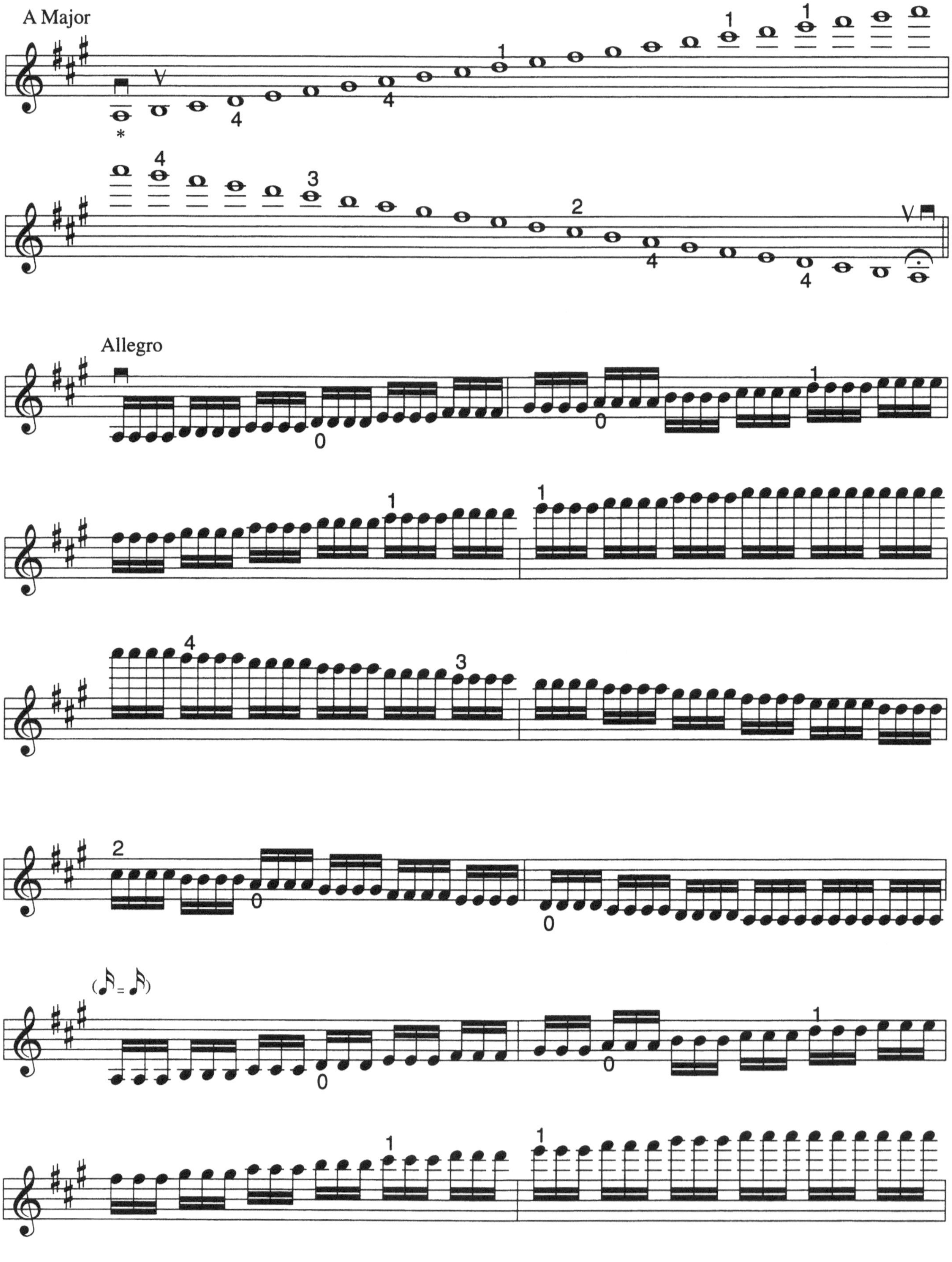

*each note as long as possible (10-20 seconds)

4 times detache/ 4 times spiccato

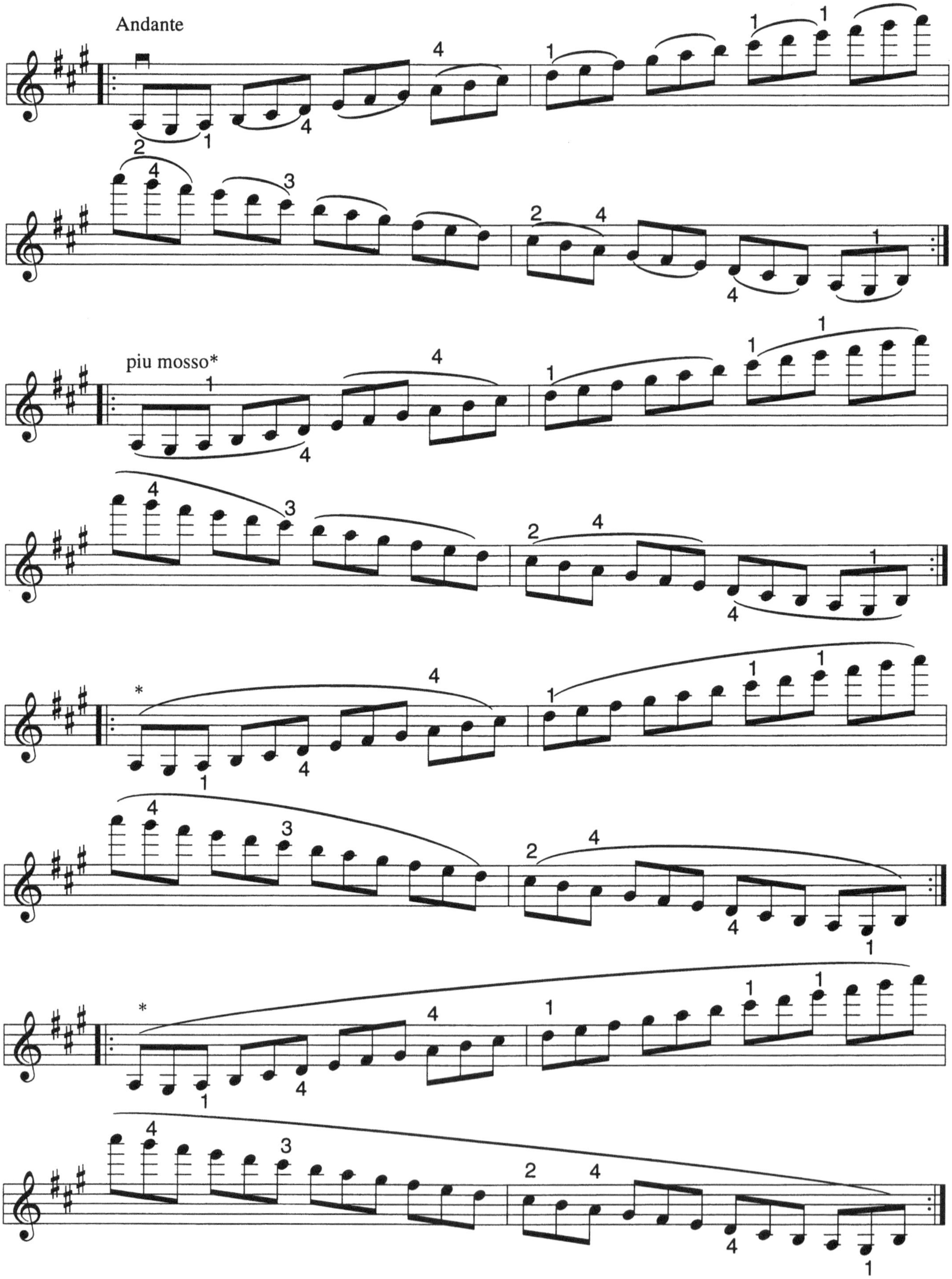

*tempo increases with each successive exercise

Four-octave scales

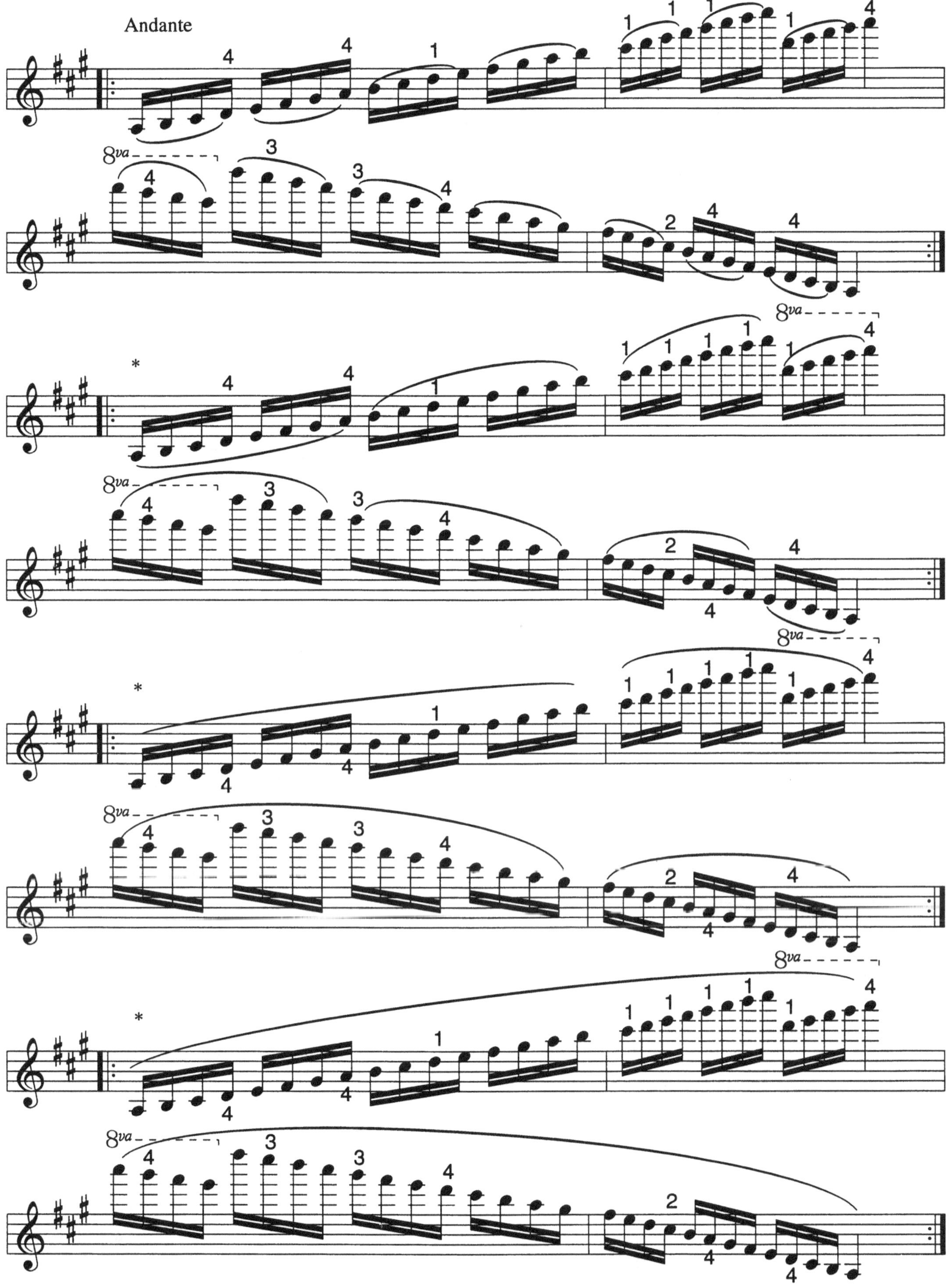

*tempo increases with each successive exercise

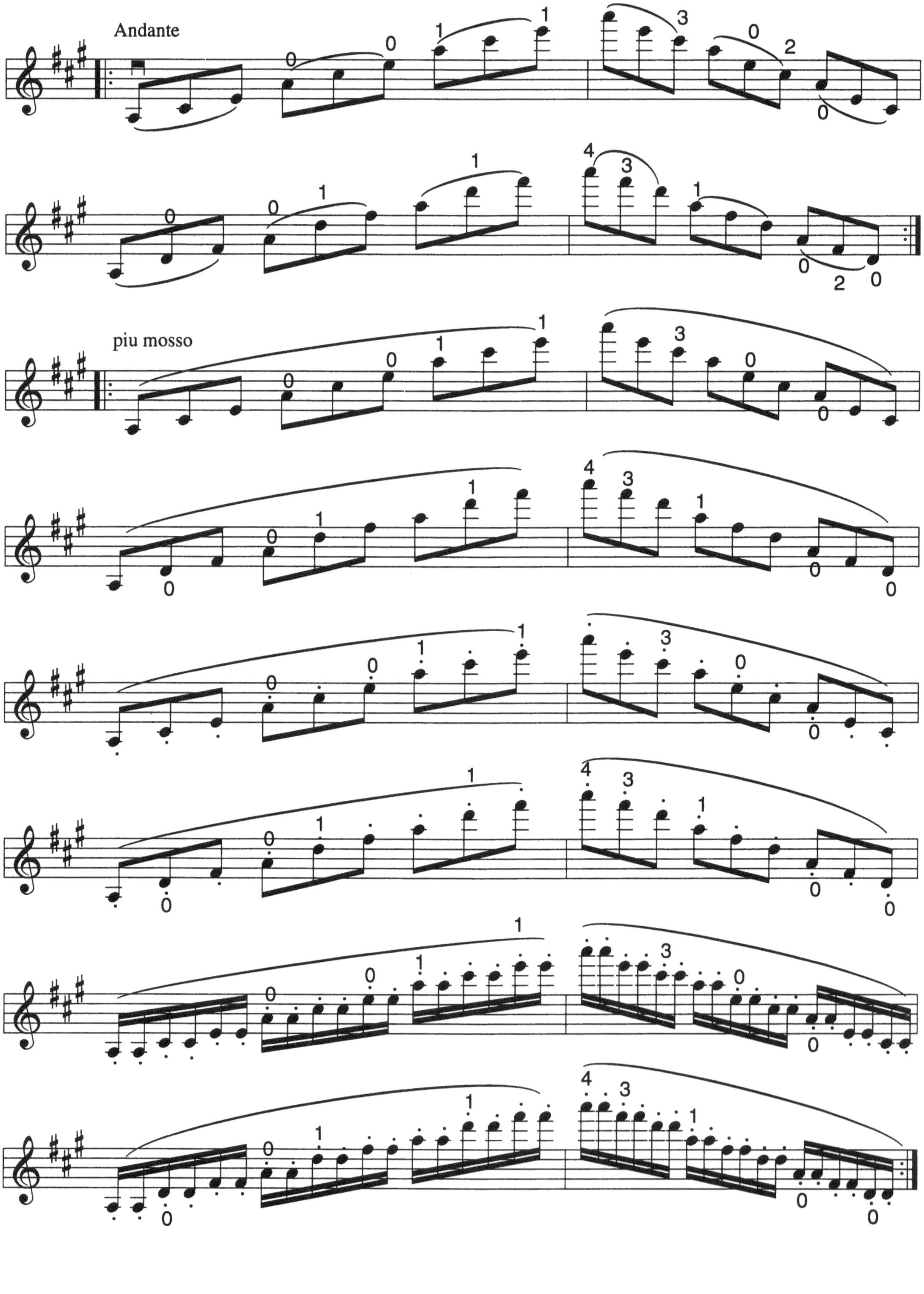
Andante
piu mosso

Four-octave arpeggios

*tempo increases with each successive exercise

*tempo increases with each successive exercise

*tempo increases with each successive exercise

*tempo increases with each successive exercise

*tempo increases with each successive exercise

E-Flat Major

E-Flat Major

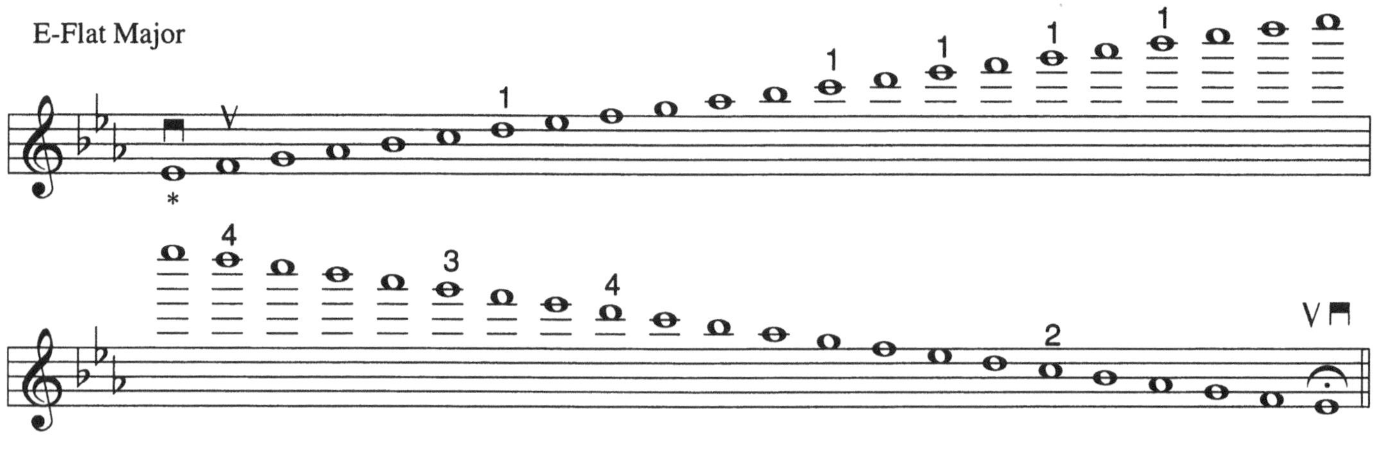

Allegro

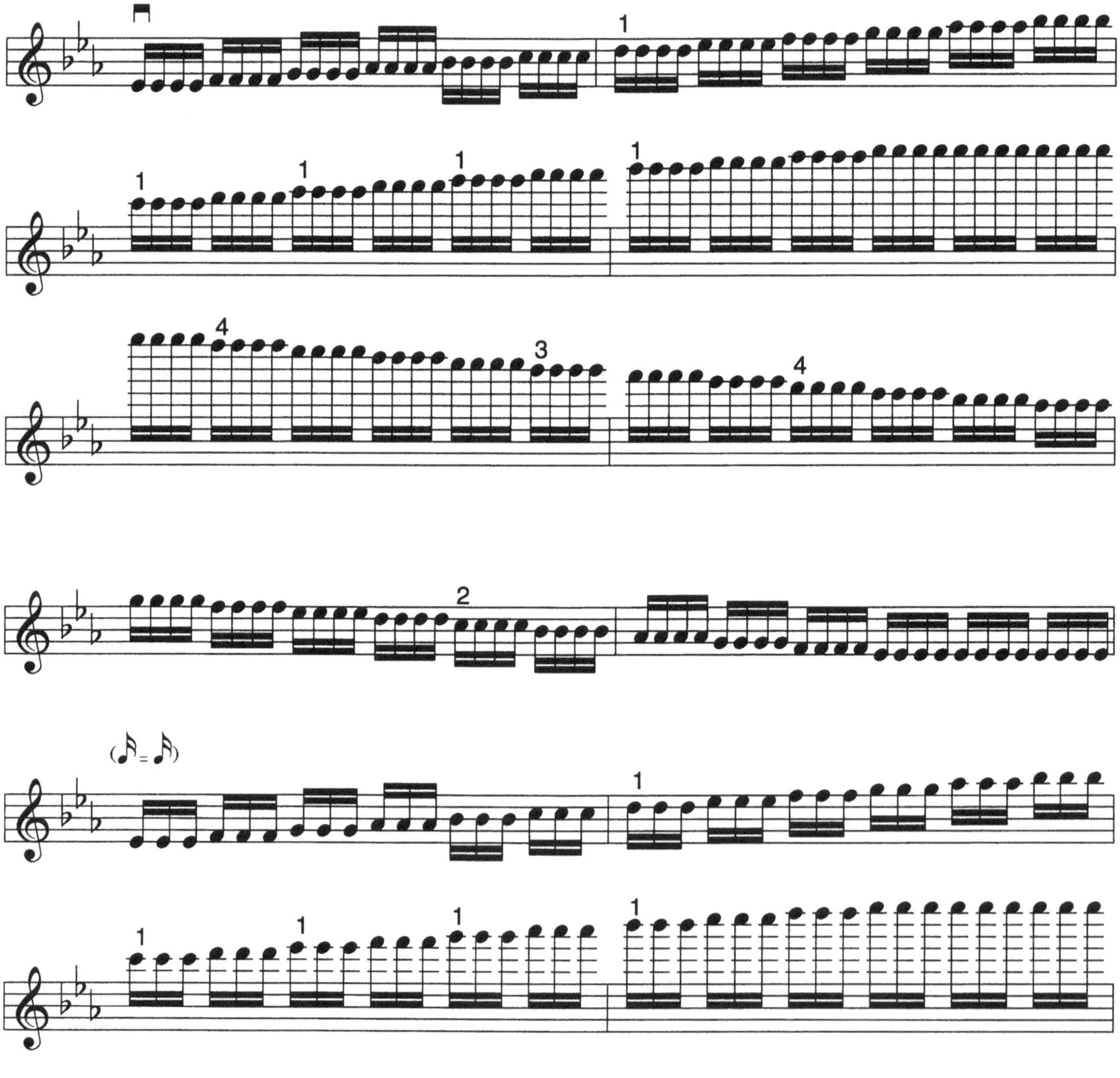

*each note as long as possible (10-20 seconds)

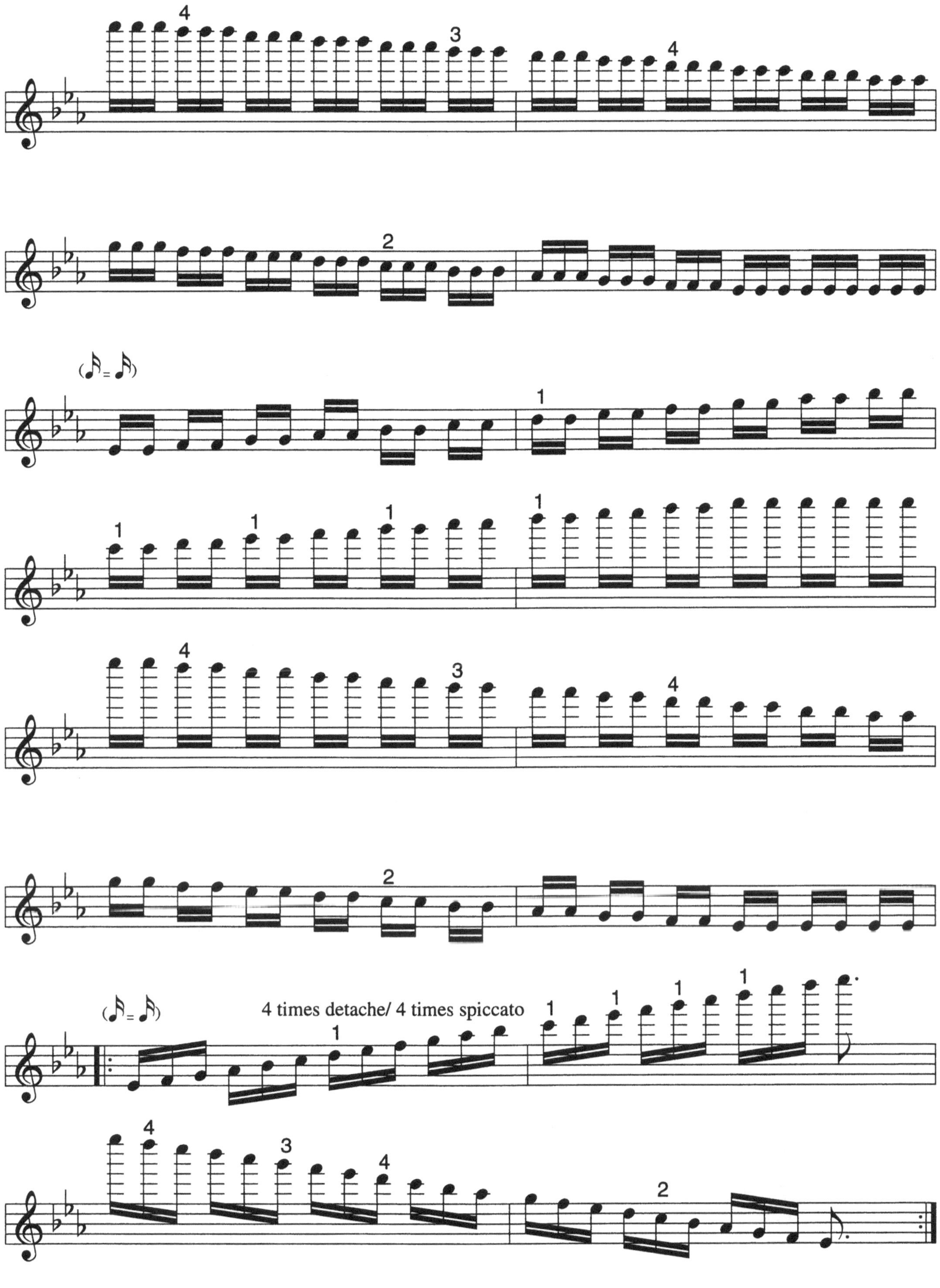
4 times detache/ 4 times spiccato

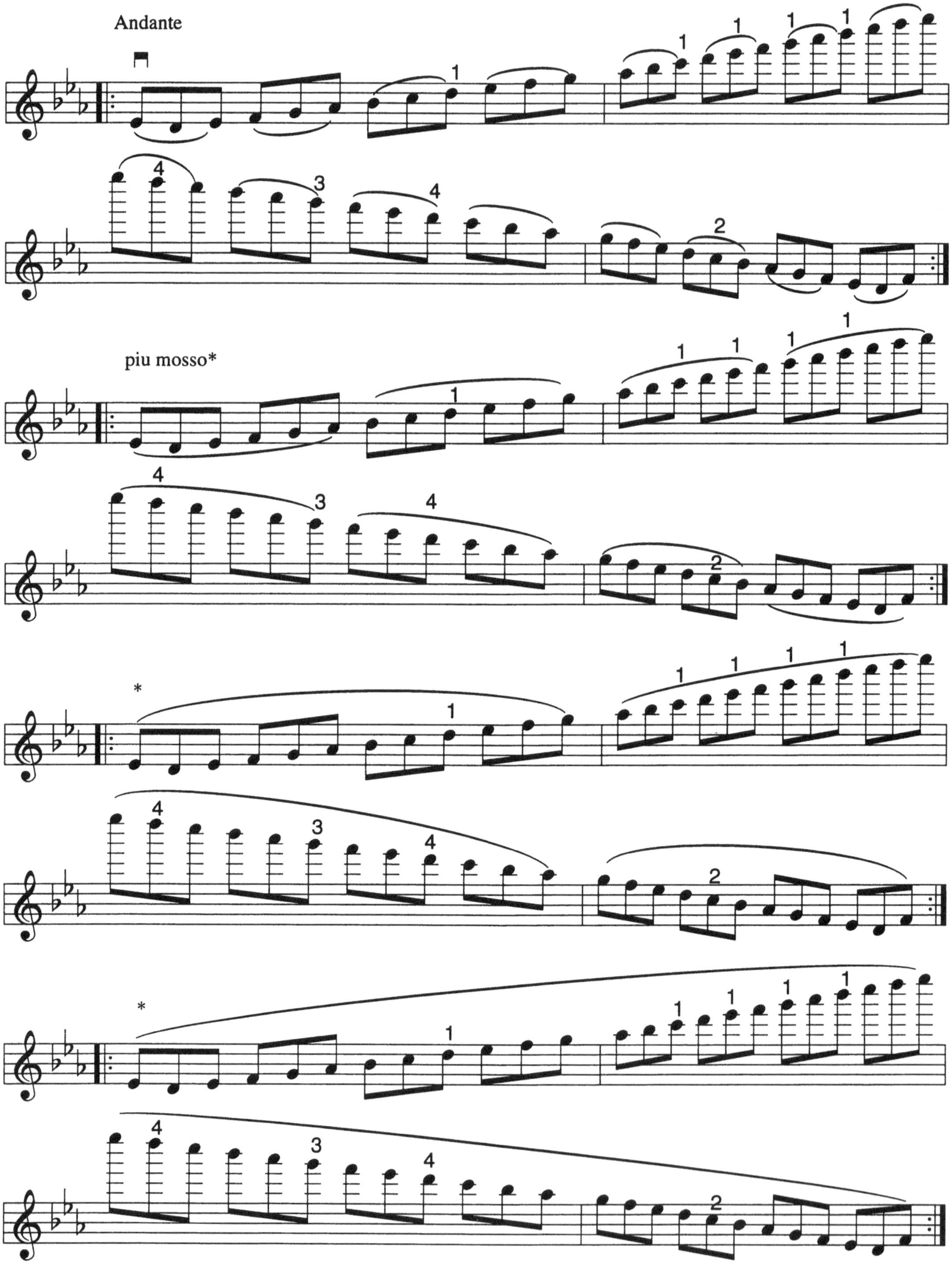

*tempo increases with each successive exercise

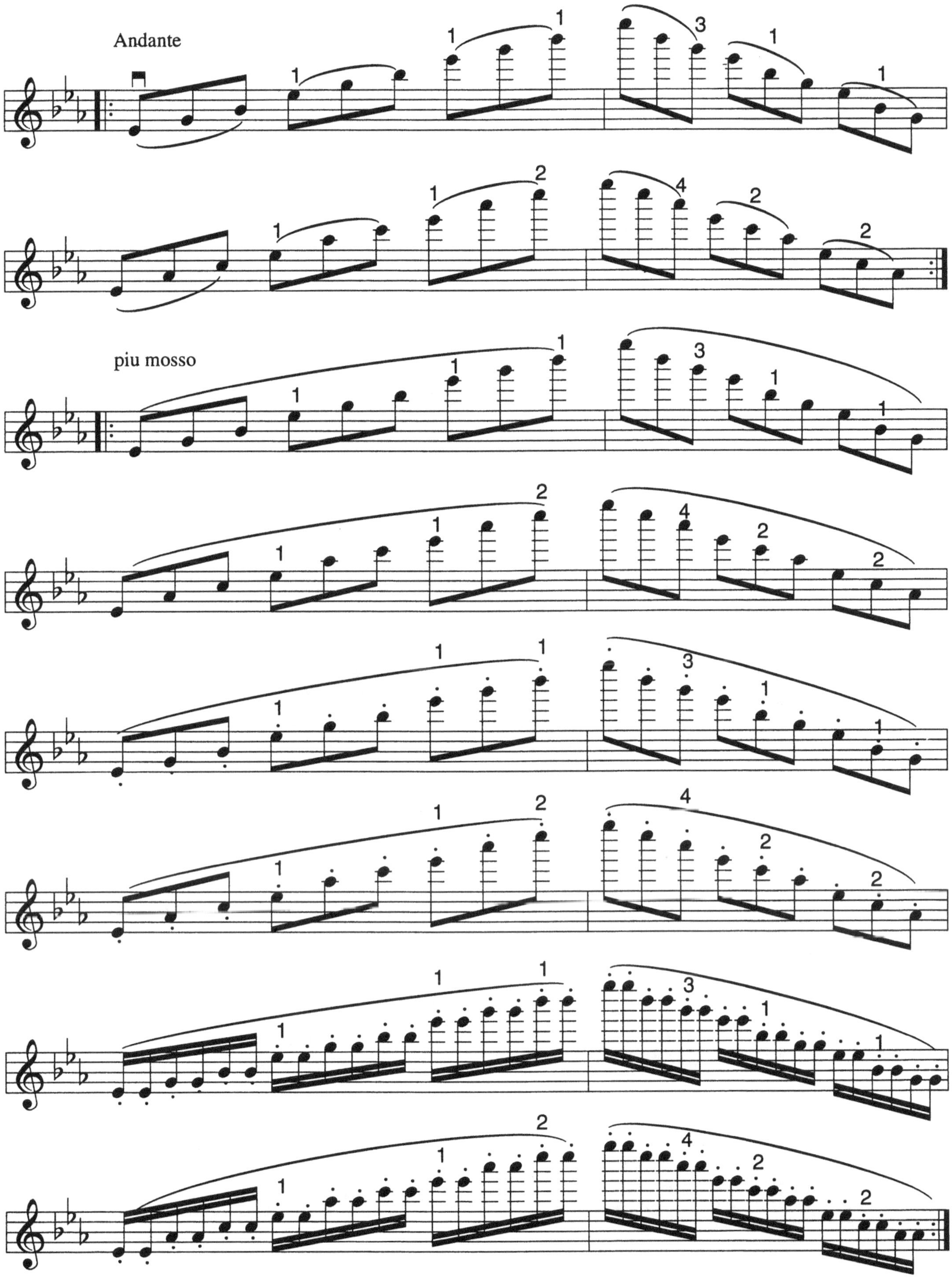
Andante
piu mosso

*tempo increases with each successive exercise

*tempo increases with each successive exercise

*tempo increases with each successive exercise

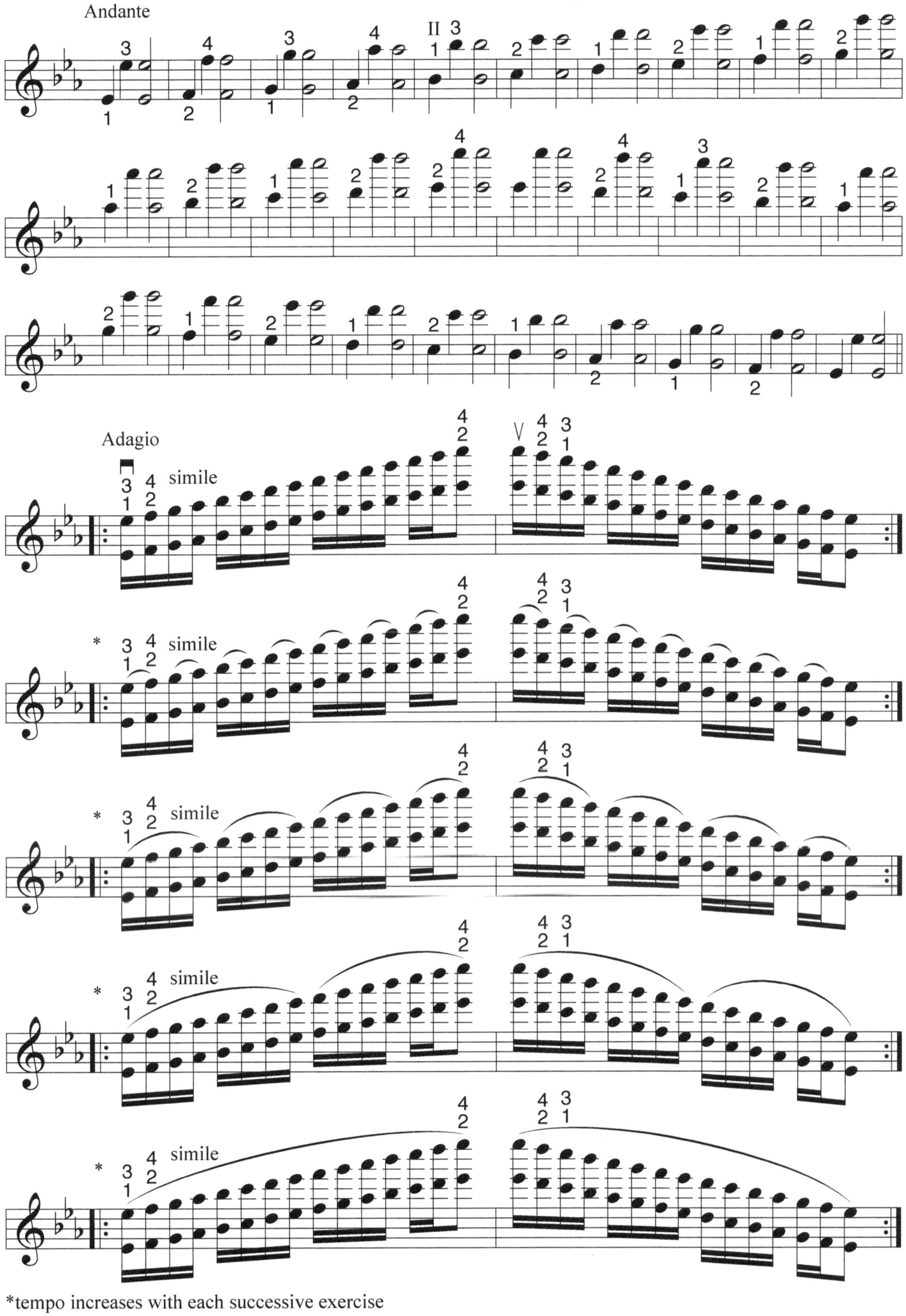

*tempo increases with each successive exercise

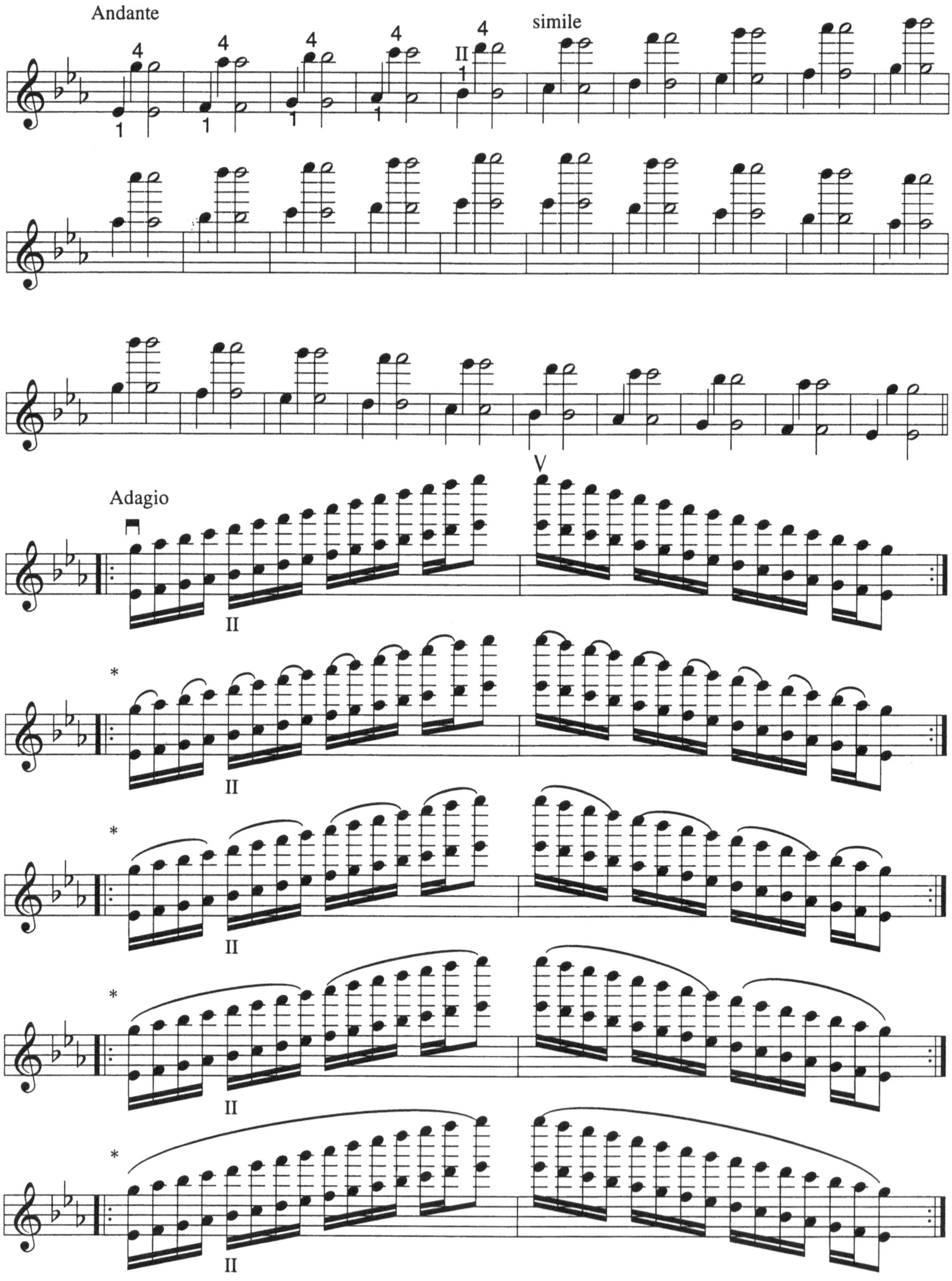

*tempo increases with each successive exercise

E Major

E Major

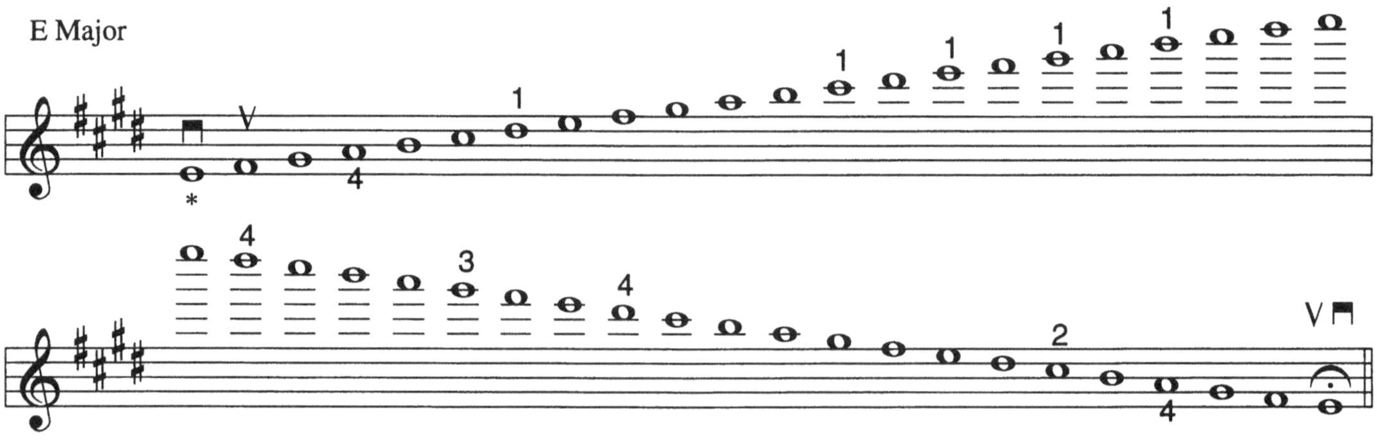

Allegro

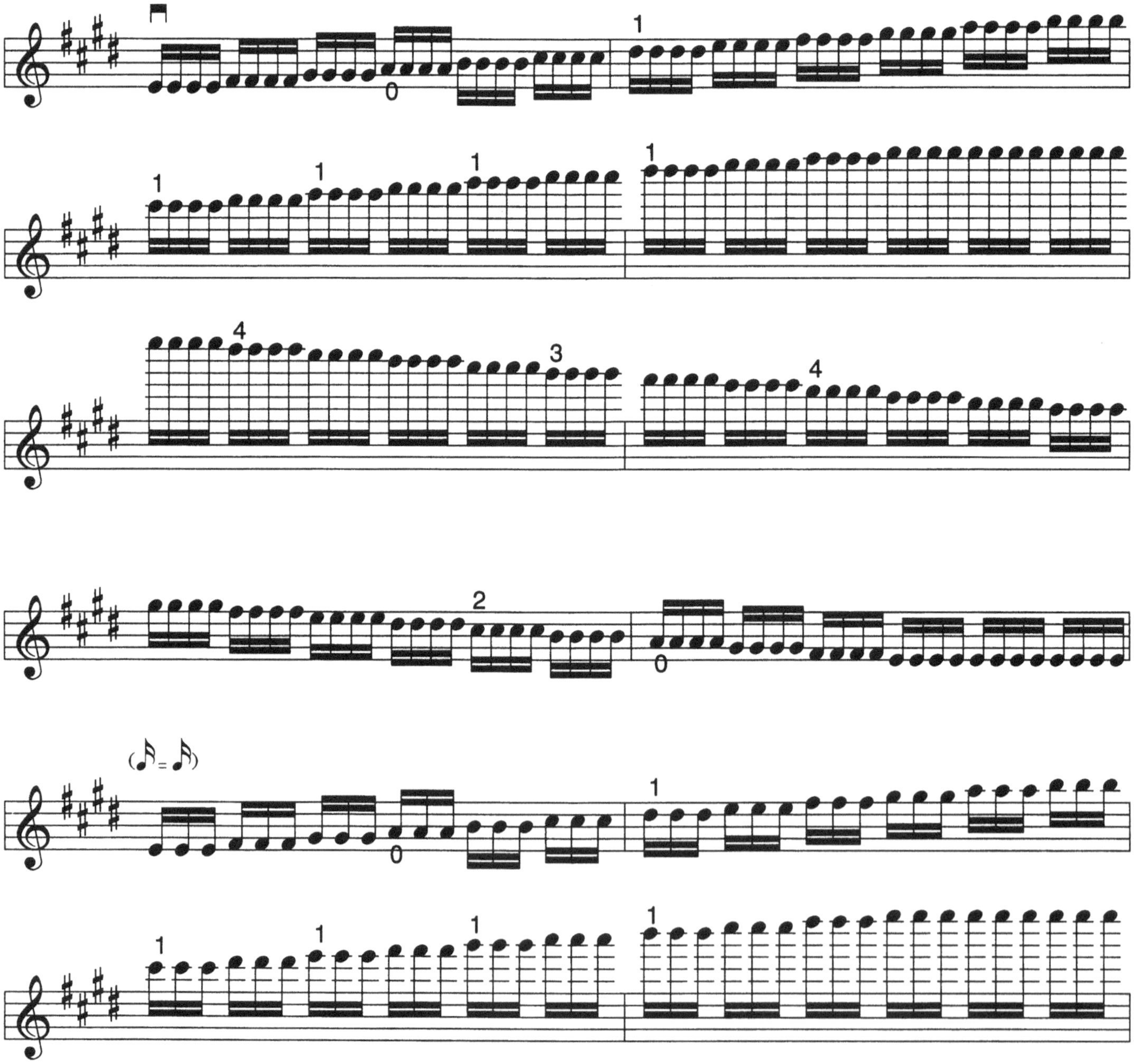

*each note as long as possible (10-20 seconds)

4 times detache/ 4 times spiccato

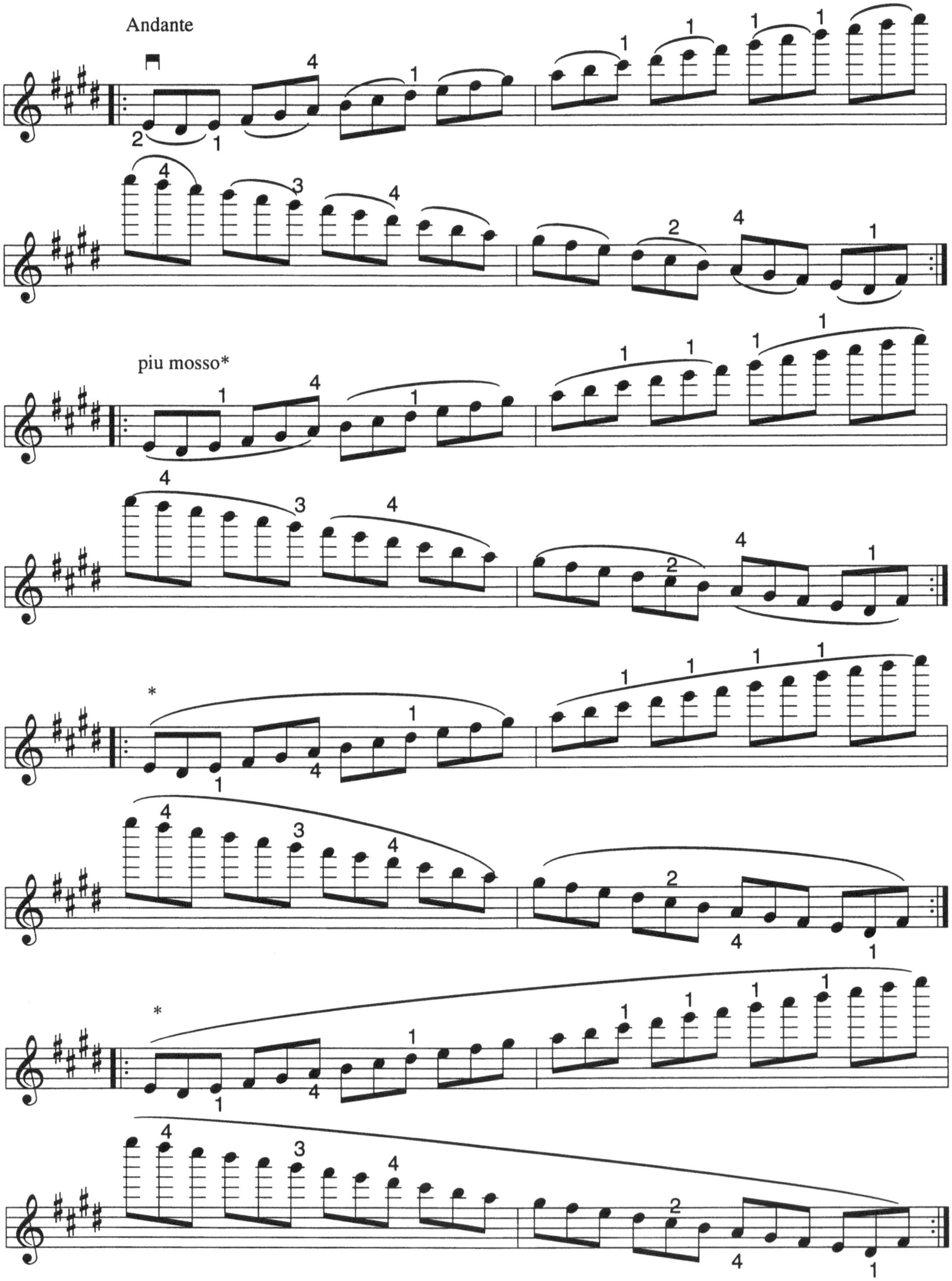

*tempo increases with each successive exercise

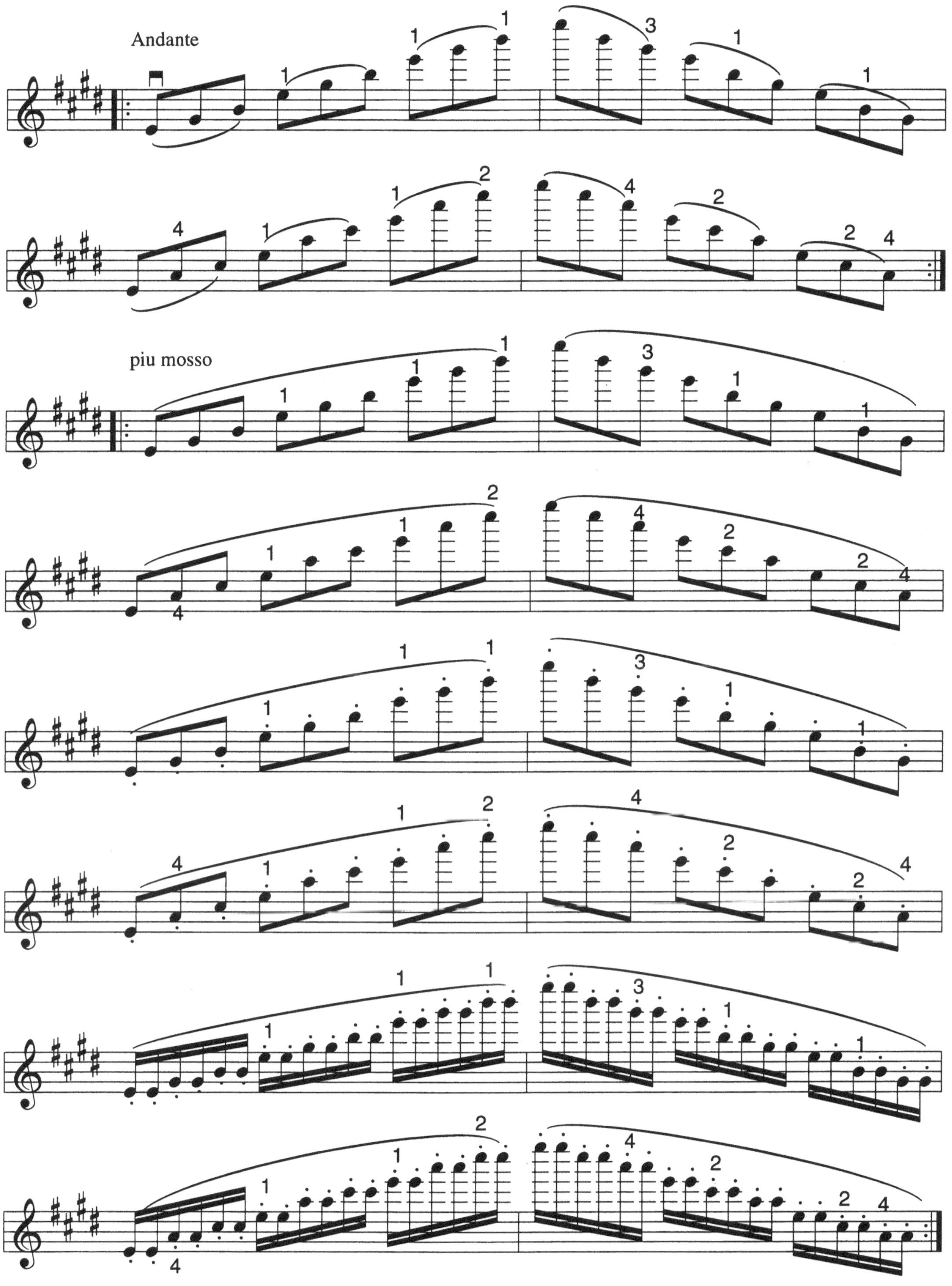
Andante
piu mosso

*tempo increases with each successive exercise

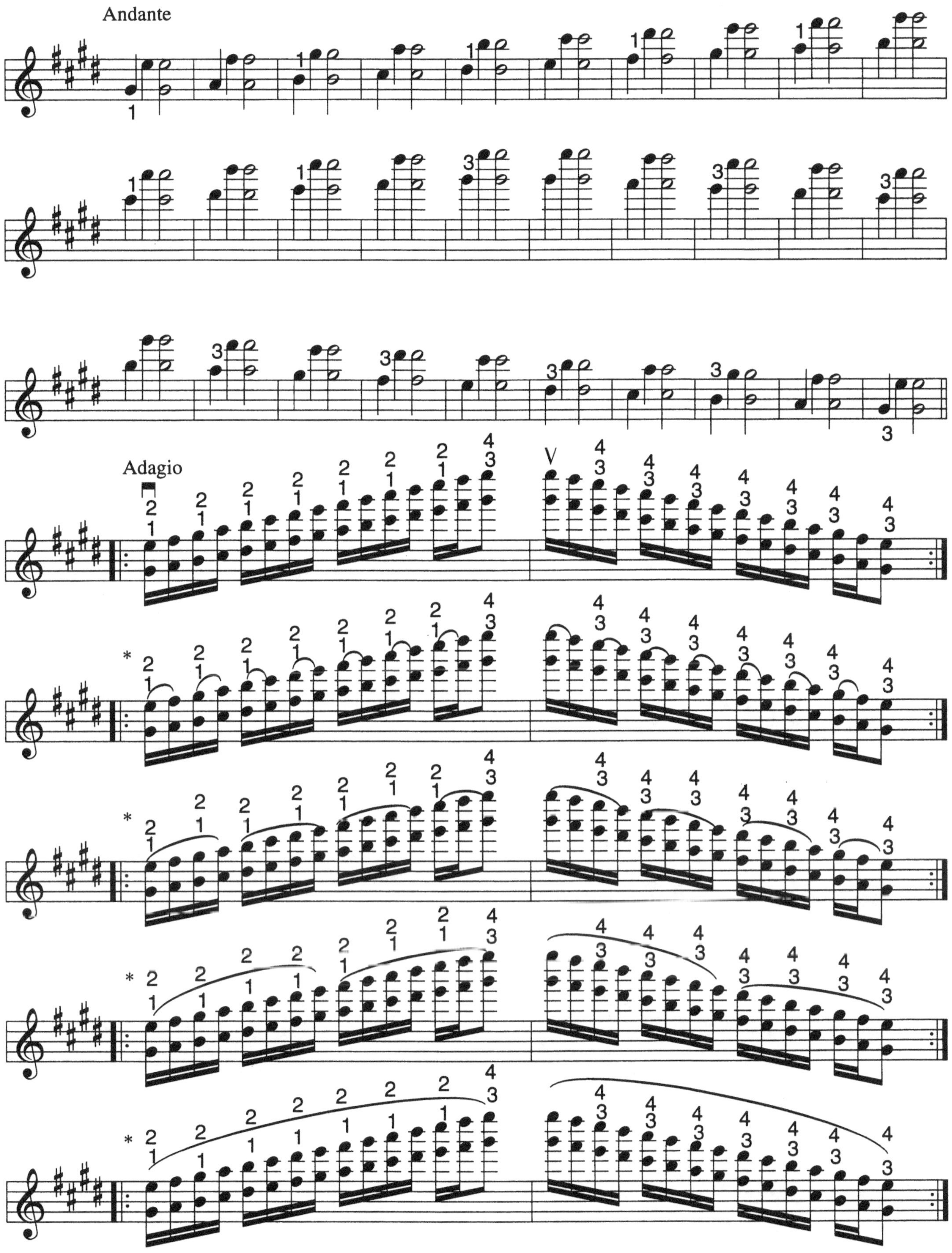

*tempo increases with each successive exercise

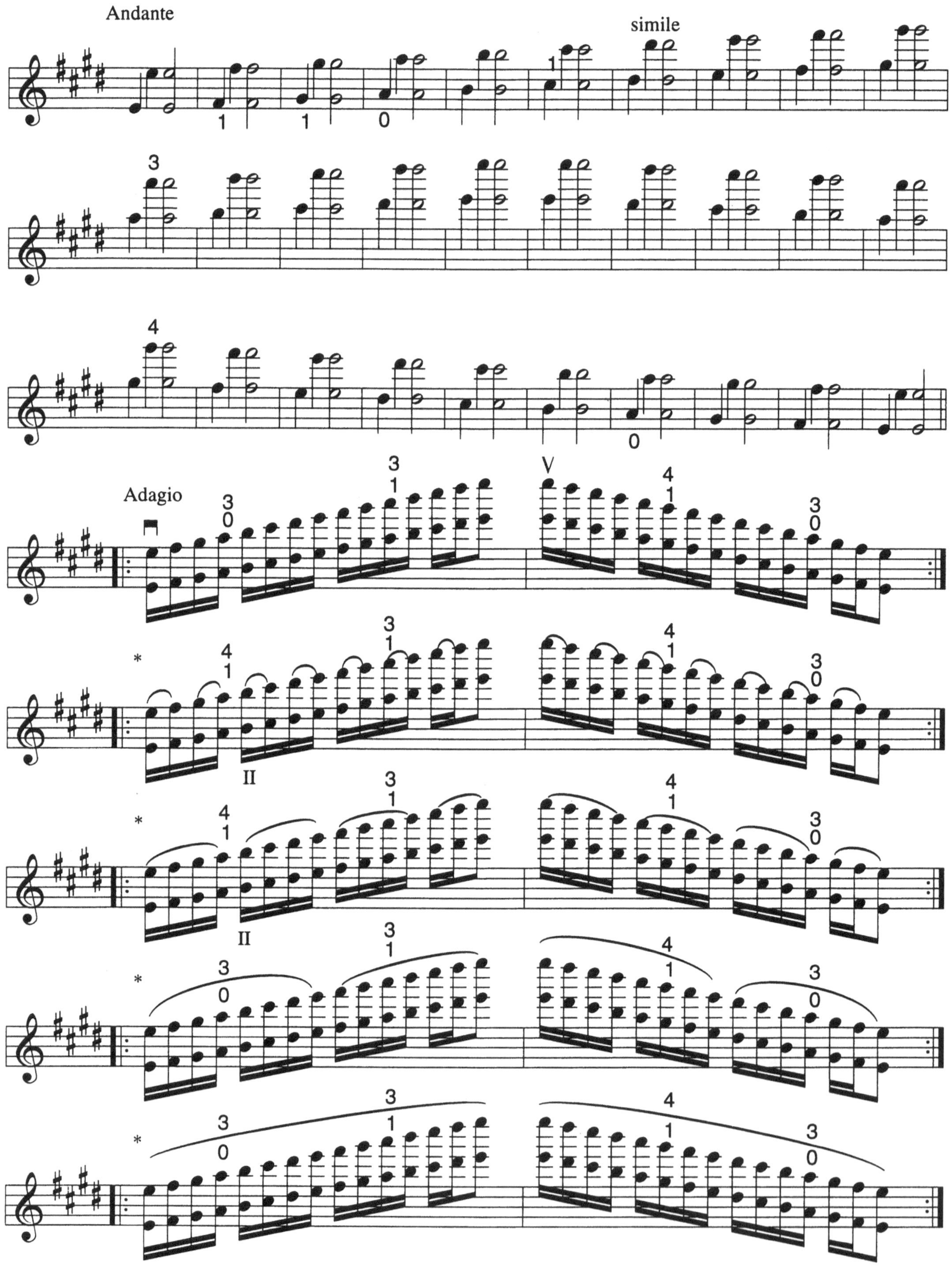

*tempo increases with each successive exercise

*tempo increases with each successive exercise

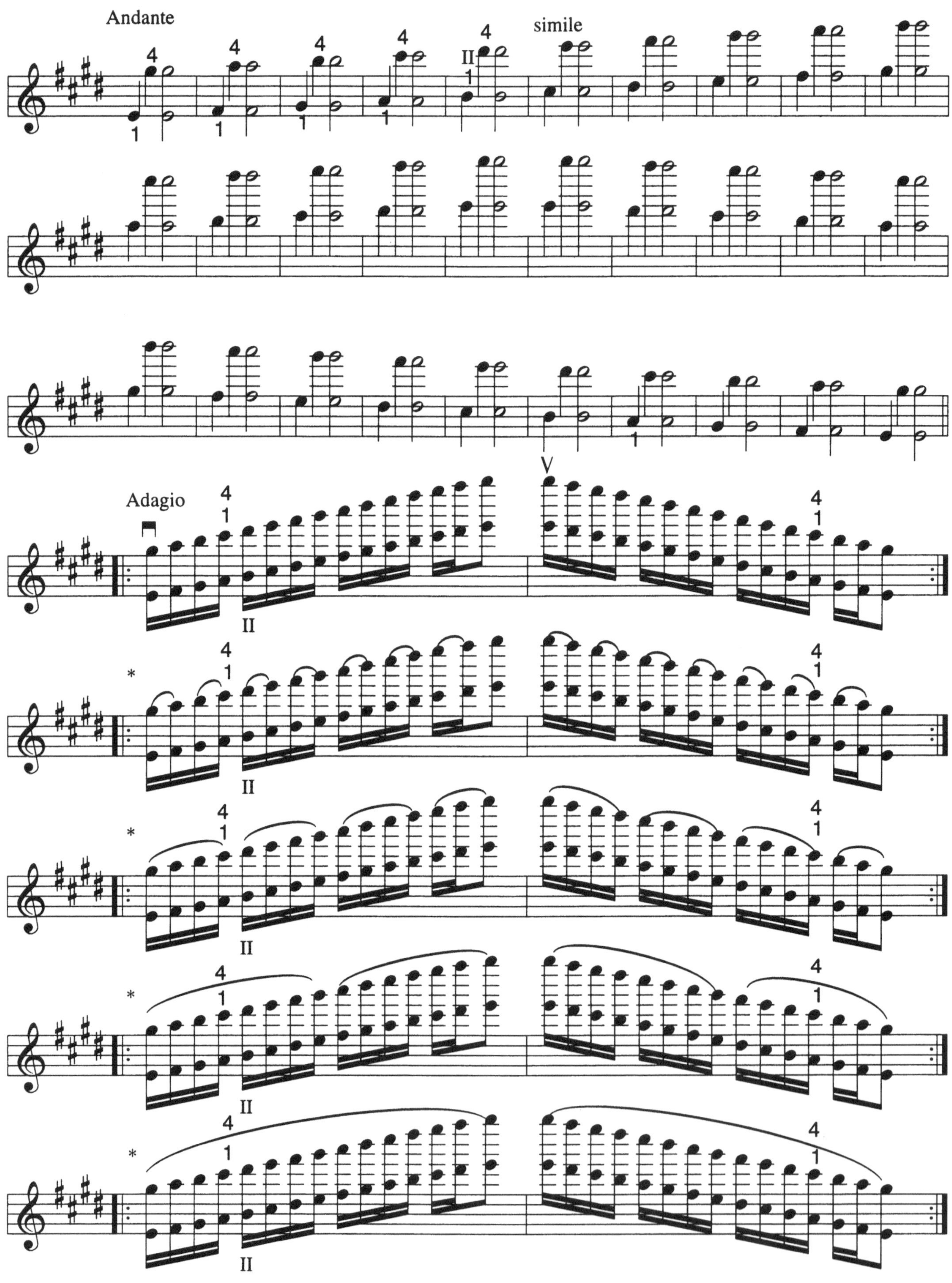

*tempo increases with each successive exercise

A-Flat Major

A-Flat Major

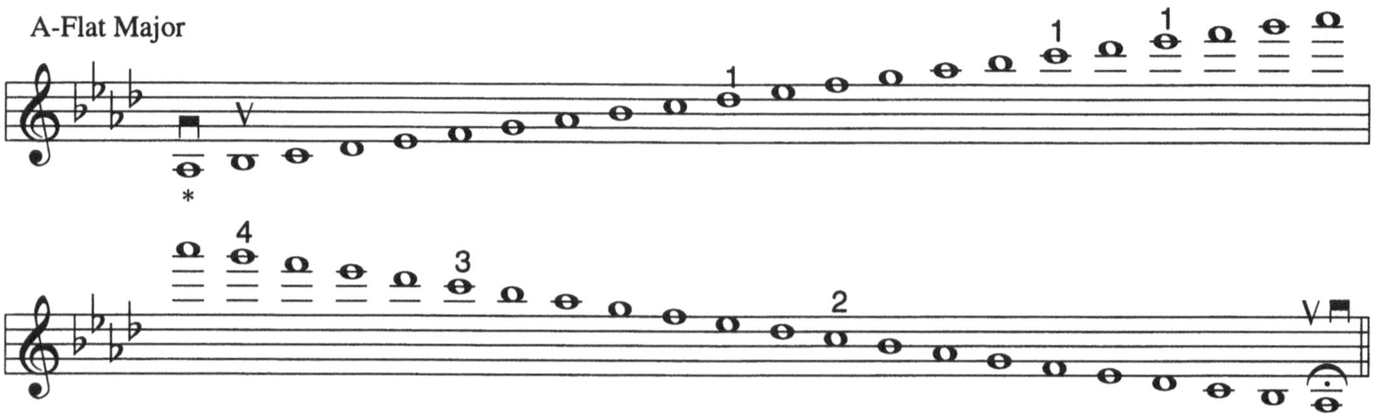

Allegro

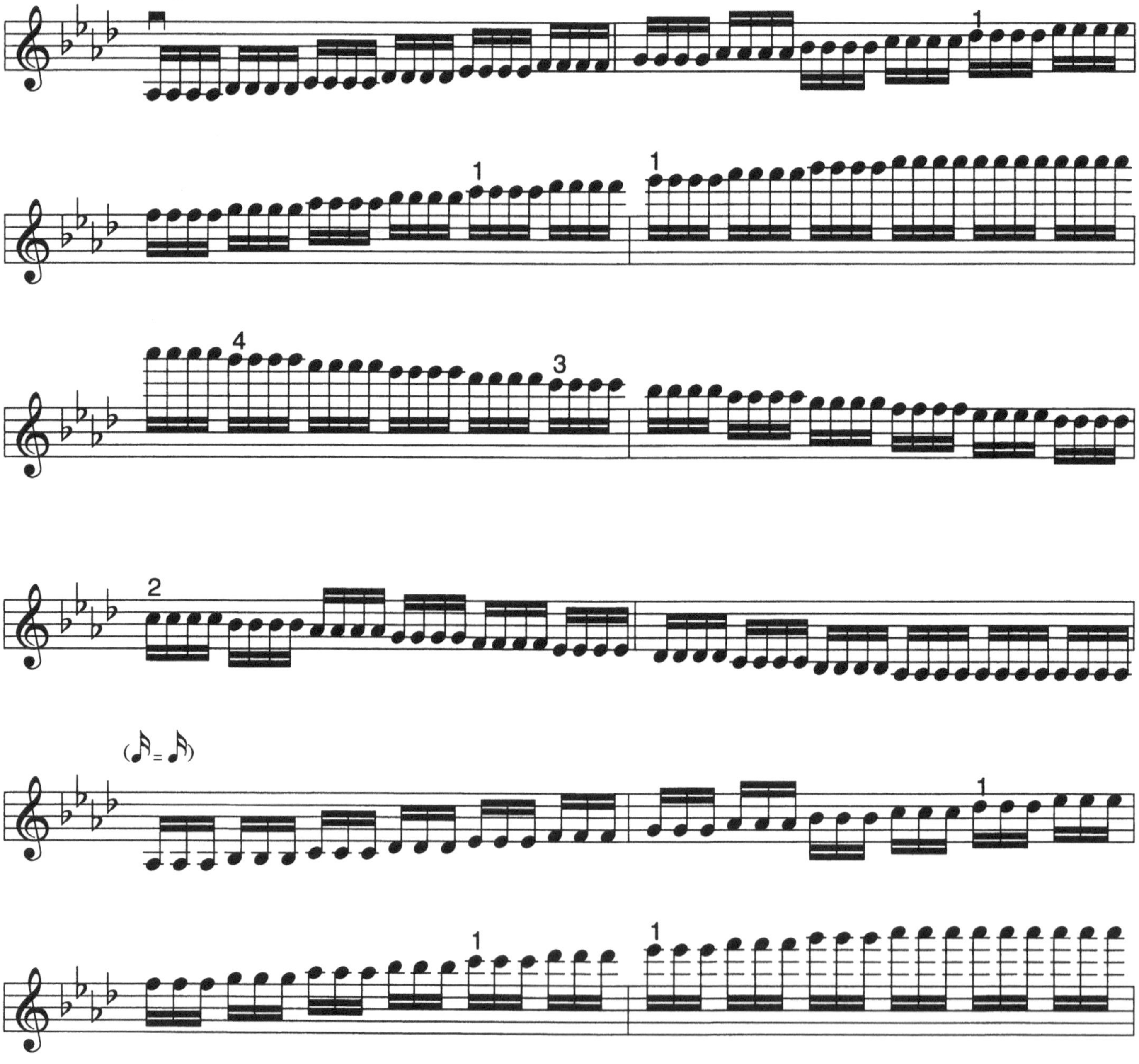

*each note as long as possible (10-20 seconds)

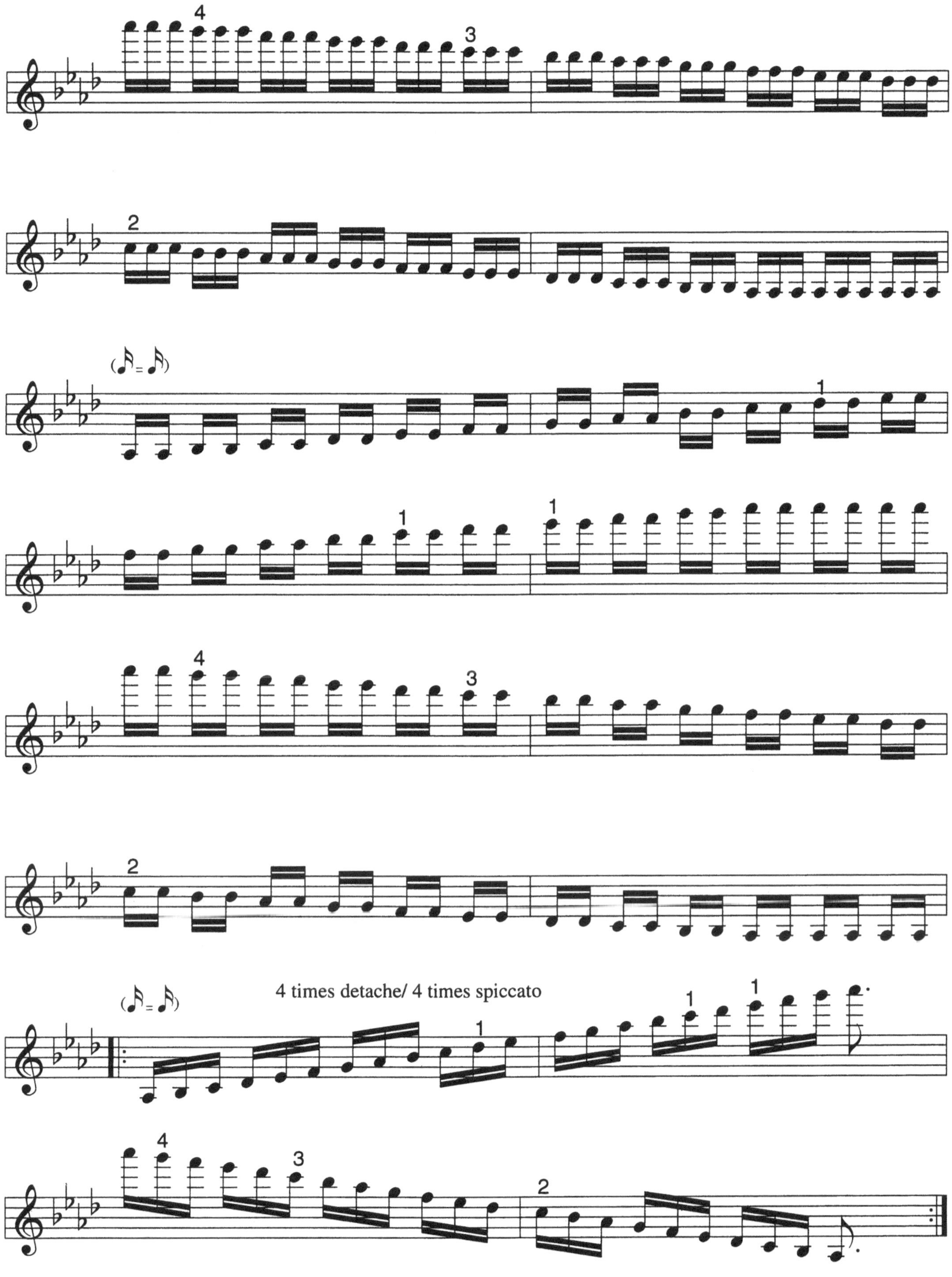
4 times detache/ 4 times spiccato

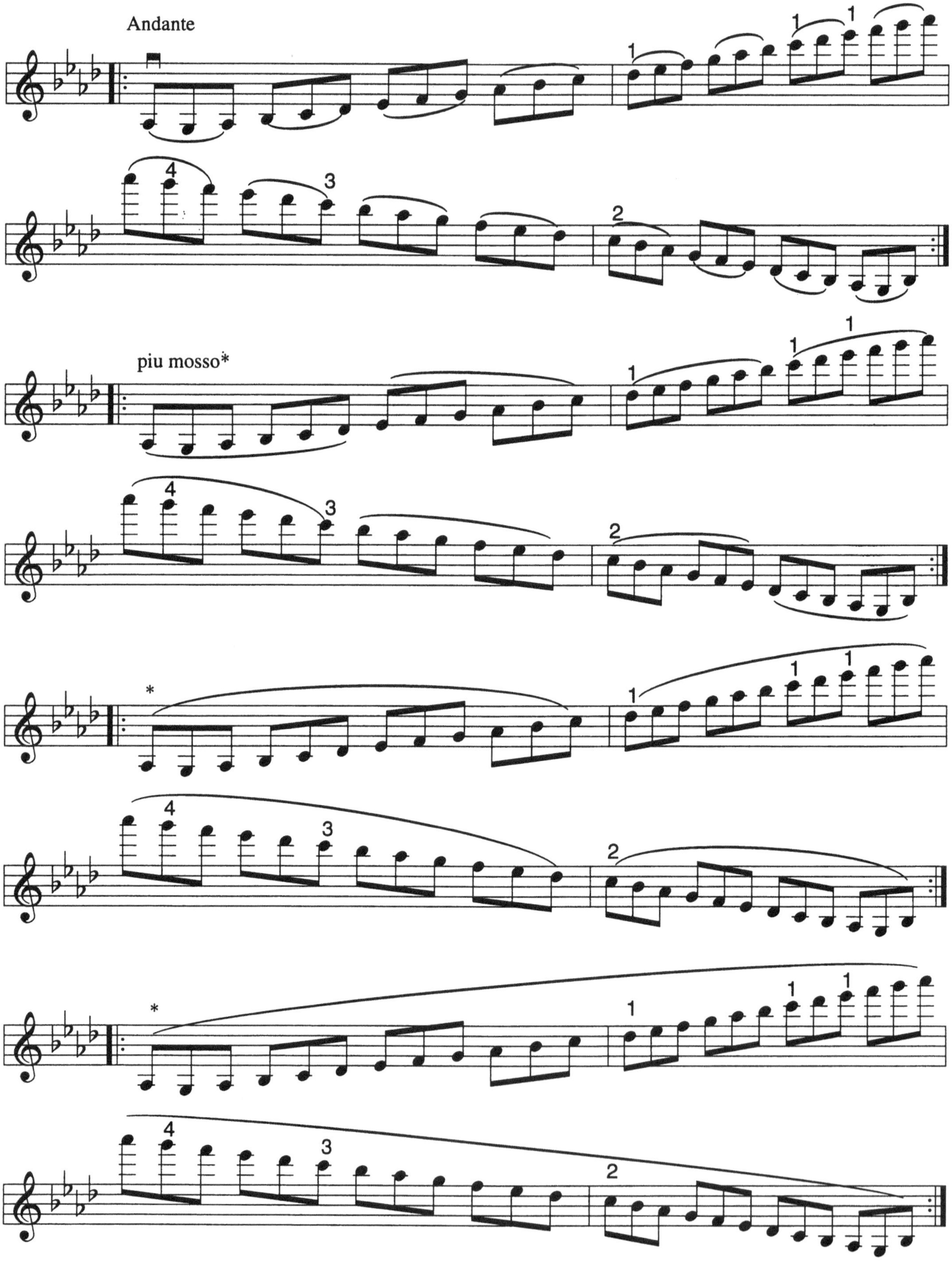

*tempo increases with each successive exercise

Four-octave Scales

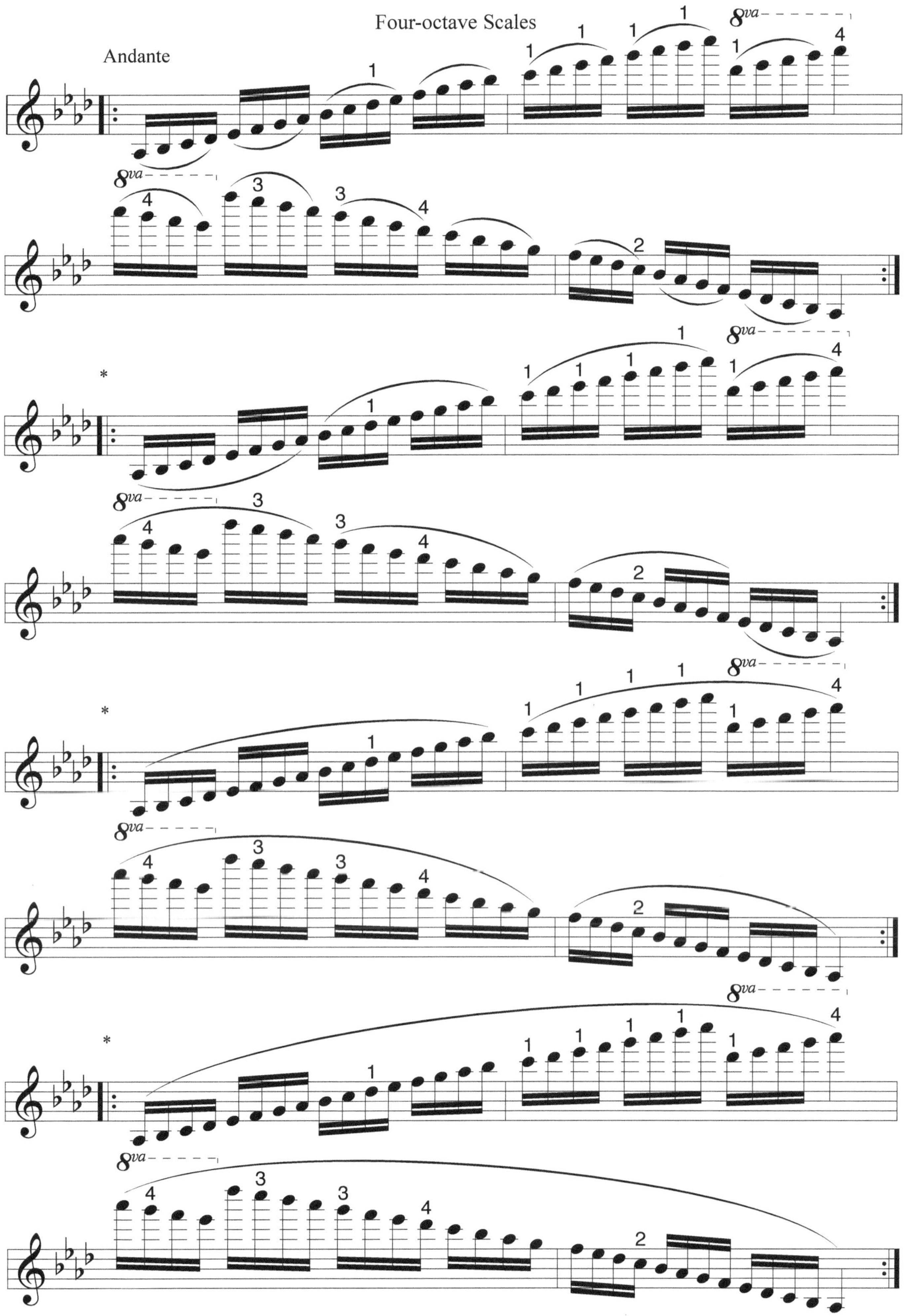

*tempo increases with each successive exercise

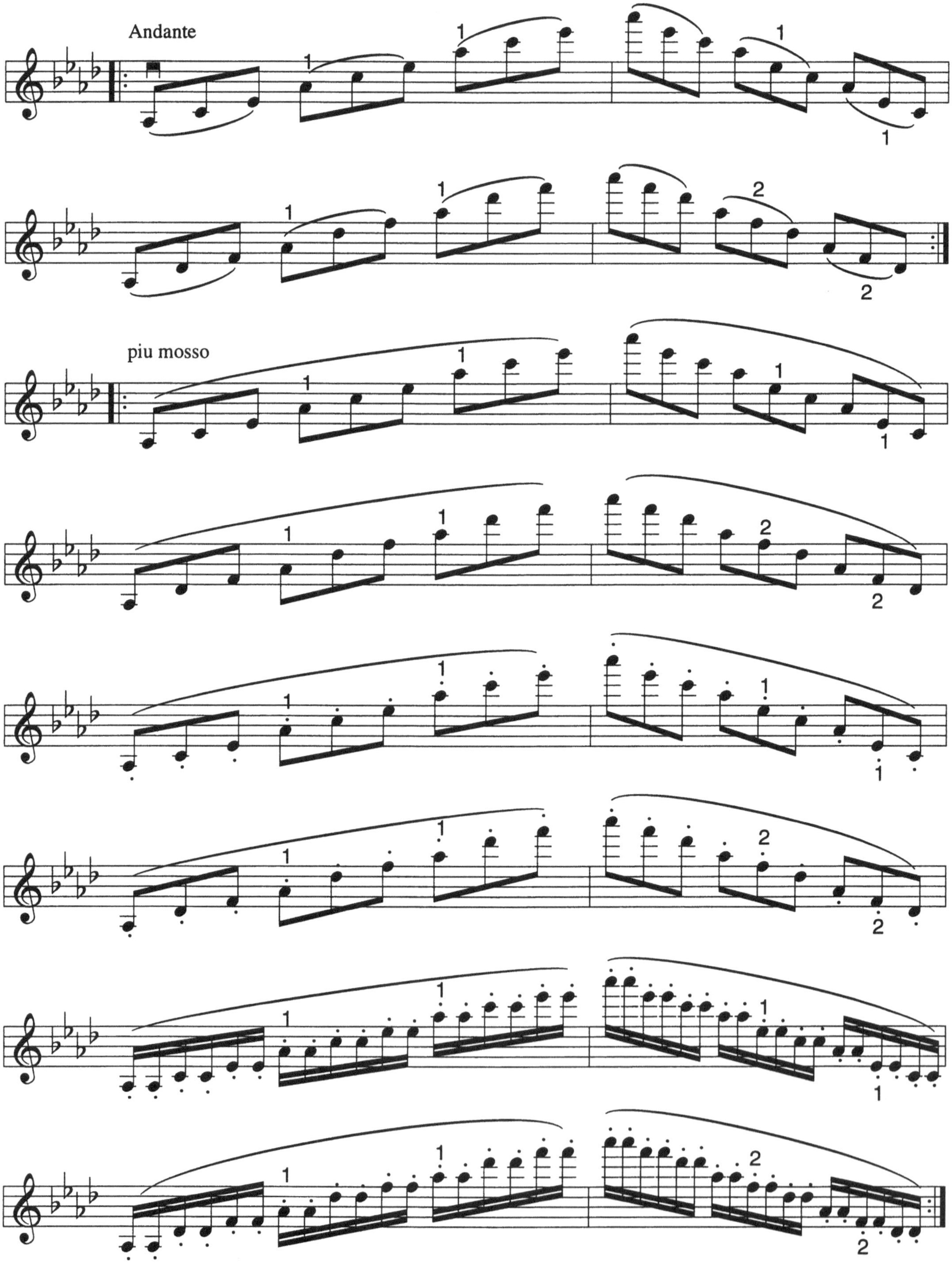
Andante
piu mosso

Four-octave arpeggios

*tempo increases with each successive exercise

*tempo increases with each successive exercise

*tempo increases with each successive exercise

*tempo increases with each successive exercise

*tempo increases with each successive exercise

B Major

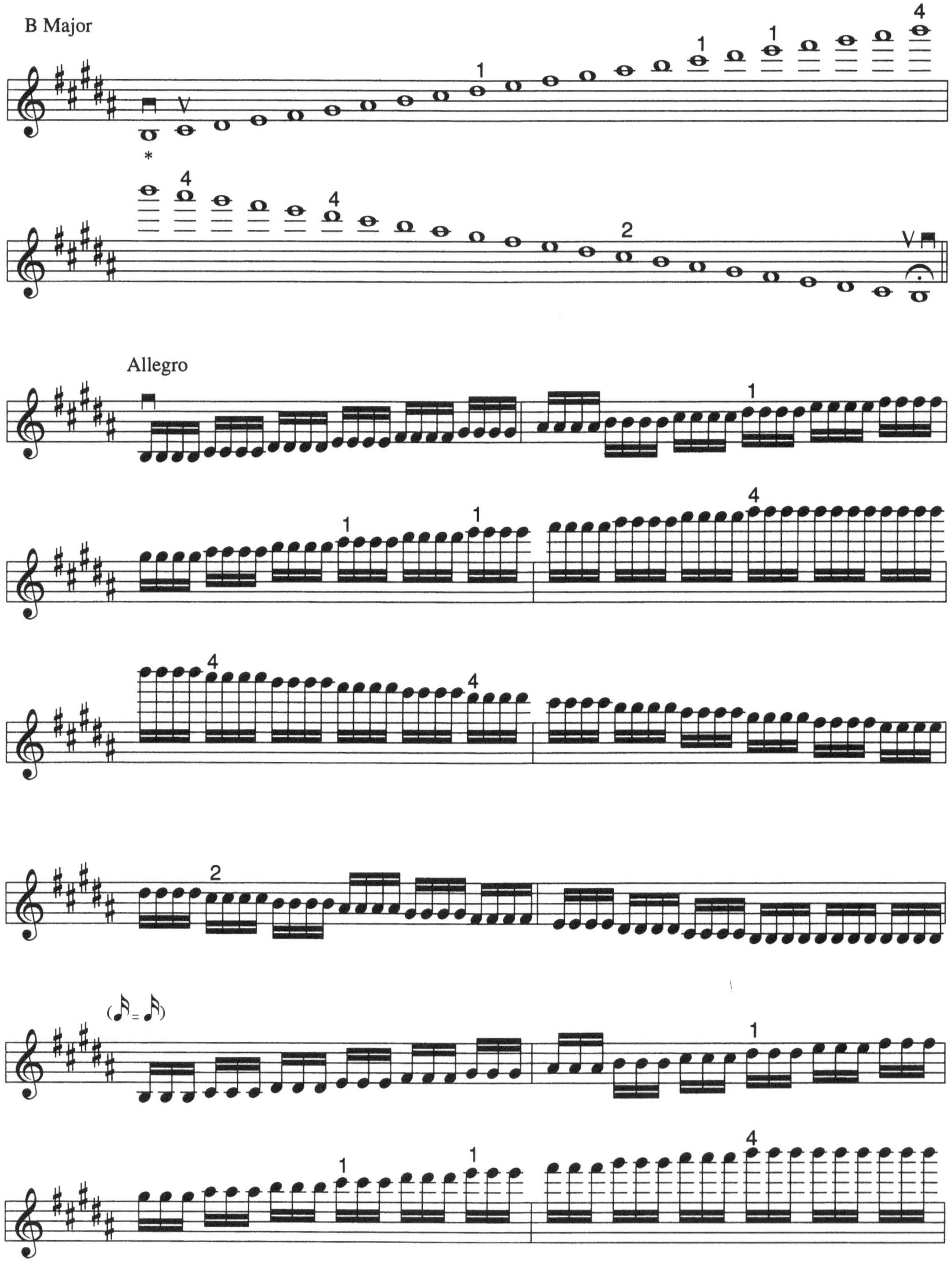

*each note as long as possible (10-20 seconds)

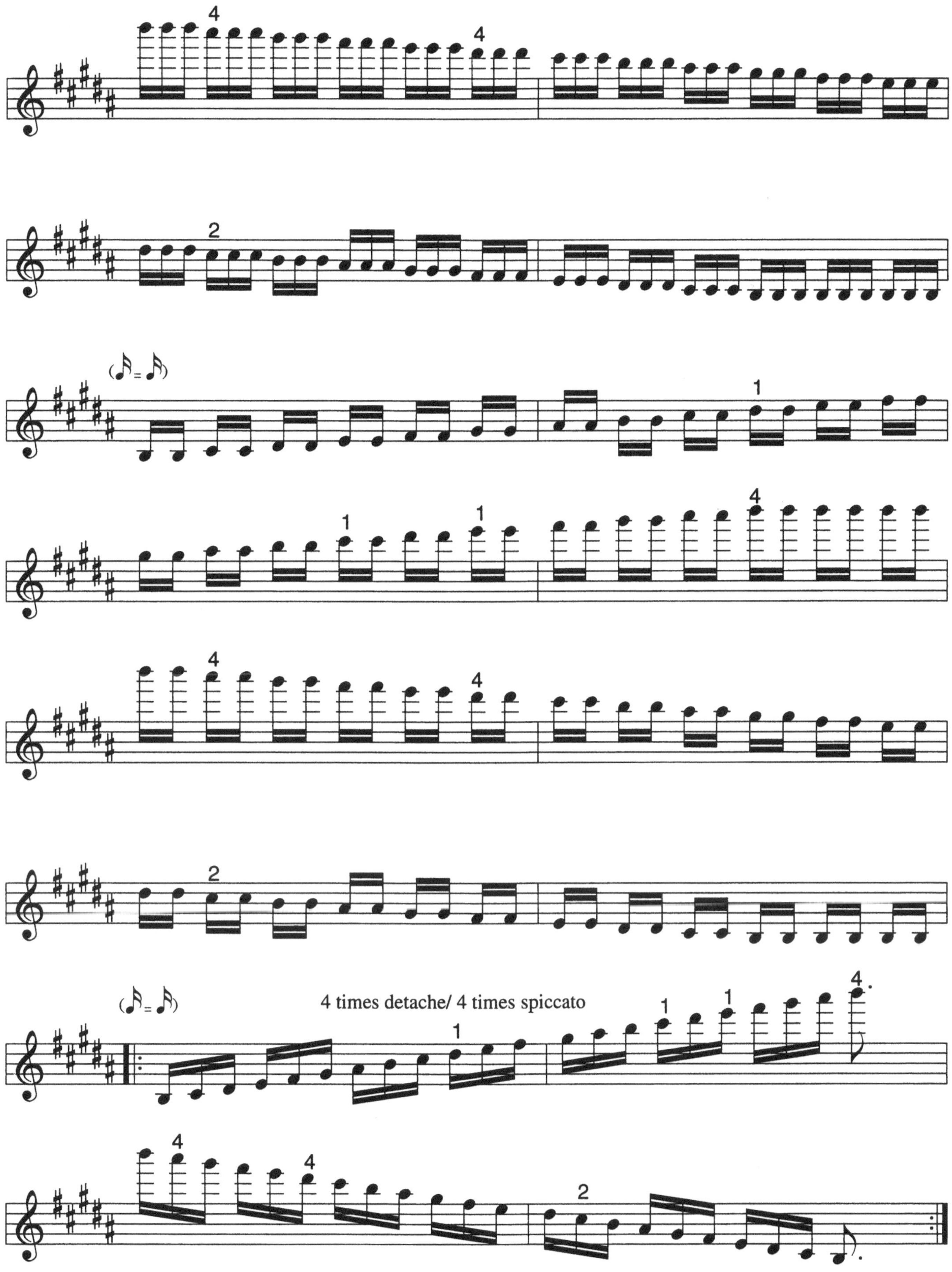
4 times detache/ 4 times spiccato

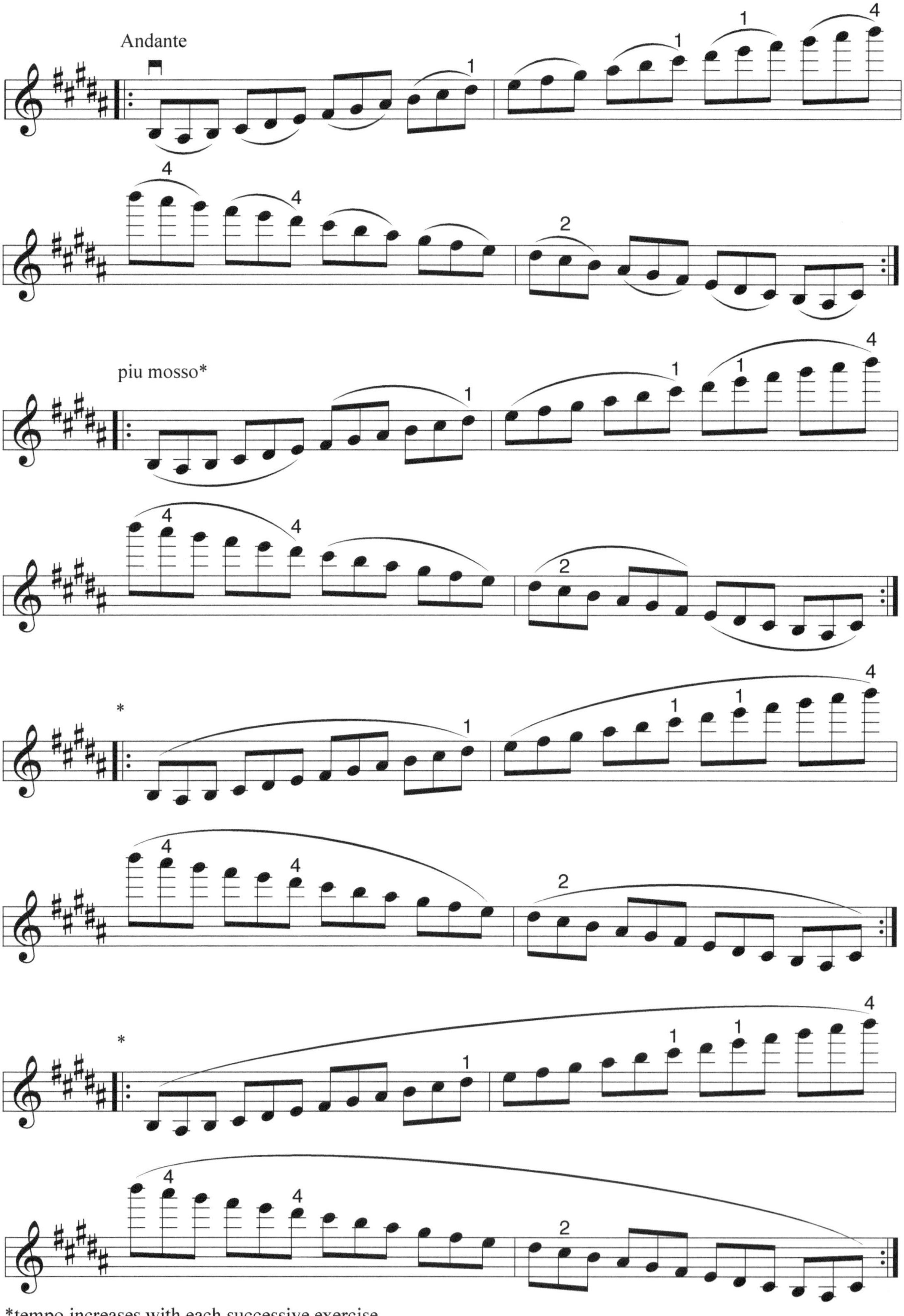

*tempo increases with each successive exercise

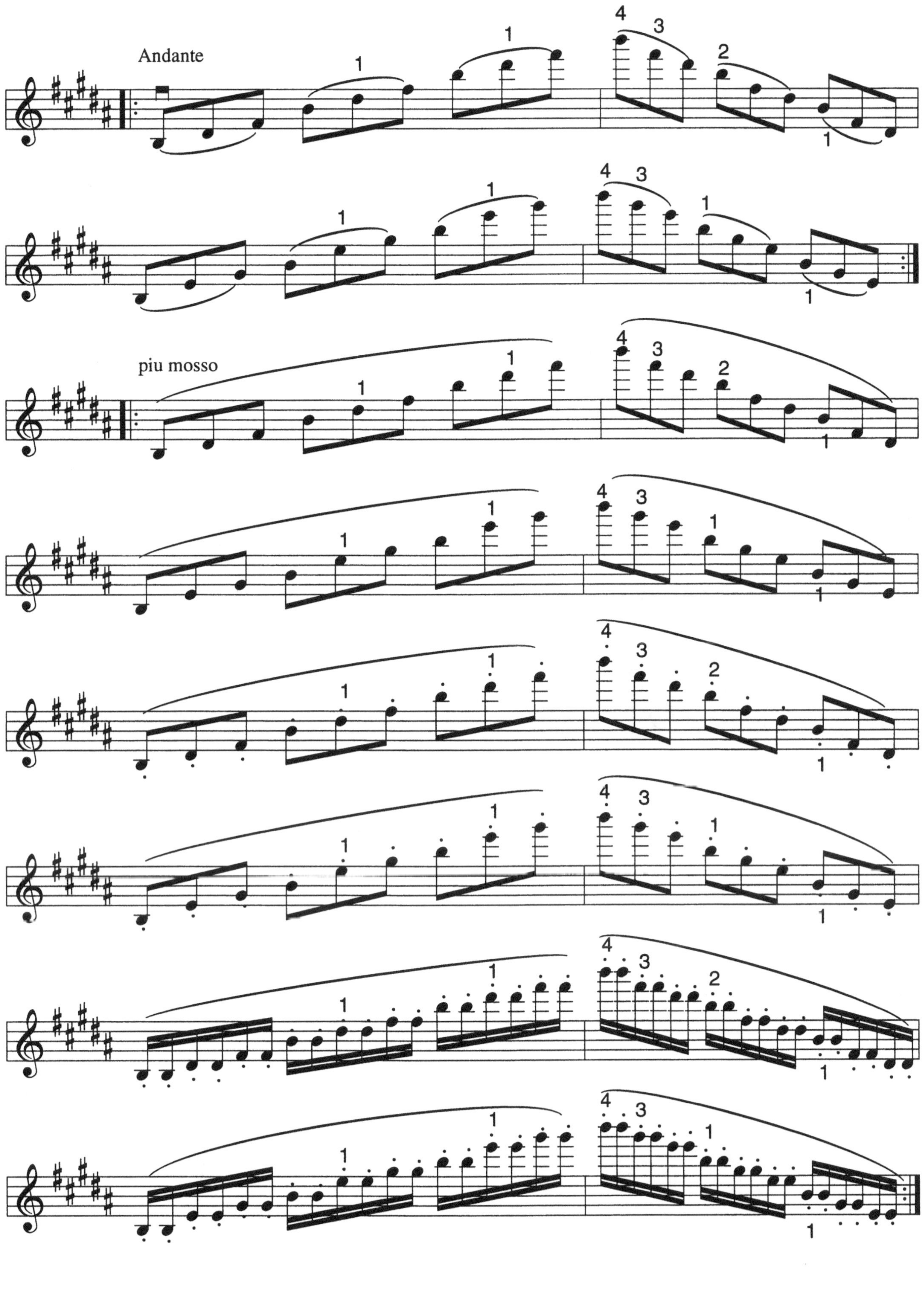
Andante
piu mosso

*tempo increases with each successive exercise

*tempo increases with each successive exercise

*tempo increases with each successive exercise

*tempo increases with each successive exercise

*tempo increases with each successive exercise

D-Flat Major

D-Flat Major

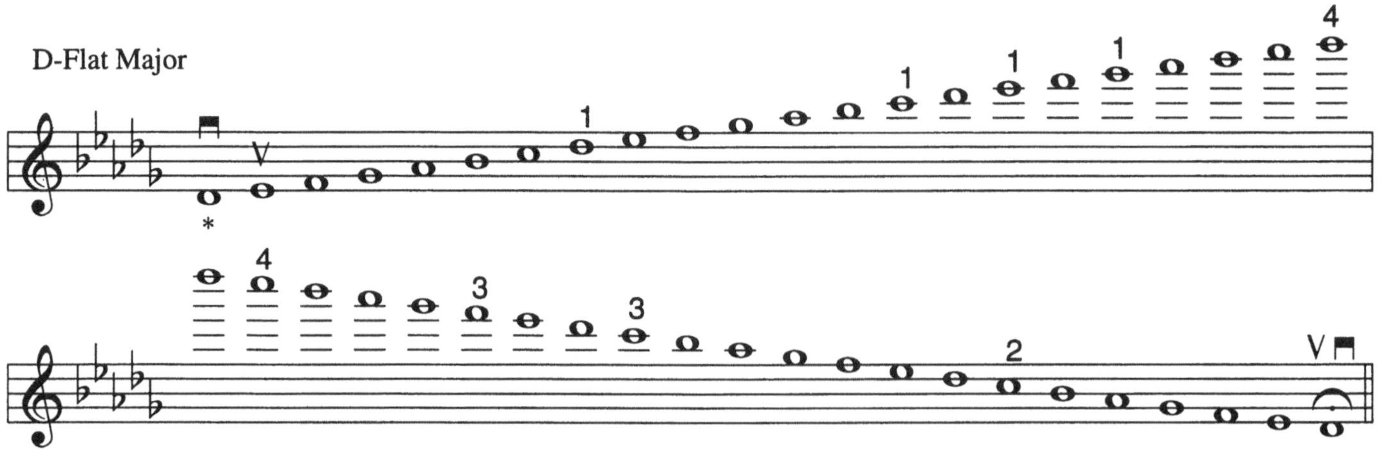

Allegro

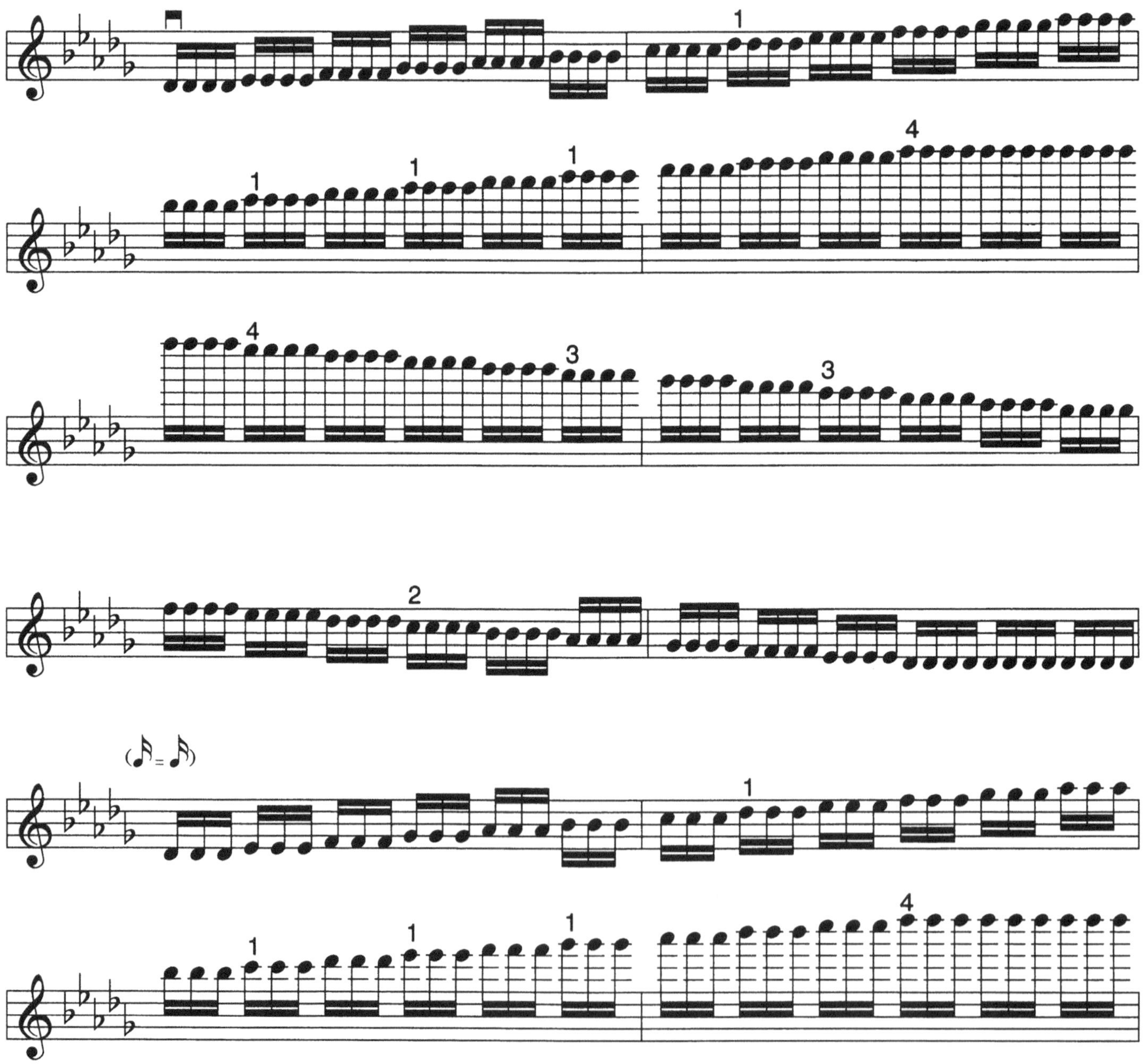

*each note as long as possible (10-20 seconds)

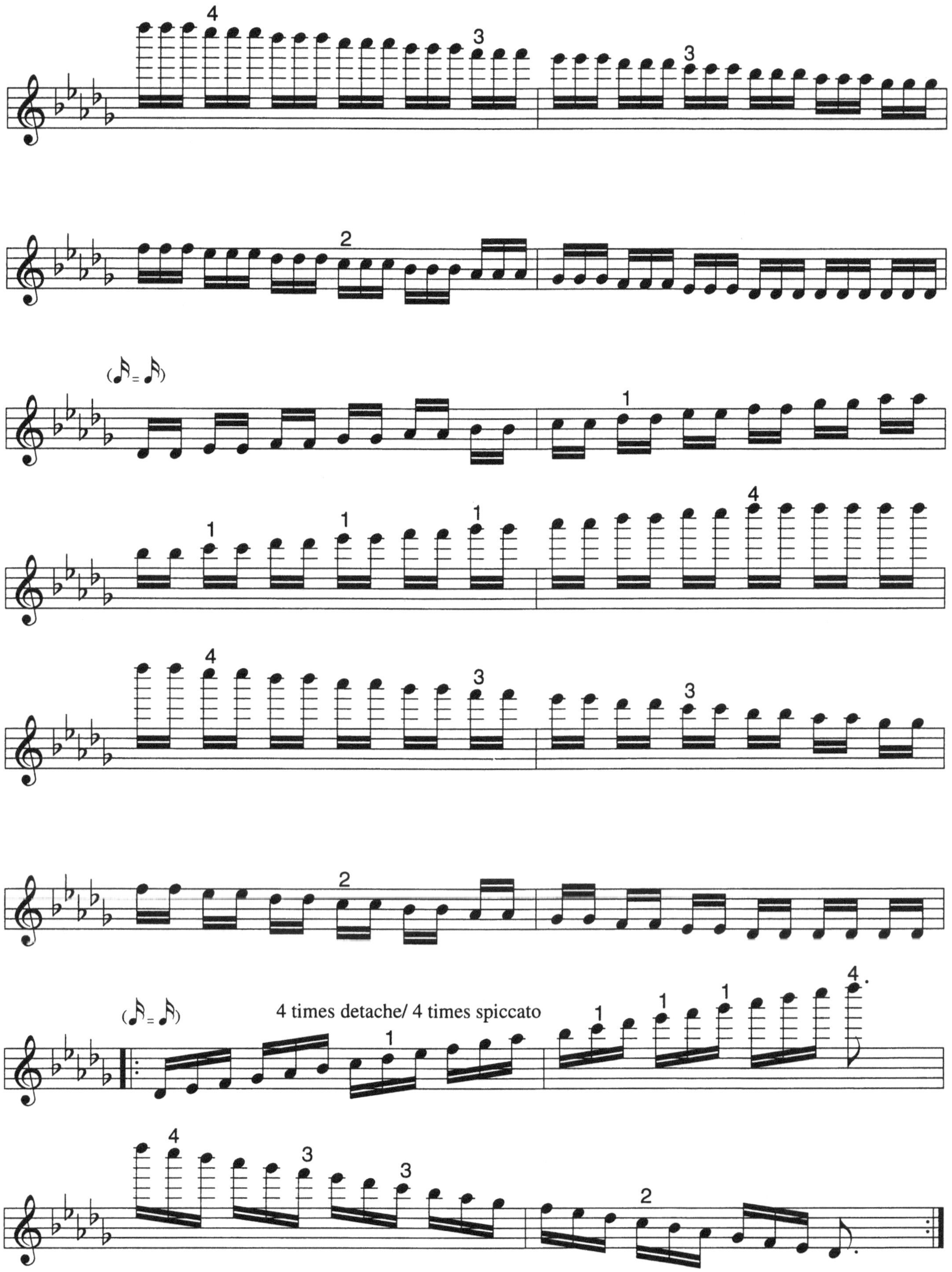
4 times detache/ 4 times spiccato

*tempo increases with each successive exercise

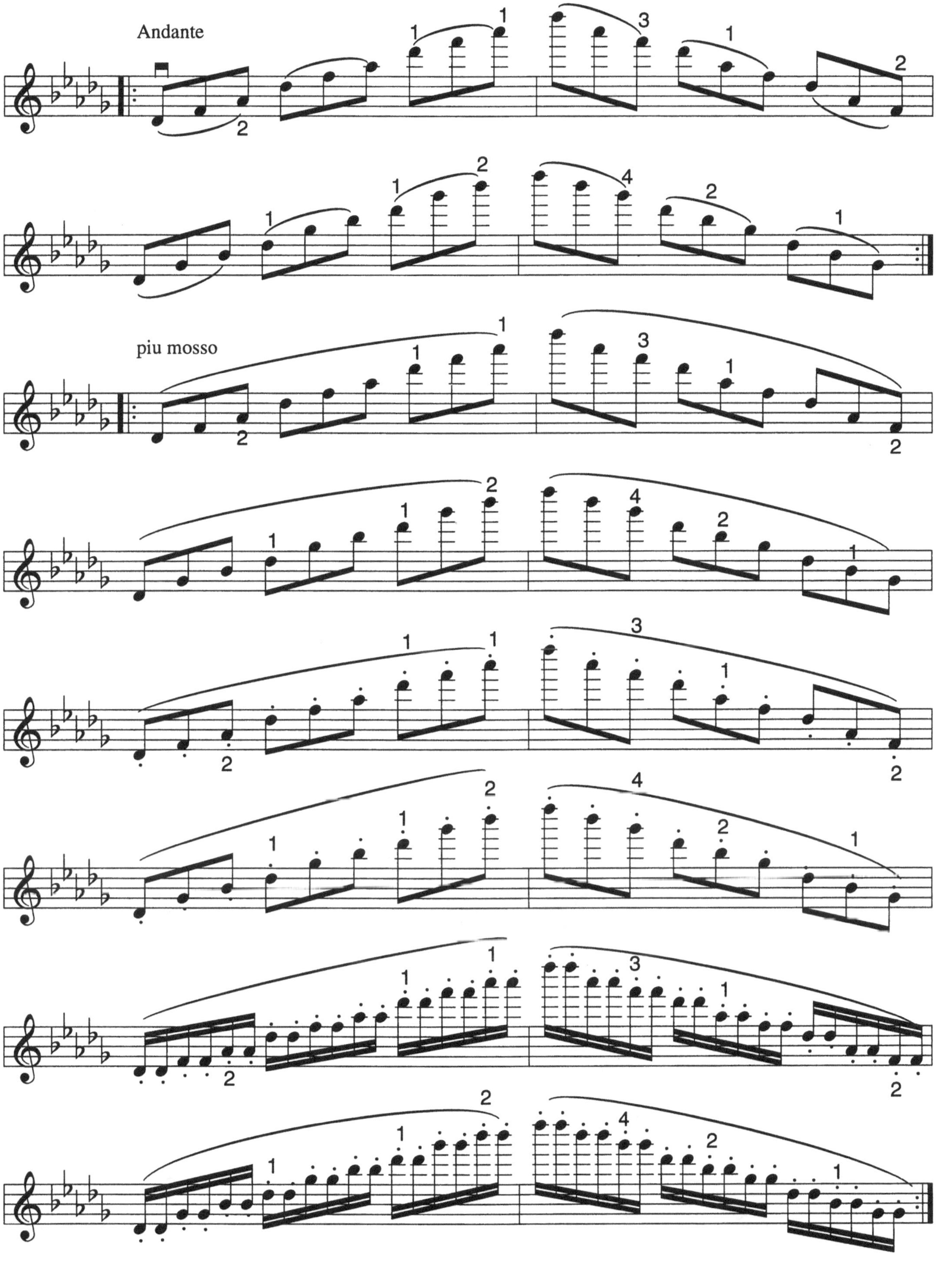
Andante
piu mosso

*tempo increases with each successive exercise

*tempo increases with each successive exercise

*tempo increases with each successive exercise

*tempo increases with each successive exercise

*tempo increases with each successive exercise

F-Sharp Major

F-Sharp Major

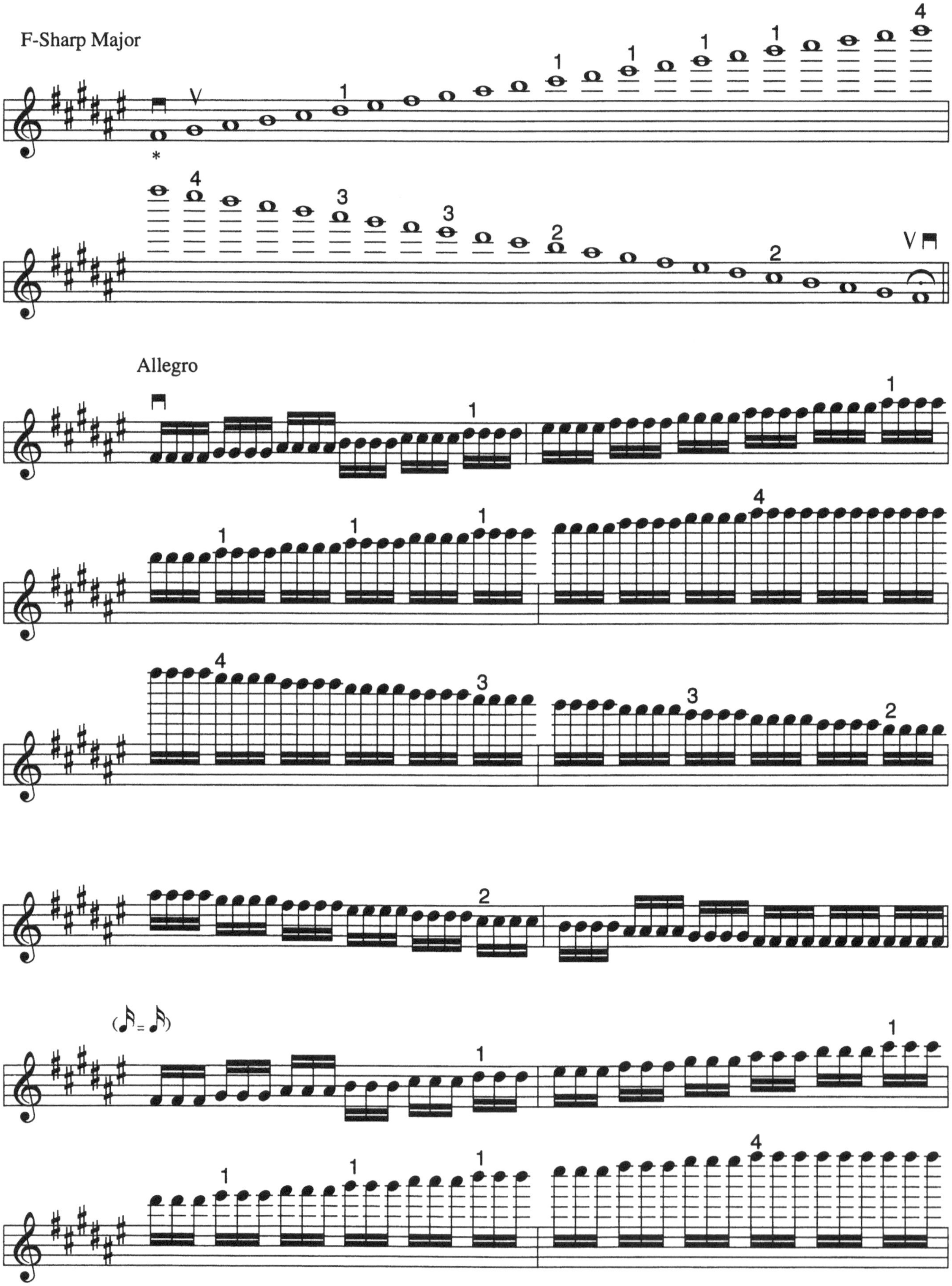

*each note as long as possible (10-20 seconds)

4 times detache/ 4 times spiccato

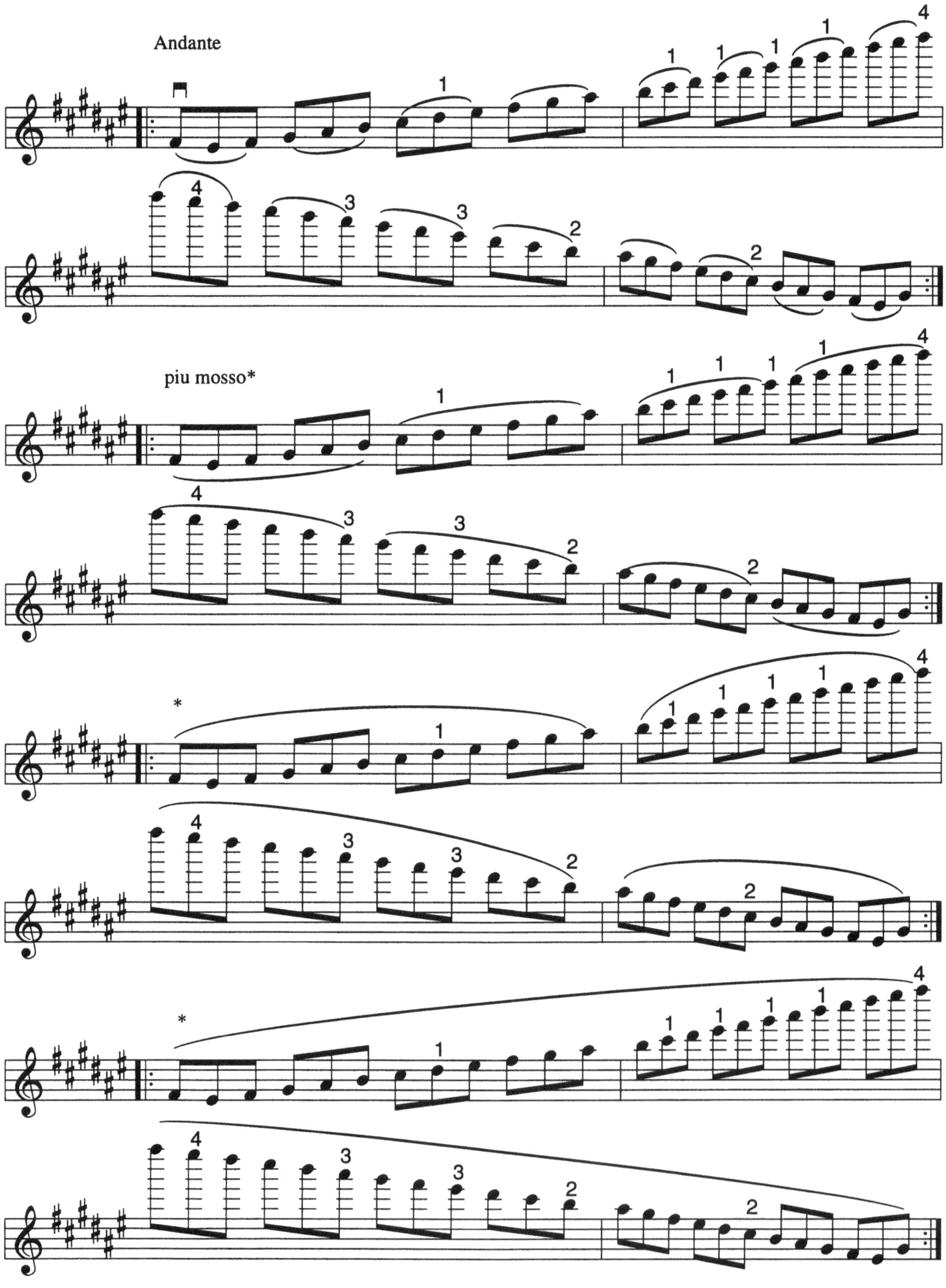

*tempo increases with each successive exercise

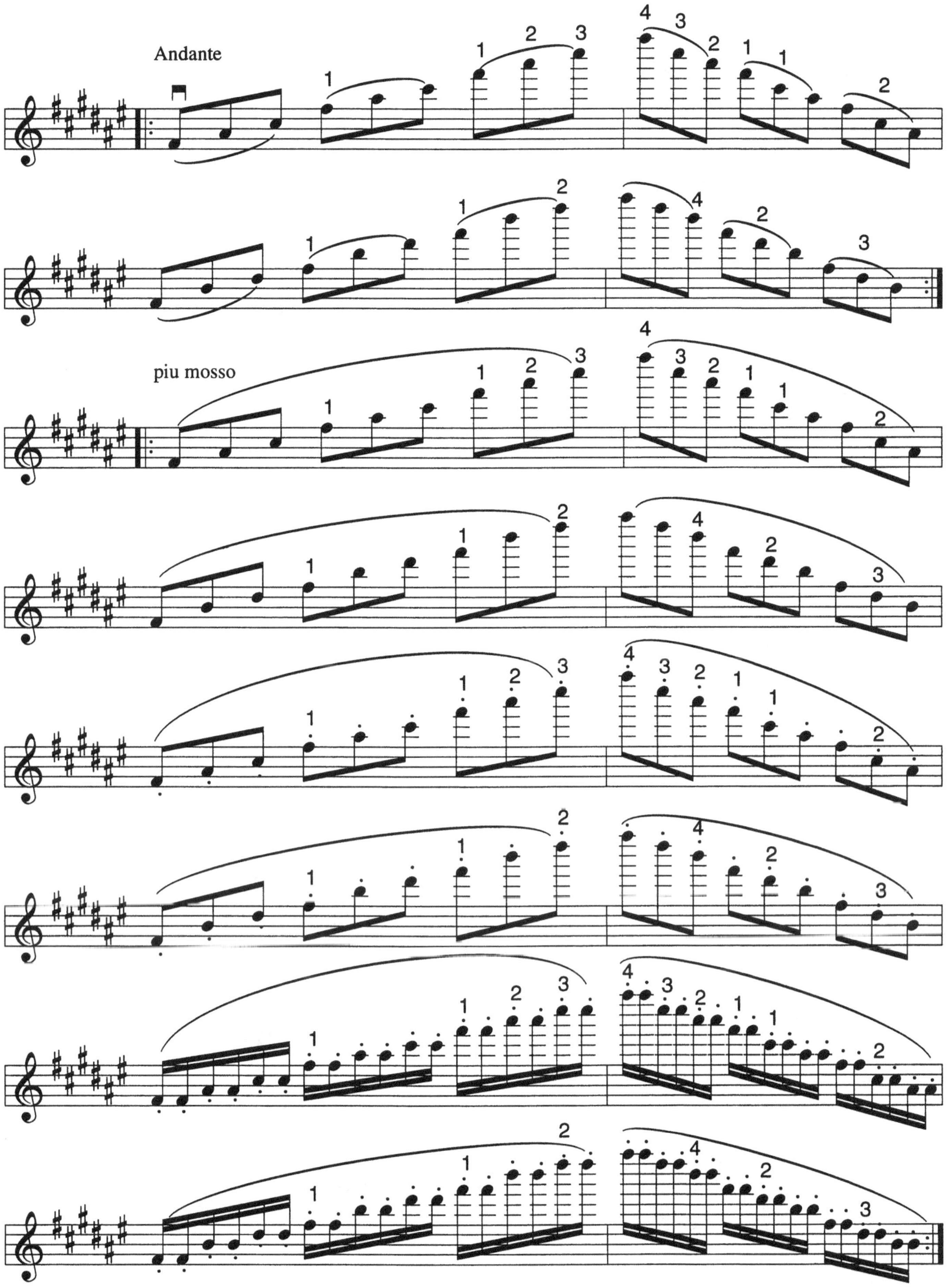
Andante
piu mosso

*tempo increases with each successive exercise

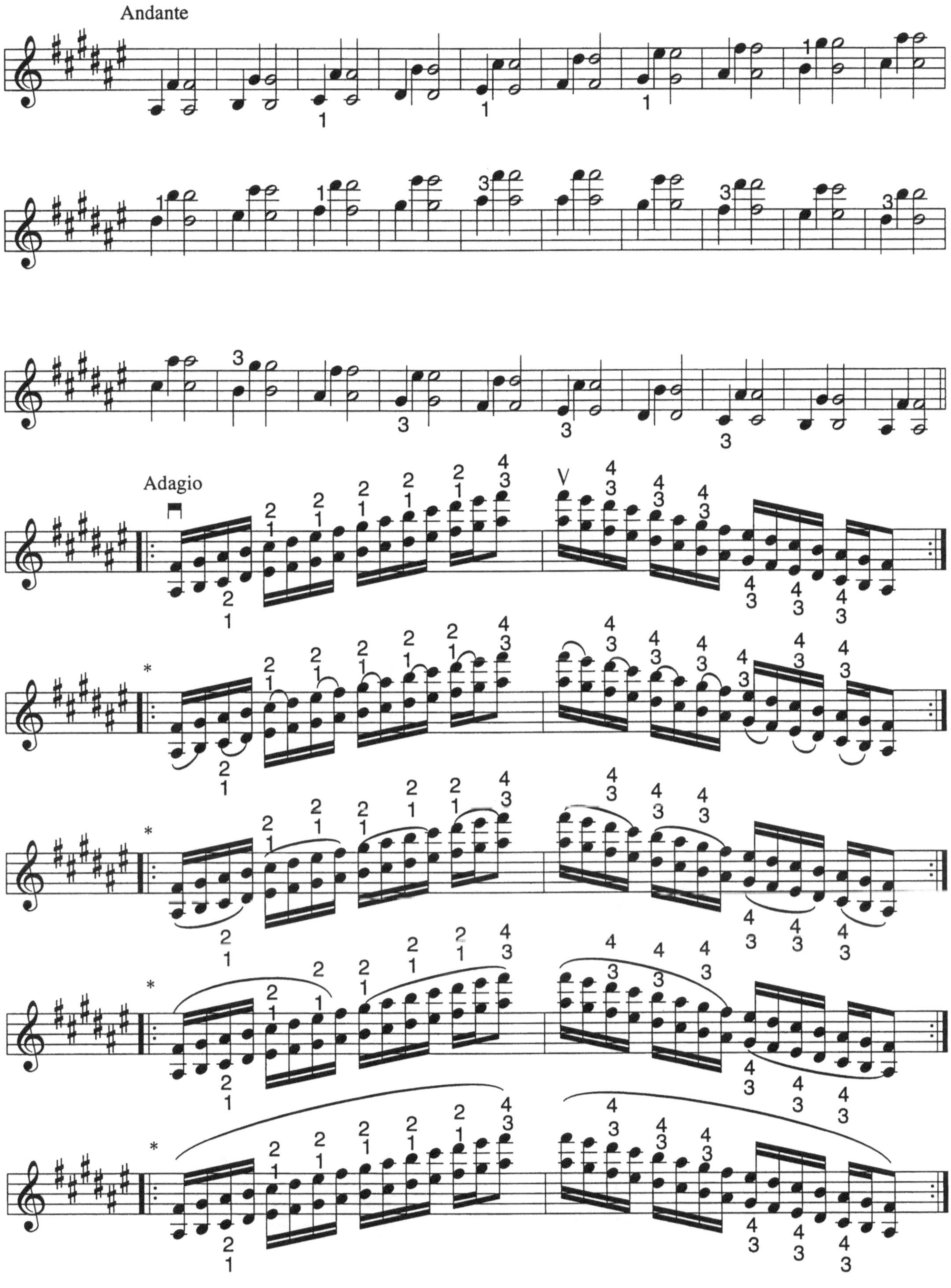

*tempo increases with each successive exercise

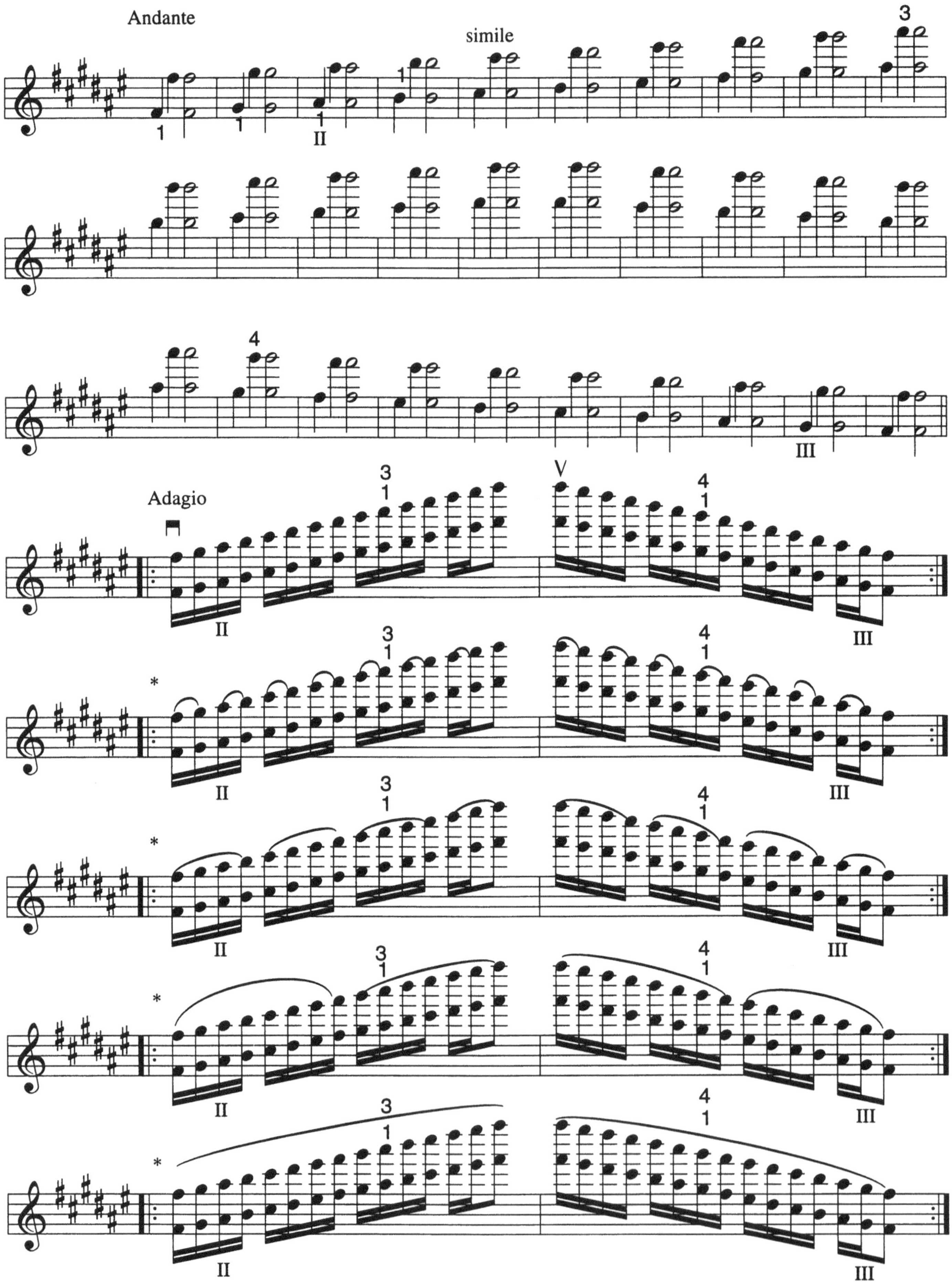

*tempo increases with each successive exercise

*tempo increases with each successive exercise

*tempo increases with each successive exercise

G-Flat Major

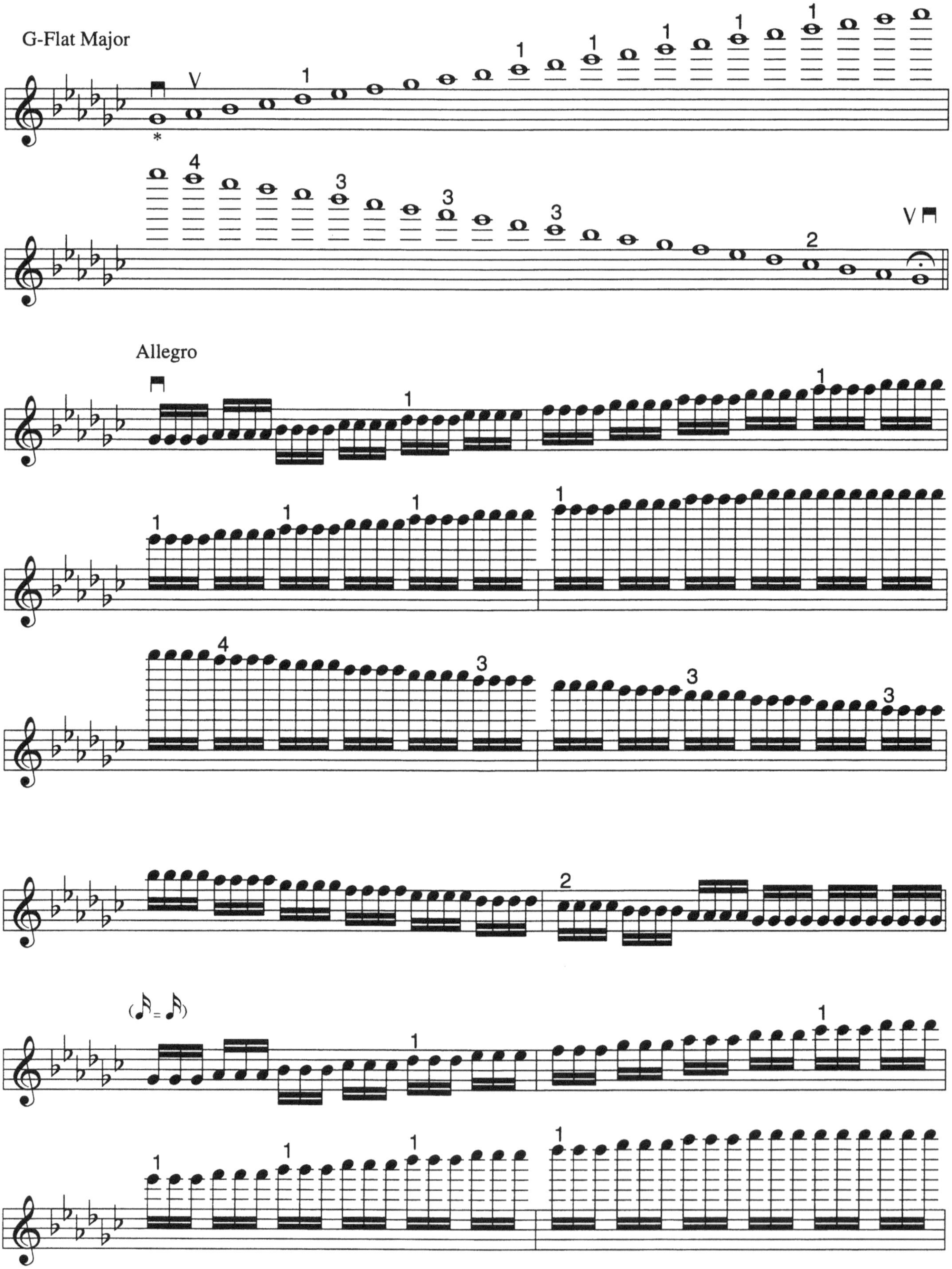

*each note as long as possible (10-20 seconds)

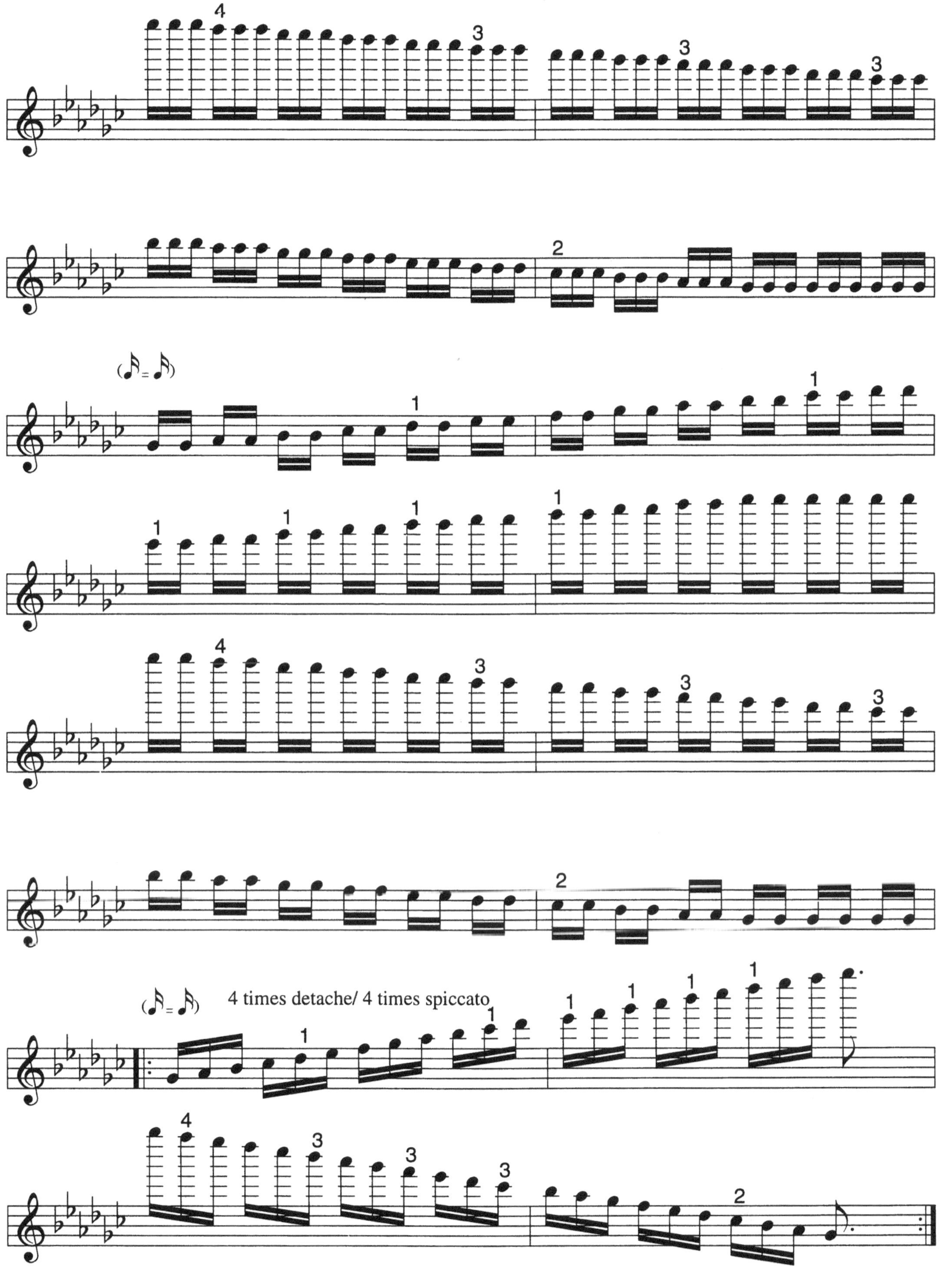
4 times detache/ 4 times spiccato

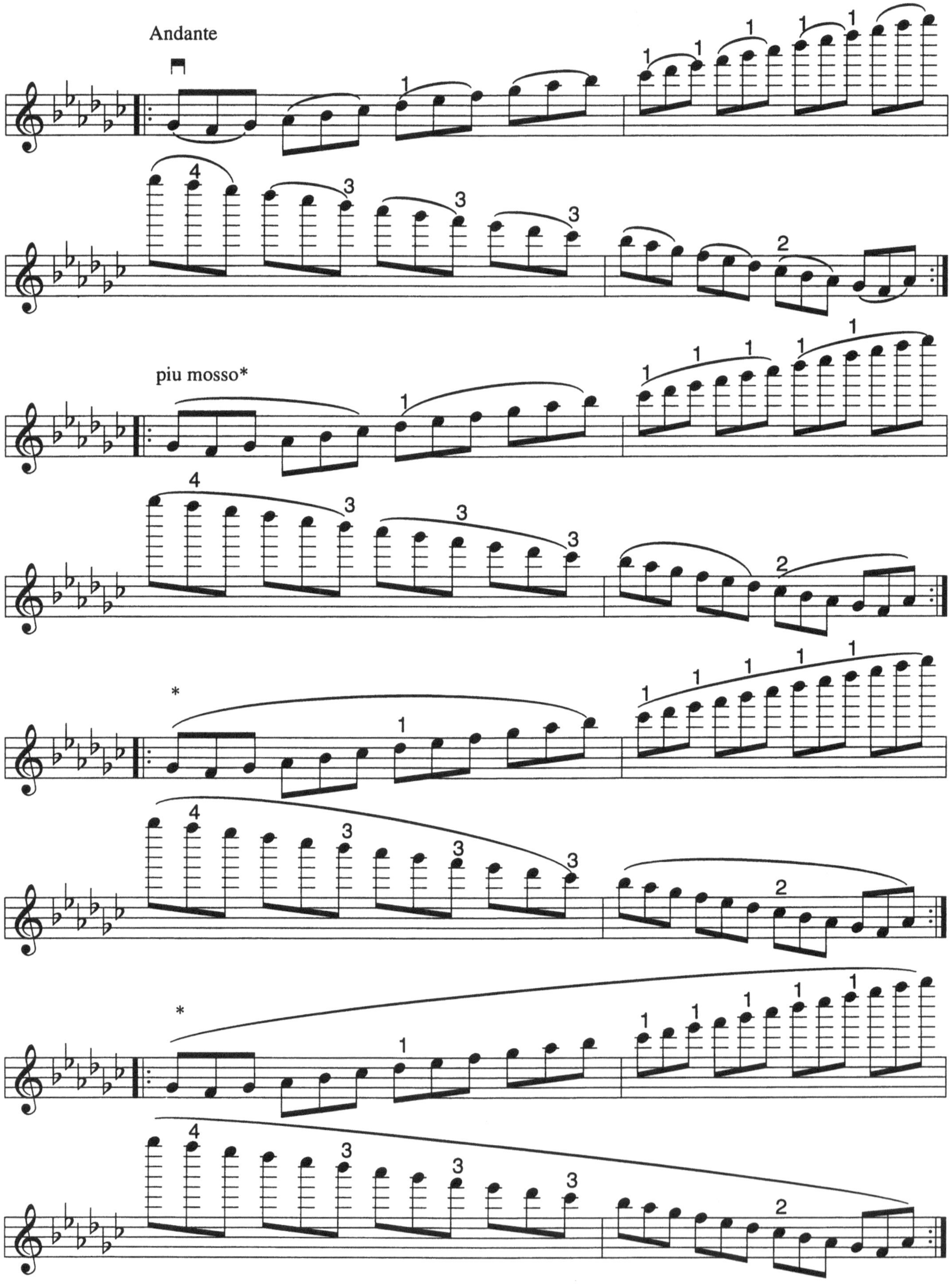

*tempo increases with each successive exercise

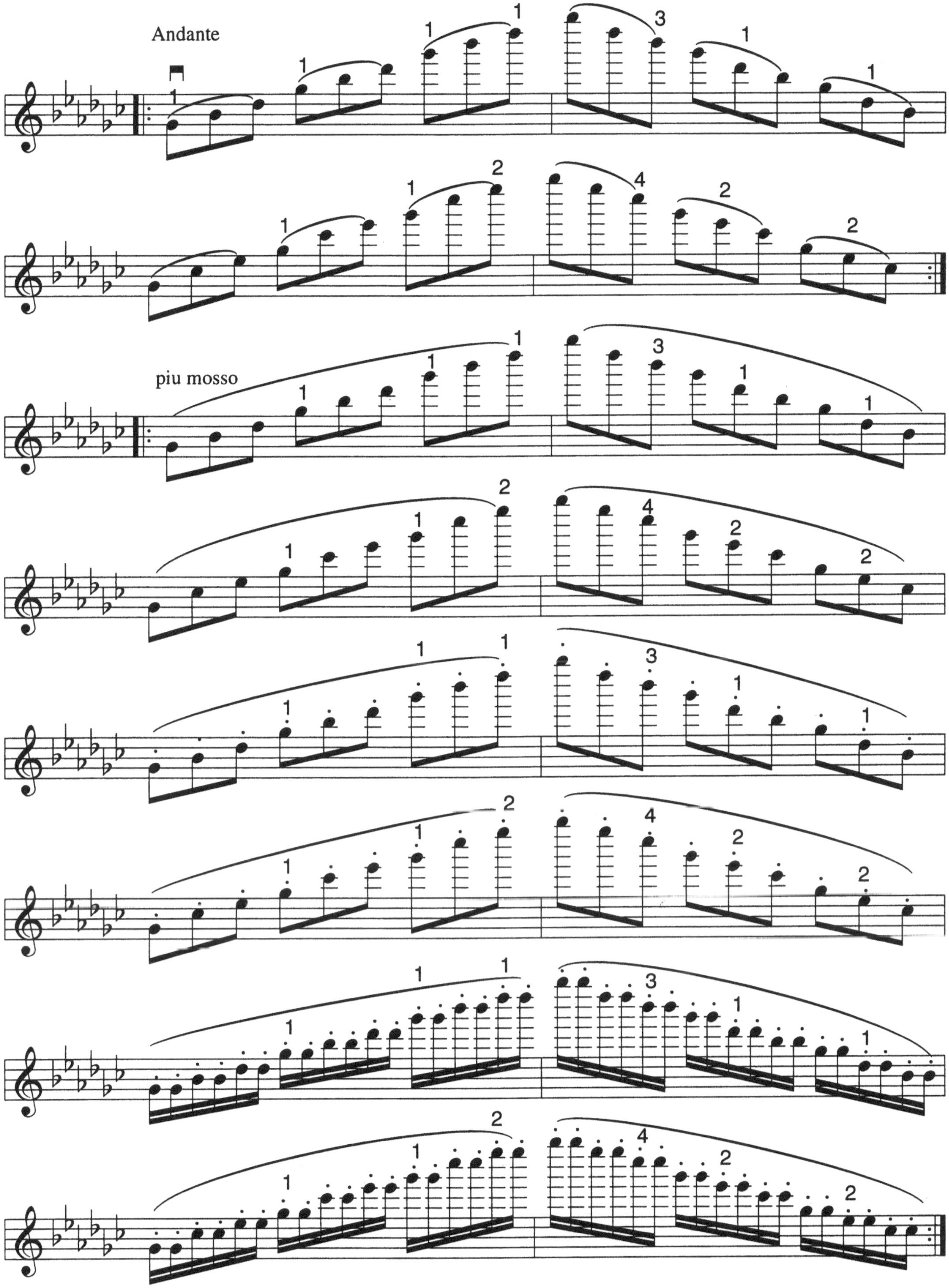
Andante
piu mosso

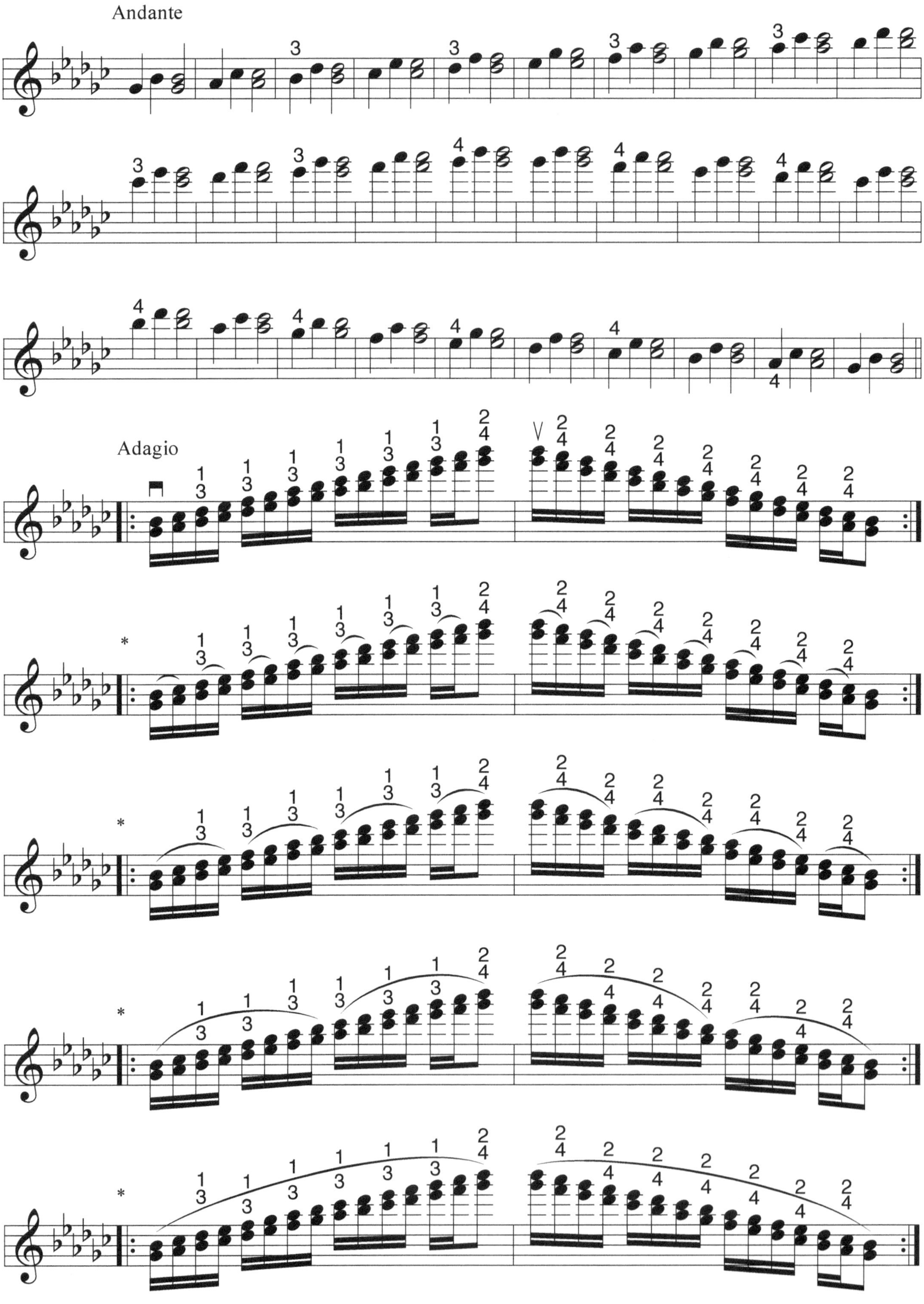

*tempo increases with each successive exercise

*tempo increases with each successive exercise

*tempo increases with each successive exercise

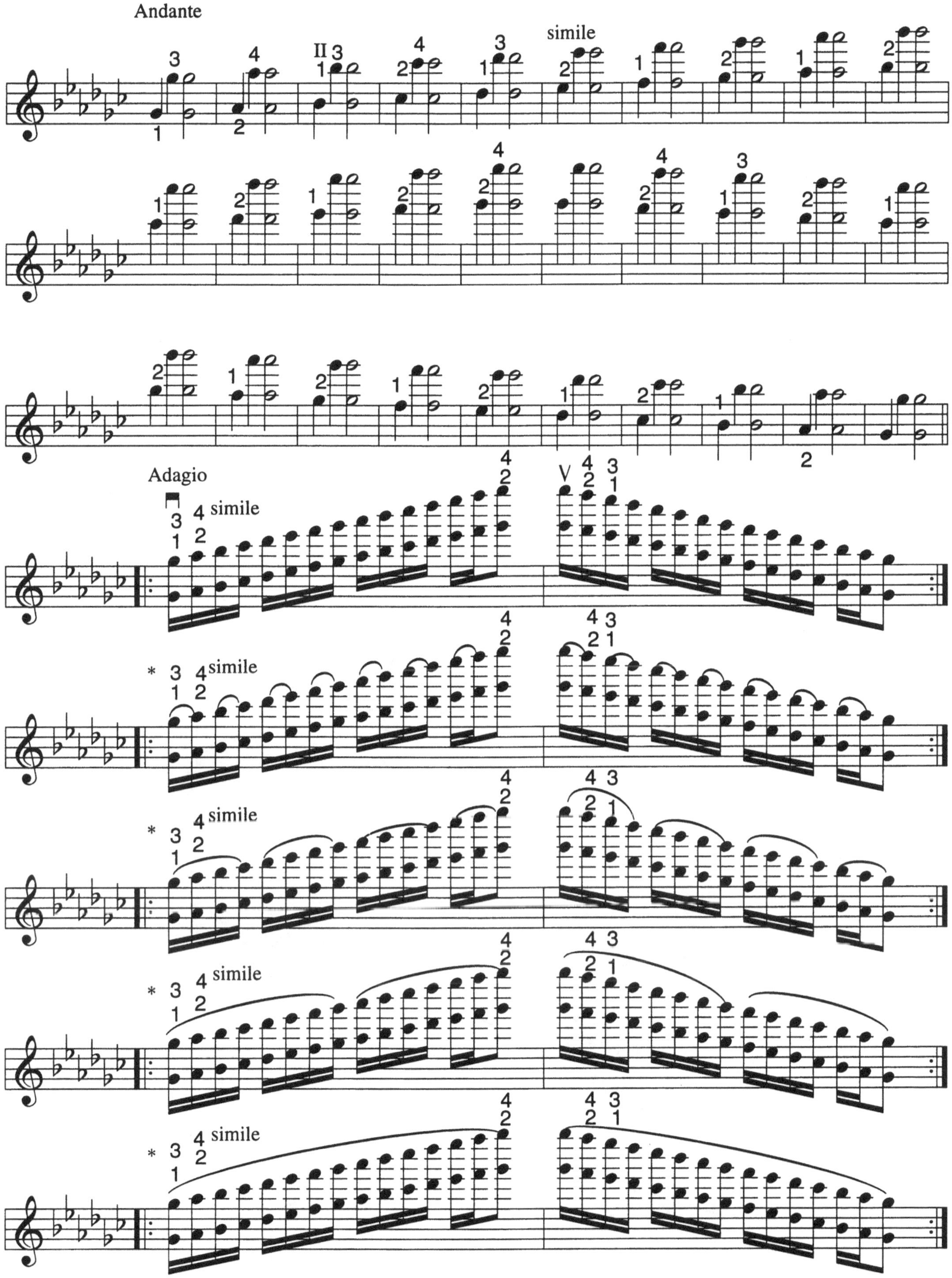

*tempo increases with each successive exercise

*tempo increases with each successive exercise

C-Sharp Major

C-Sharp Major

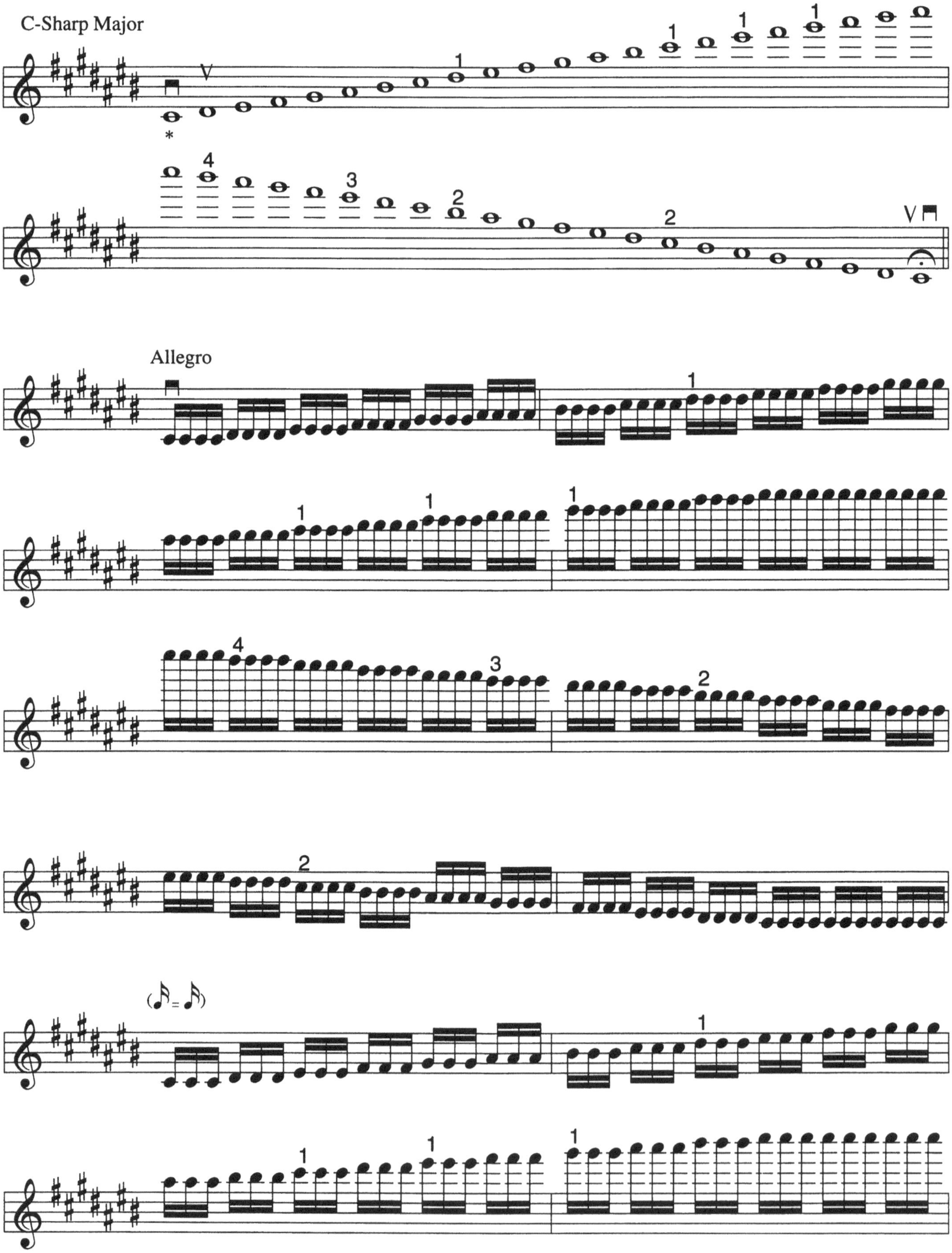

*each note as long as possible (10-20 seconds)

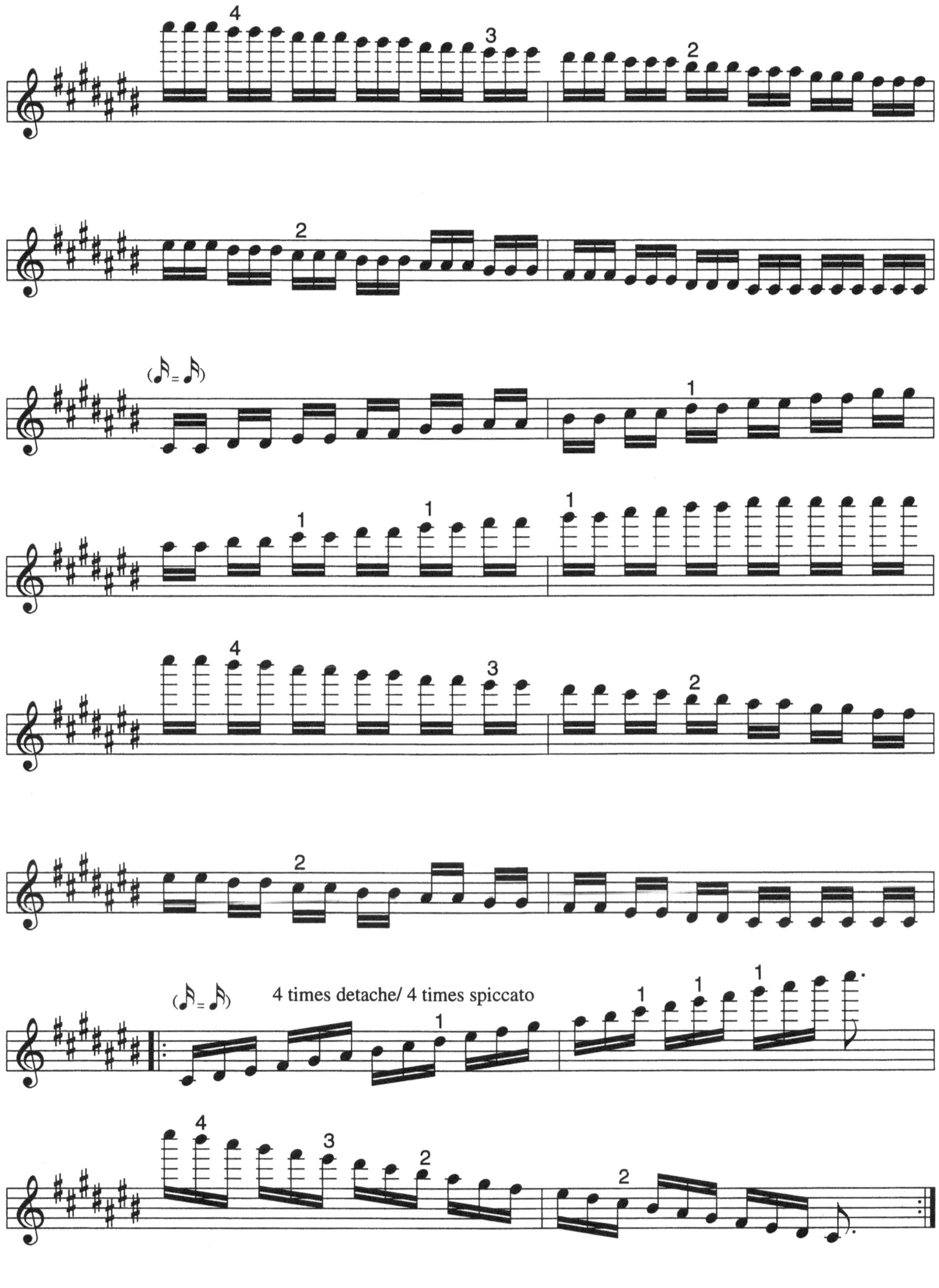
4 times detache/ 4 times spiccato

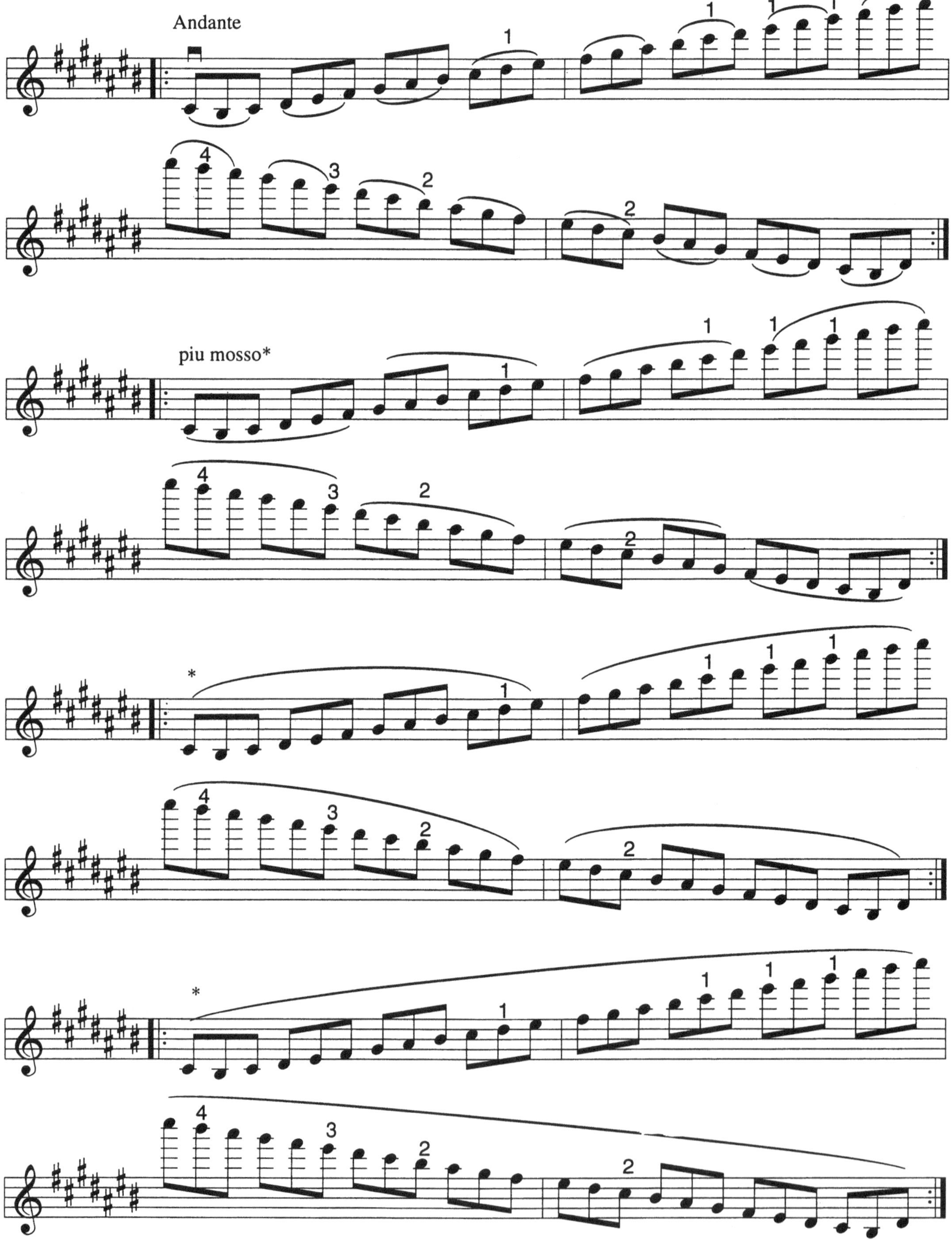

*tempo increases with each successive exercise

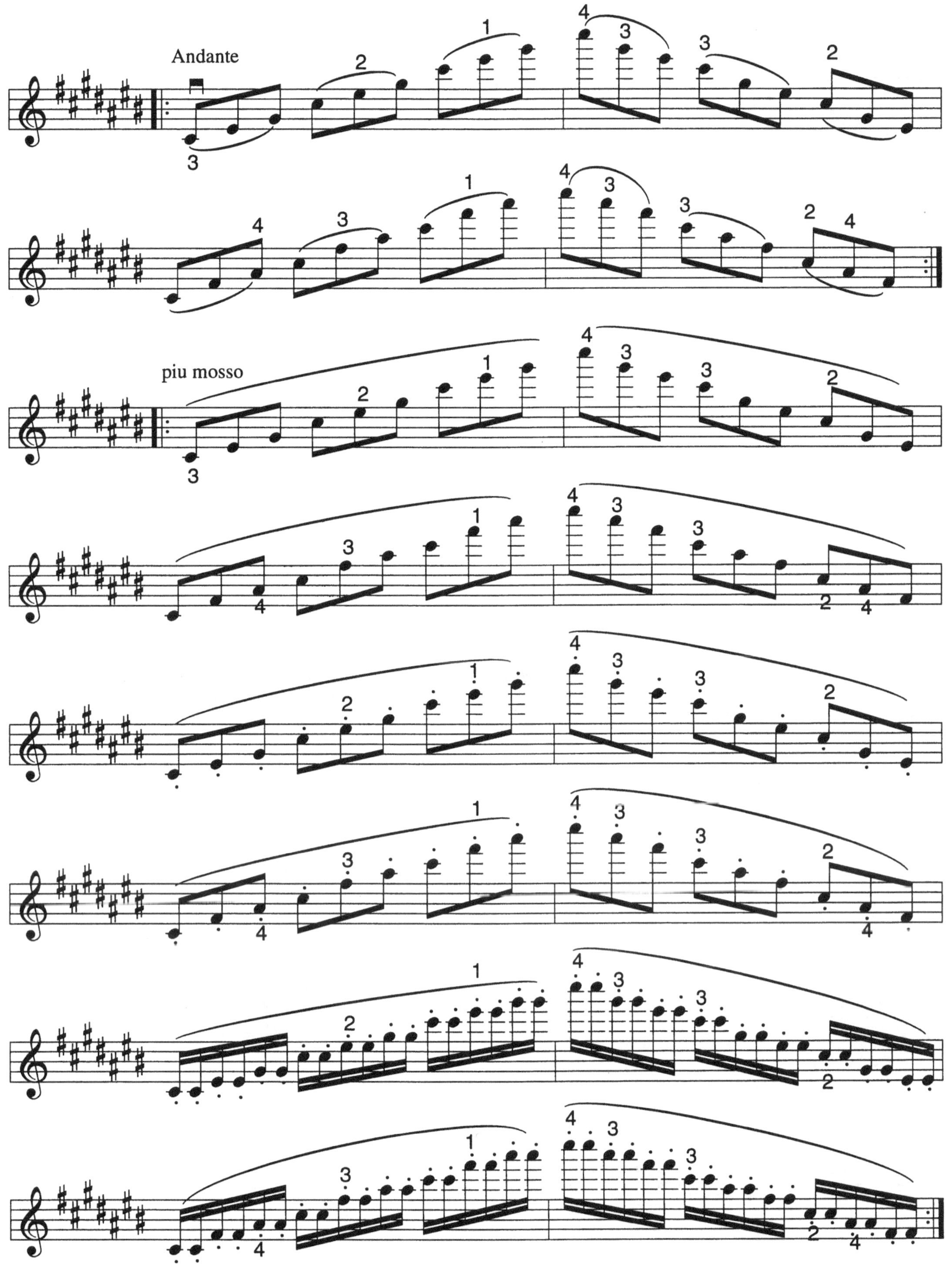
Andante
piu mosso

*tempo increases with each successive exercise

*tempo increases with each successive exercise

*tempo increases with each successive exercise

*tempo increases with each successive exercise

*tempo increases with each successive exercise

C-Flat Major

C-Flat Major

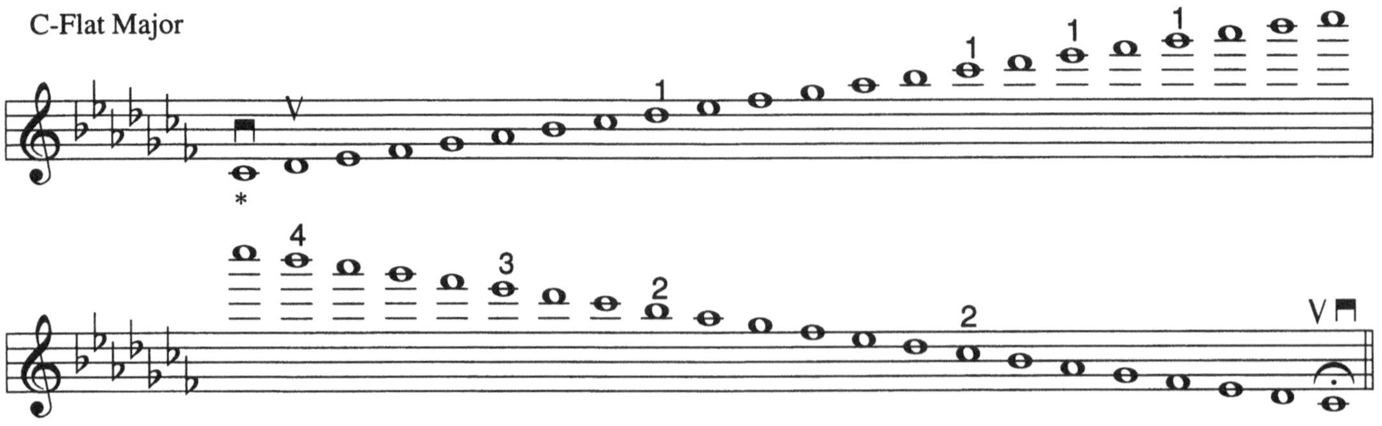

Allegro

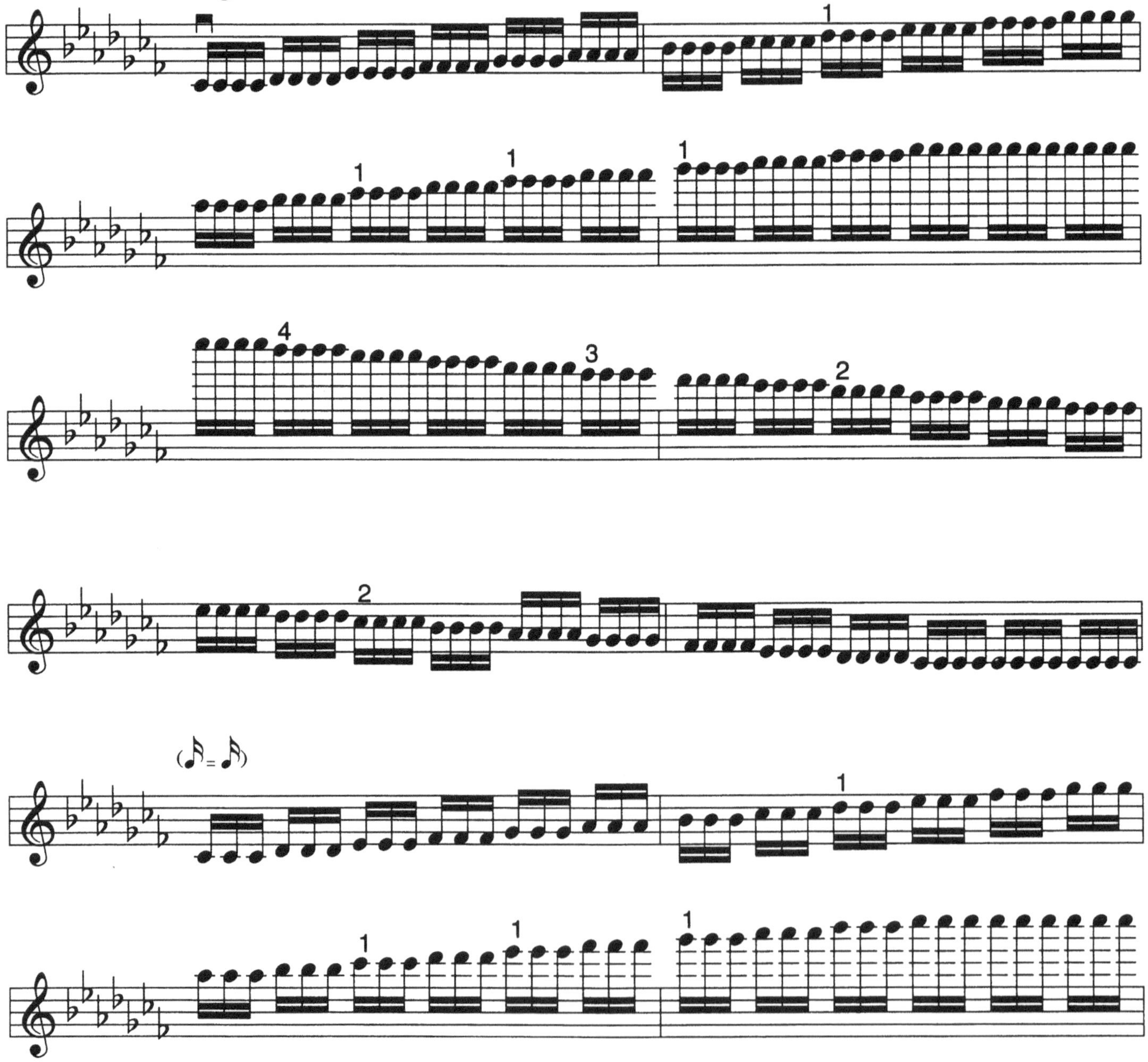

*each note as long as possible (10-20 seconds)

4 times detache/ 4 times spiccato

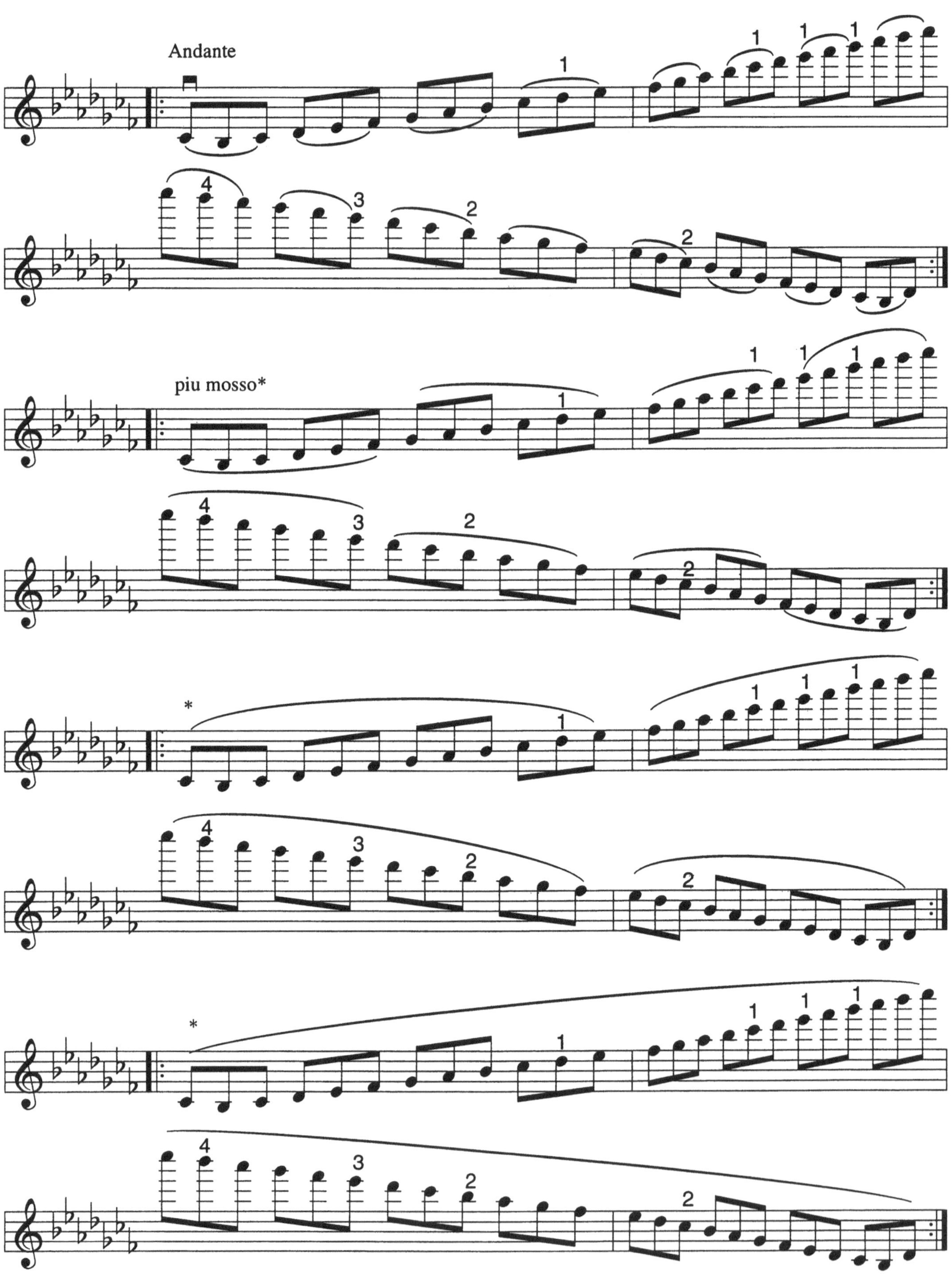

*tempo increases with each successive exercise

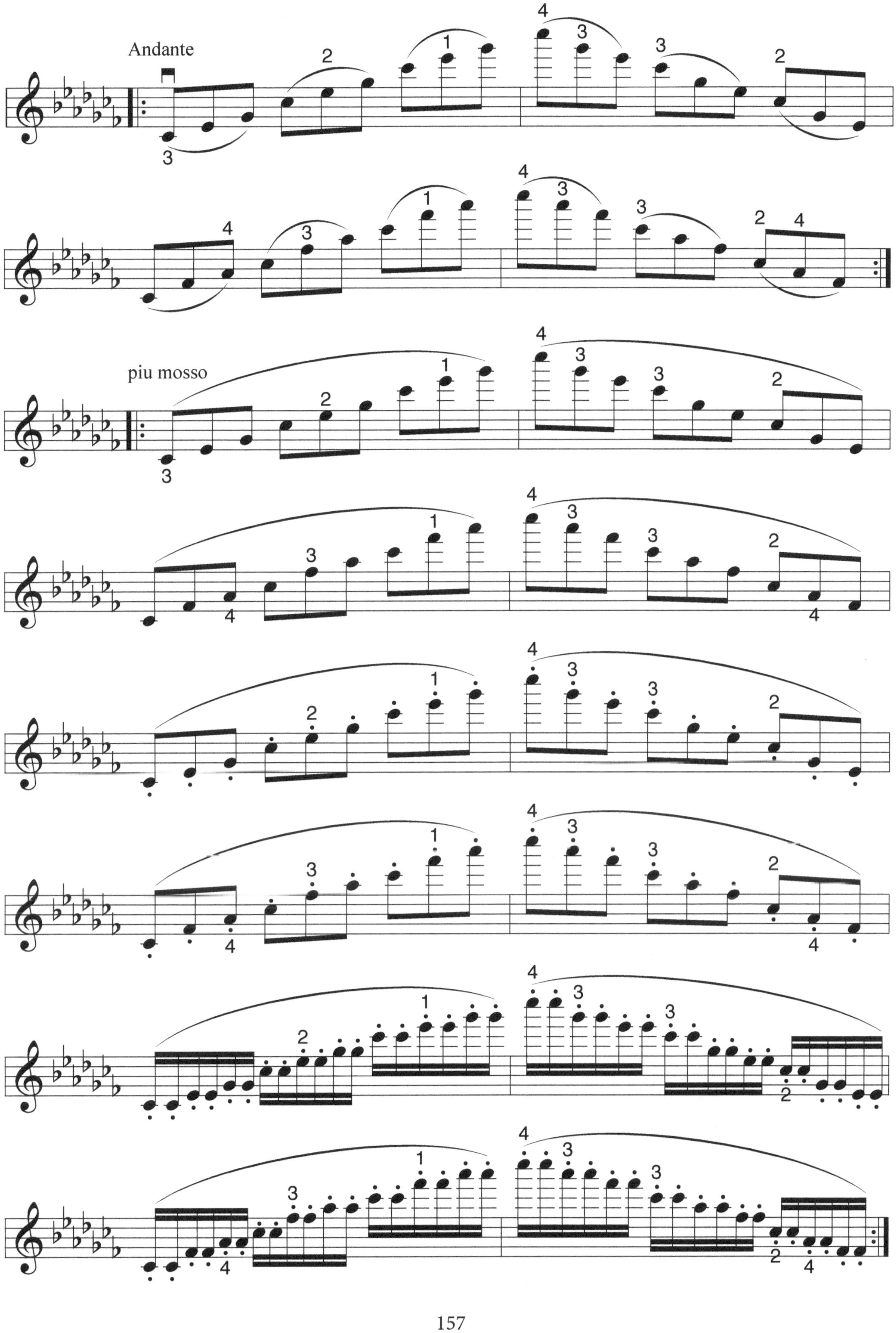
Andante
piu mosso

*tempo increases with each successive exercise

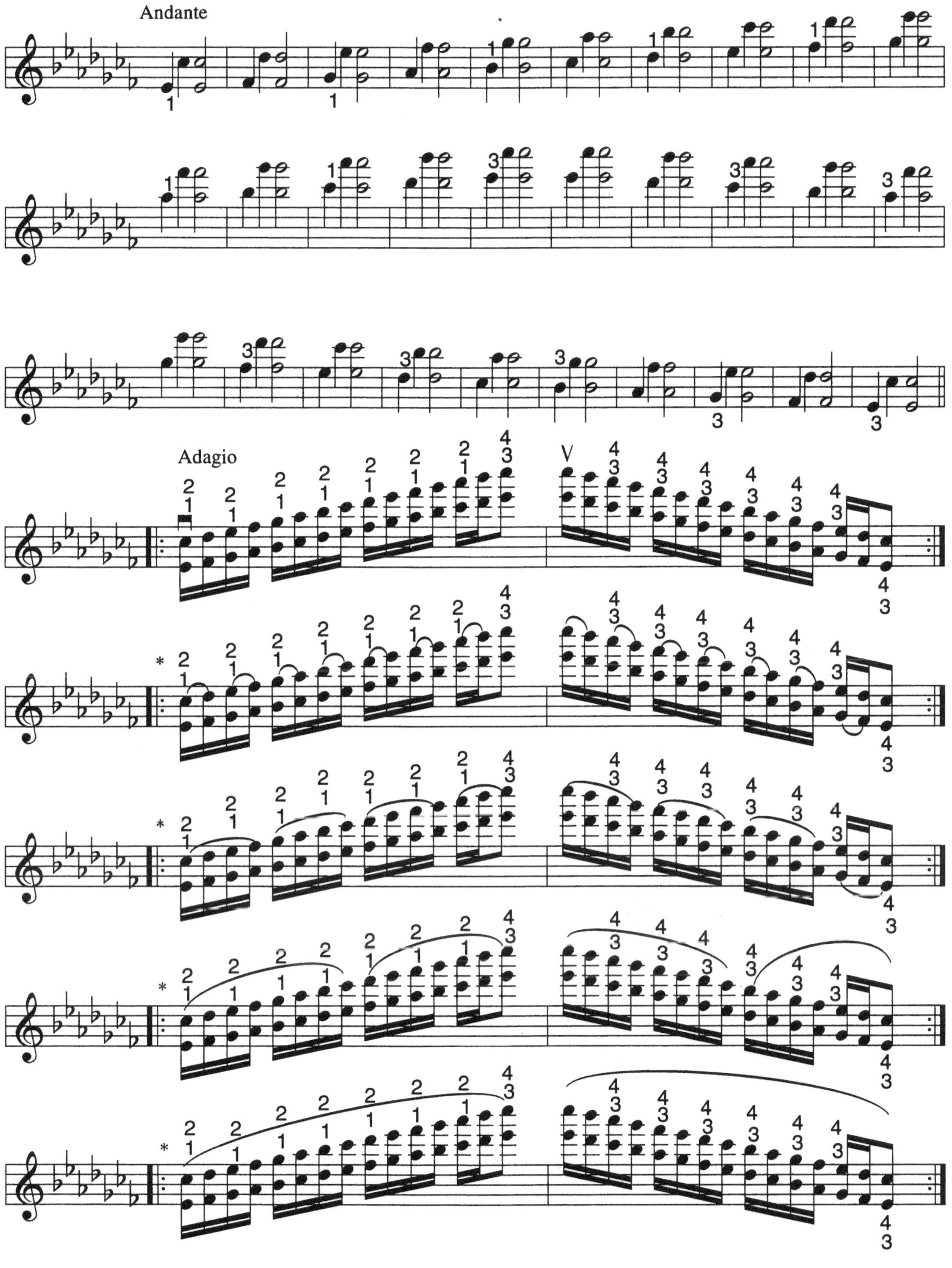

*tempo increases with each successive exercise

*tempo increases with each successive exercise

*tempo increases with each successive exercise

*tempo increases with each successive exercise

a minor

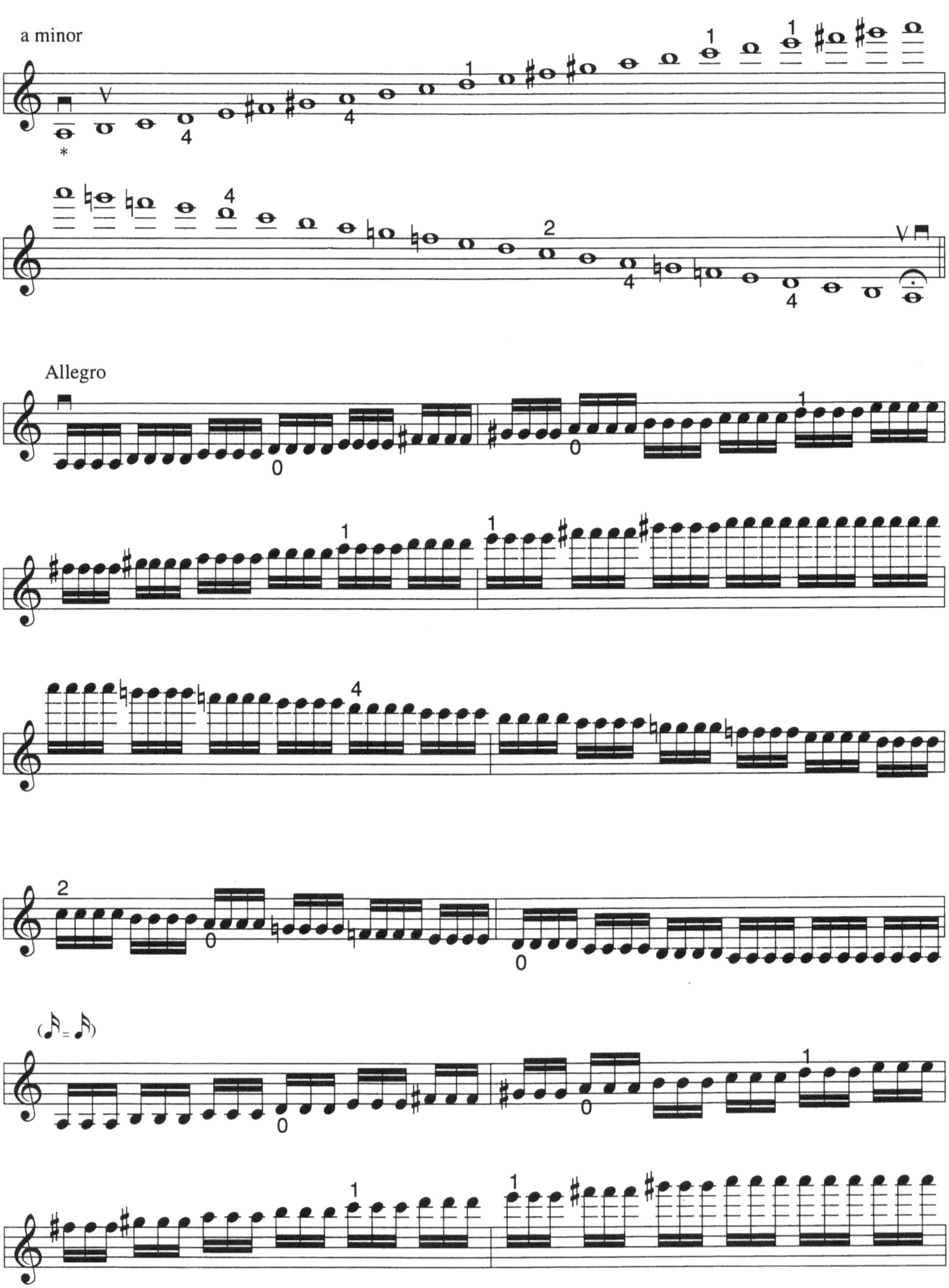

*each note as long as possible (10-20 seconds)

4 times detache/ 4 times spiccato

*tempo increases with each successive exercise

Four-octave scales

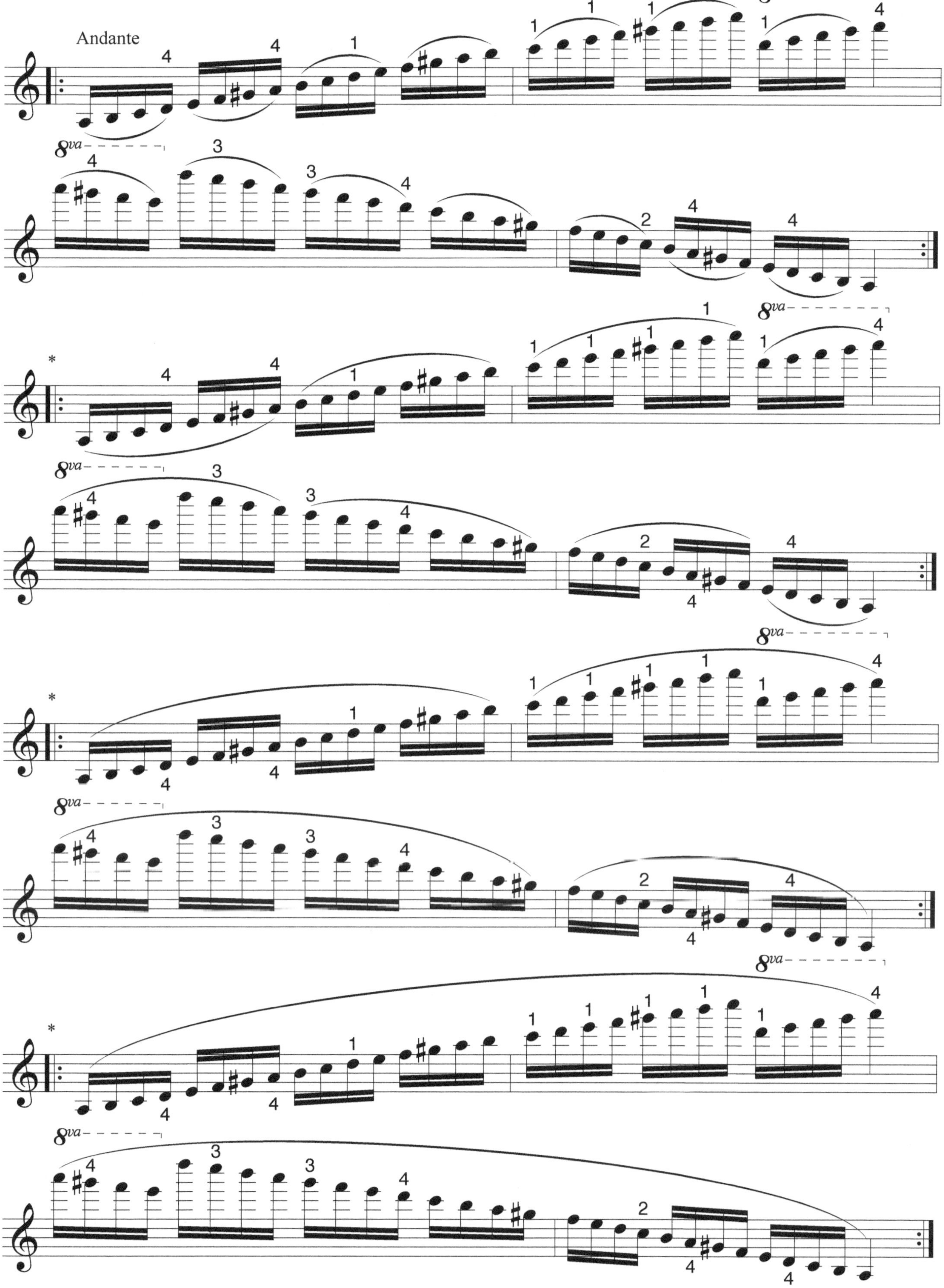

*tempo increases with each successive exercise

Andante
piu mosso

Four-octave arpeggios

*tempo increases with each successive exercise

*tempo increases with each successive exercise

*tempo increases with each successive exercise

*tempo increases with each successive exercise

*tempo increases with each successive exercise

e minor

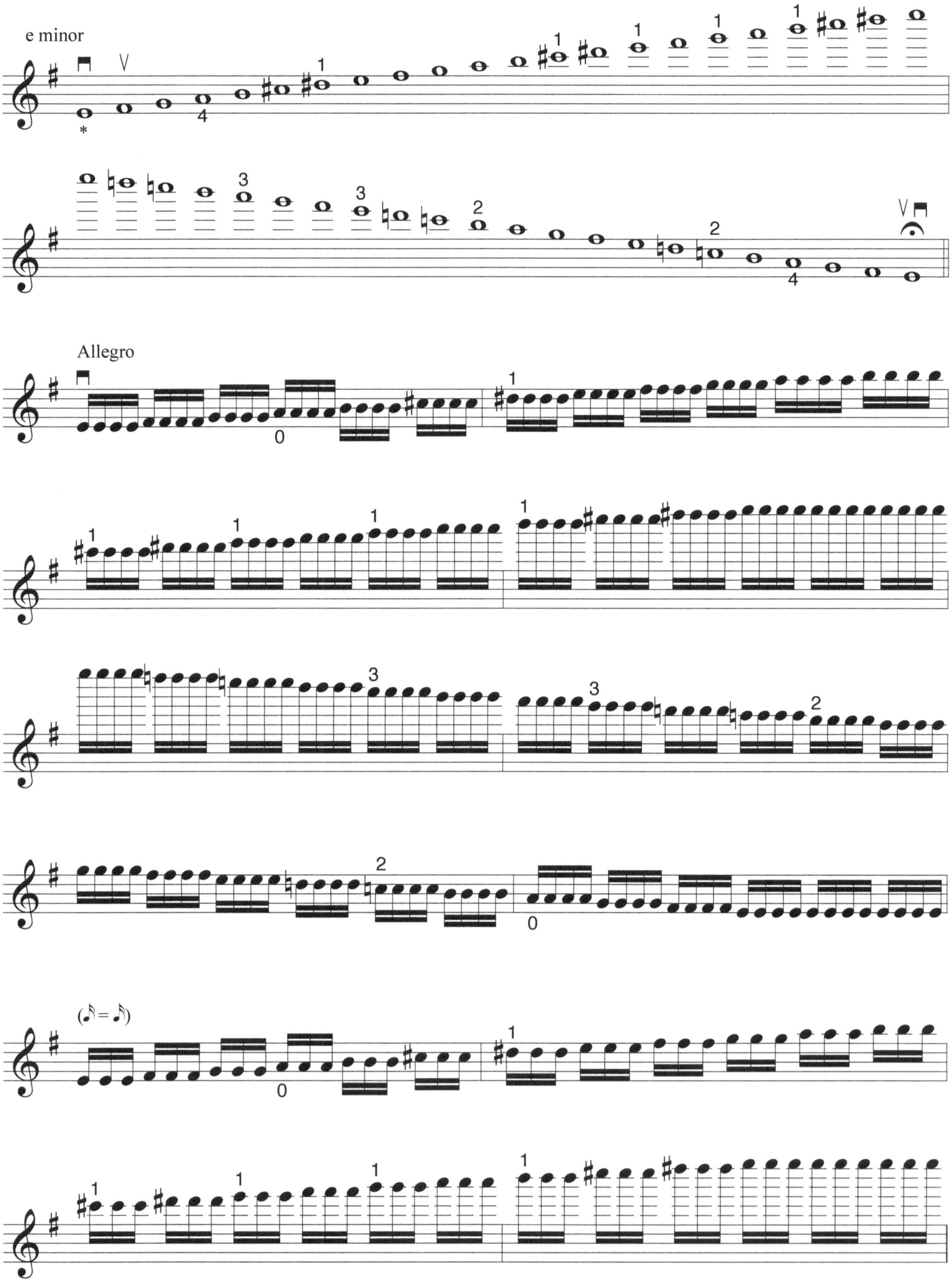

*each note as long as possible (10-20 seconds)

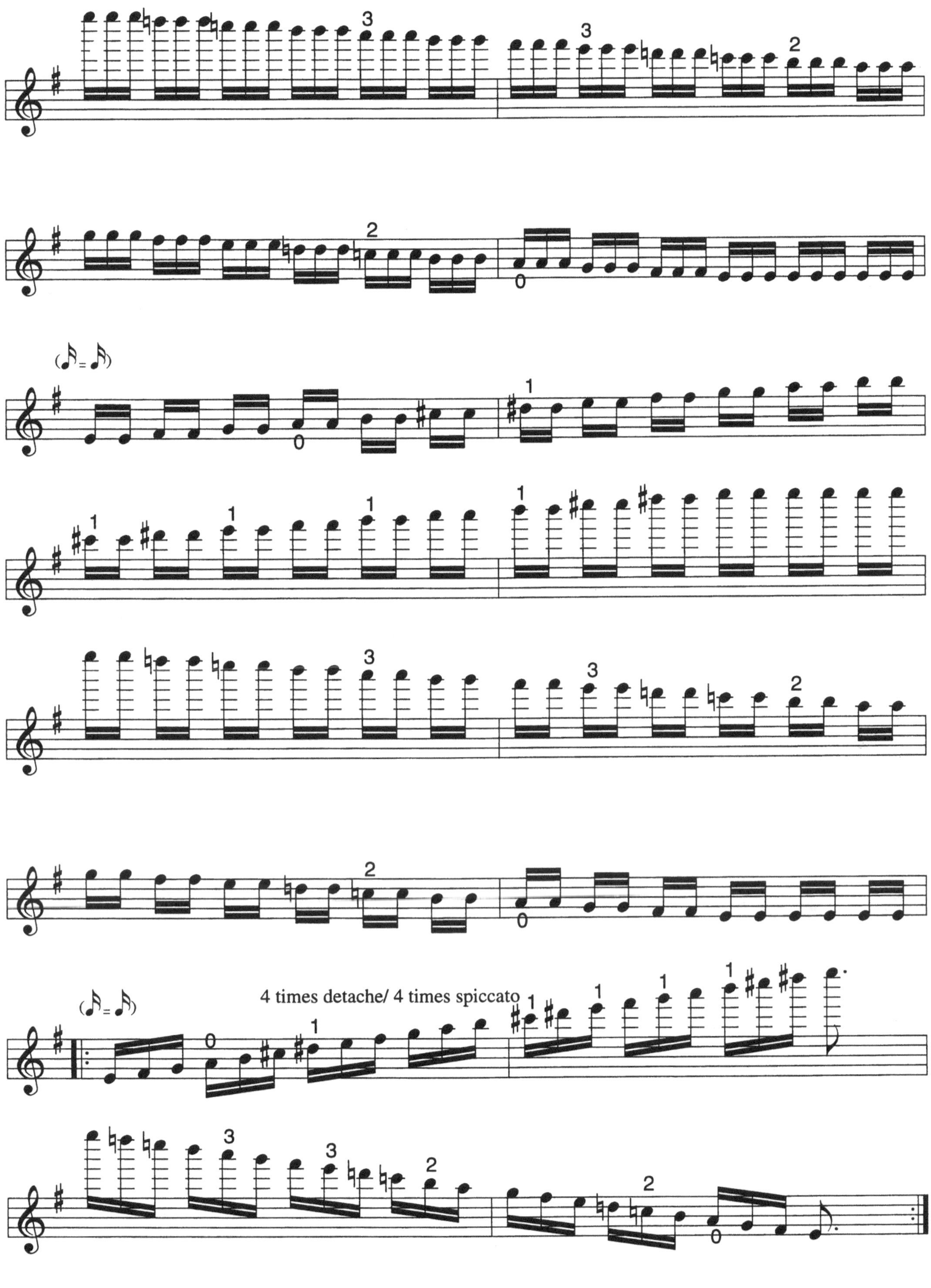
4 times detache/ 4 times spiccato

*tempo increases with each successive exercise

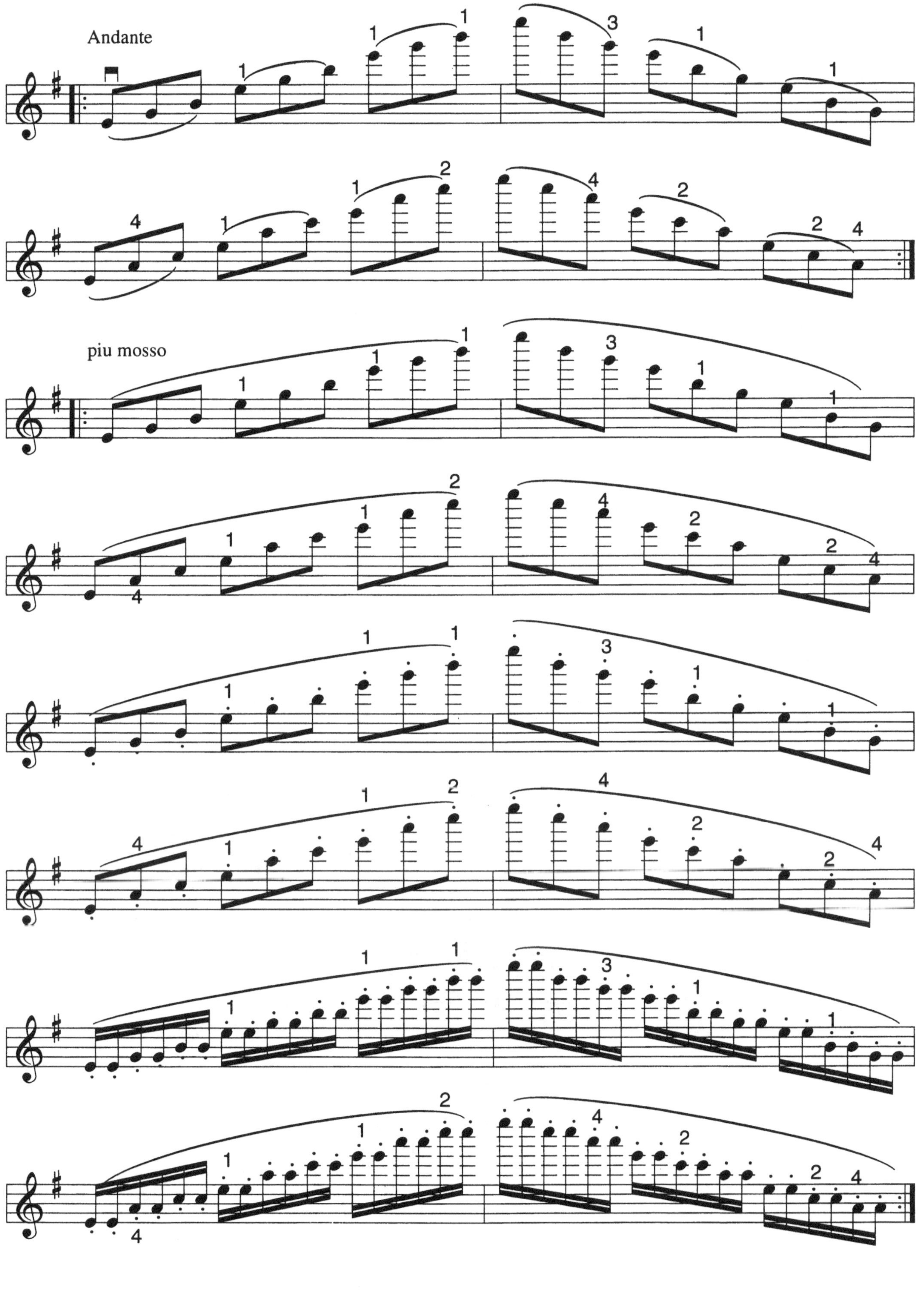
Andante
piu mosso

*tempo increases with each successive exercise

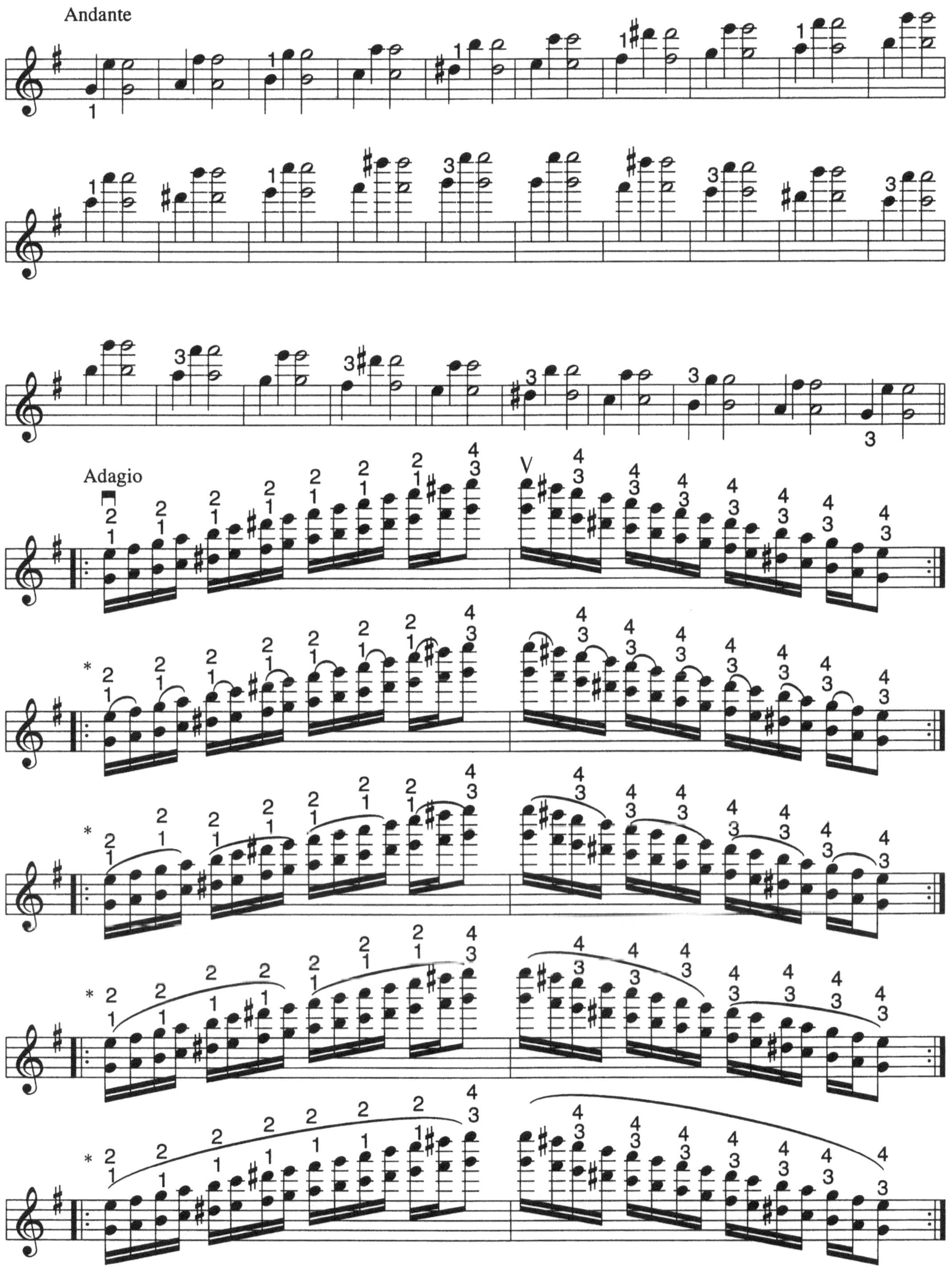

*tempo increases with each successive exercise

*tempo increases with each successive exercise

*tempo increases with each successive exercise

*tempo increases with each successive exercise

d minor

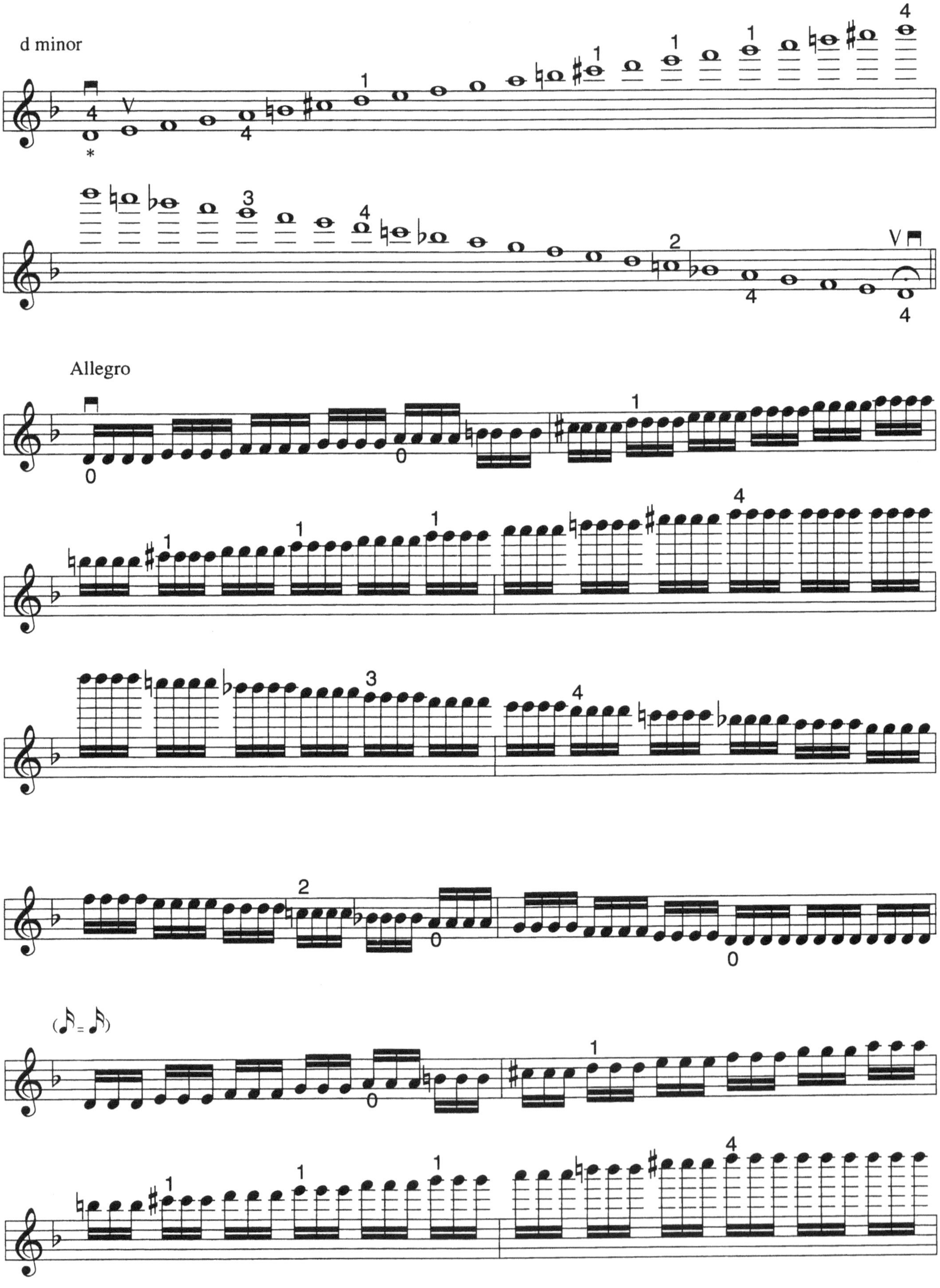

*each note as long as possible (10-20 seconds)

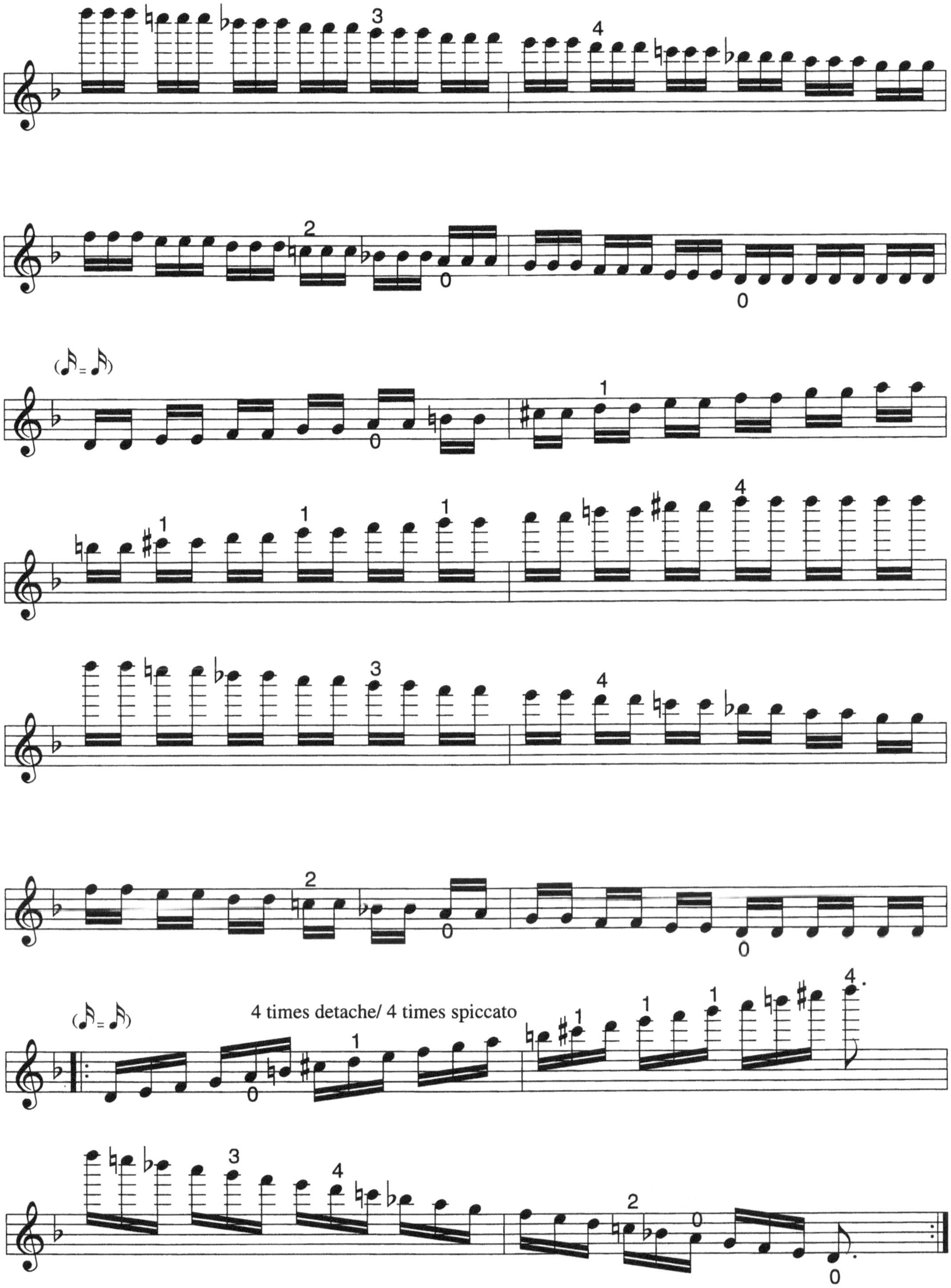
4 times detache/ 4 times spiccato

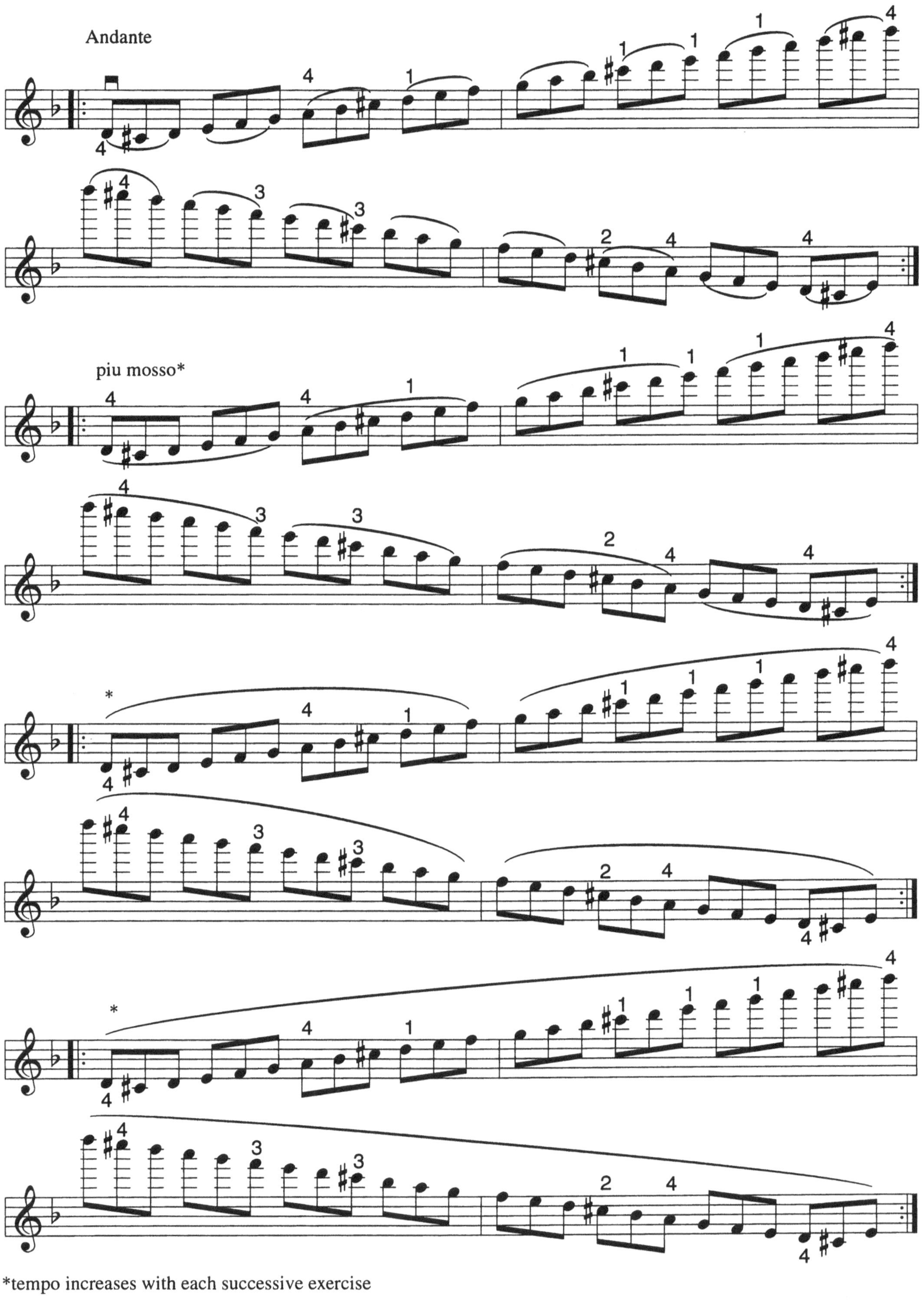

*tempo increases with each successive exercise

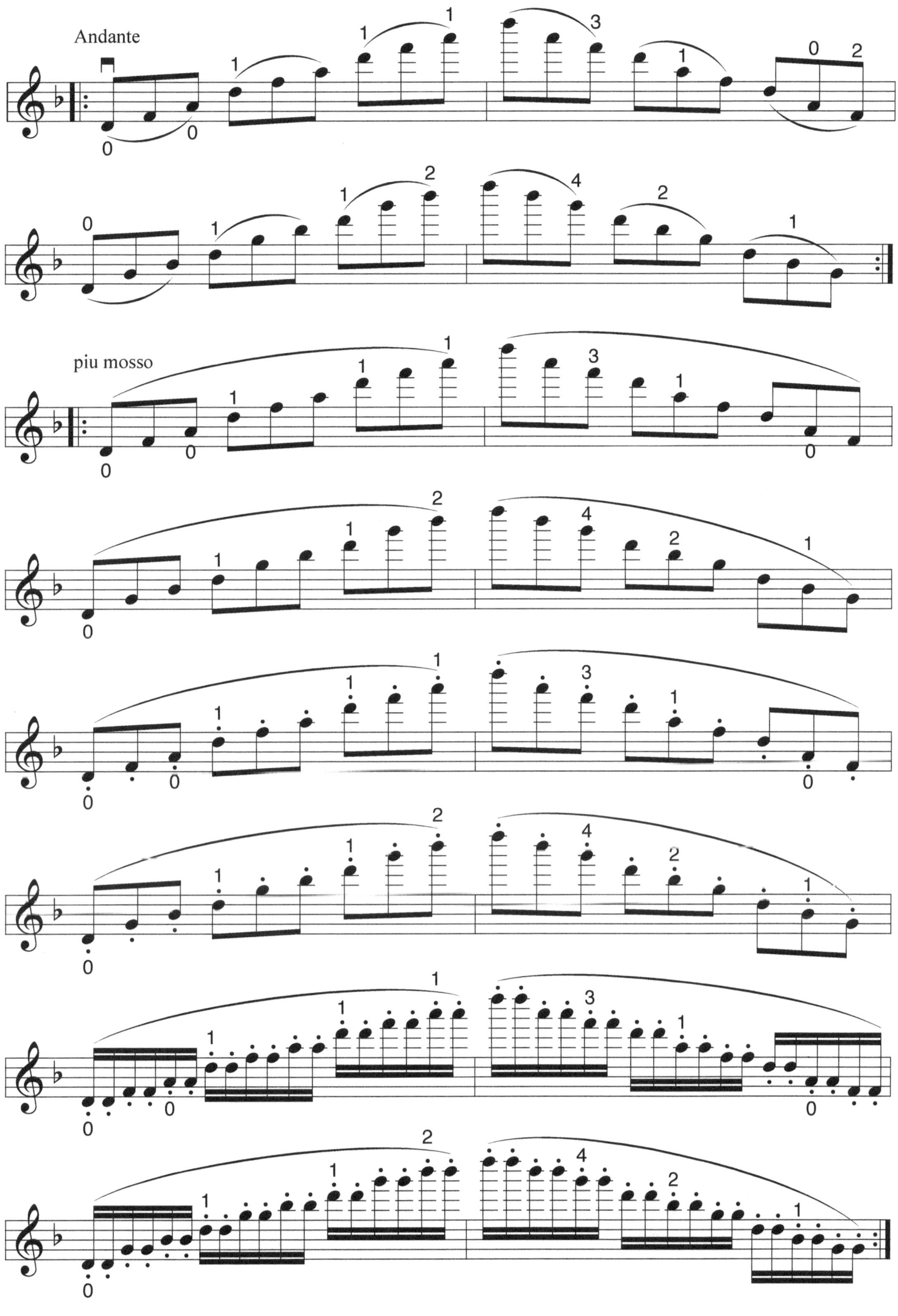
Andante
piu mosso

*tempo increases with each successive exercise

Andante

*tempo increases with each successive exercise

*tempo increases with each successive exercise

*tempo increases with each successive exercise

*tempo increases with each successive exercise

b minor

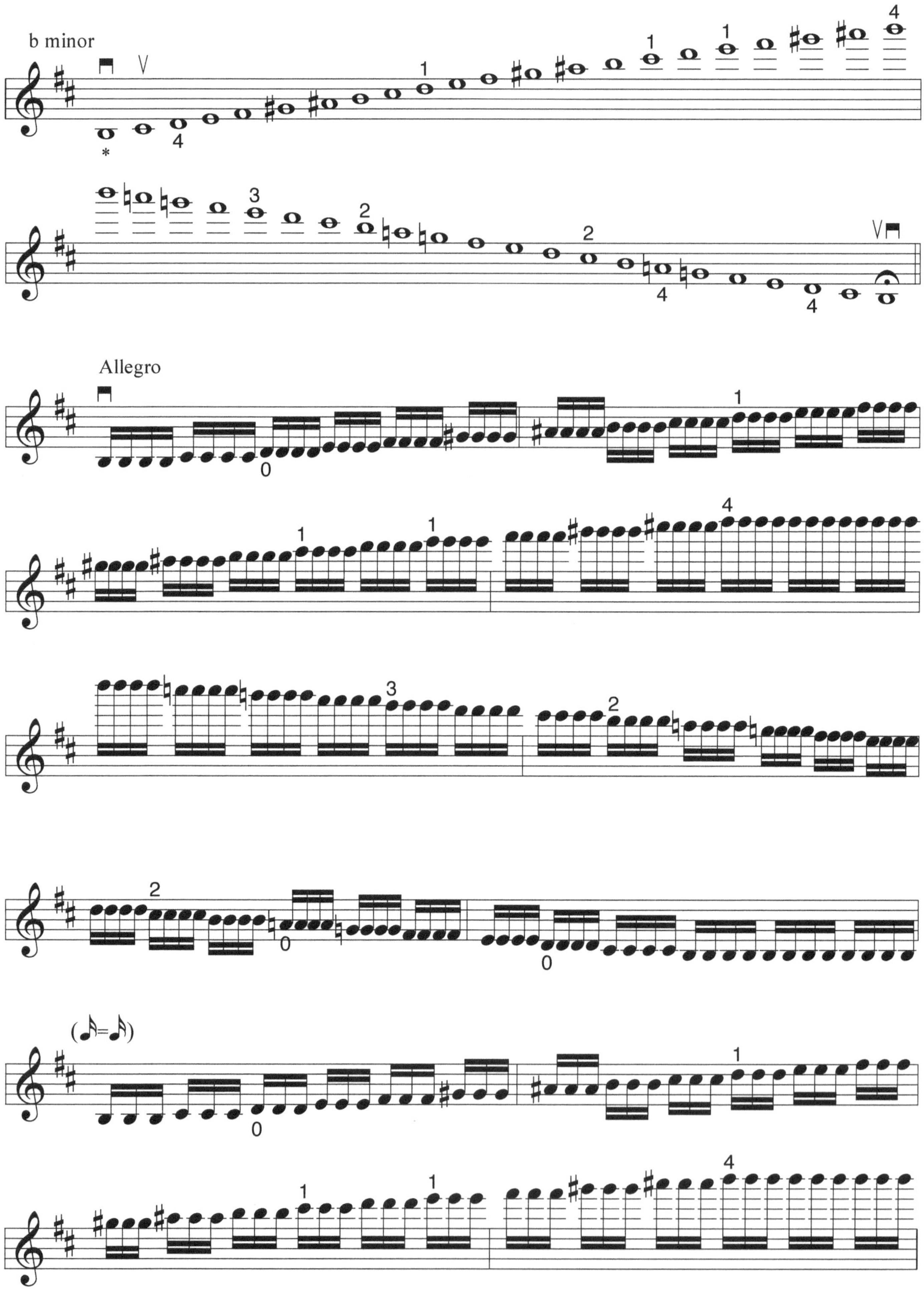

*each note as long as possible (10-20 seconds)

4 times detache/ 4 times spiccato

*tempo increases with each successive exercise

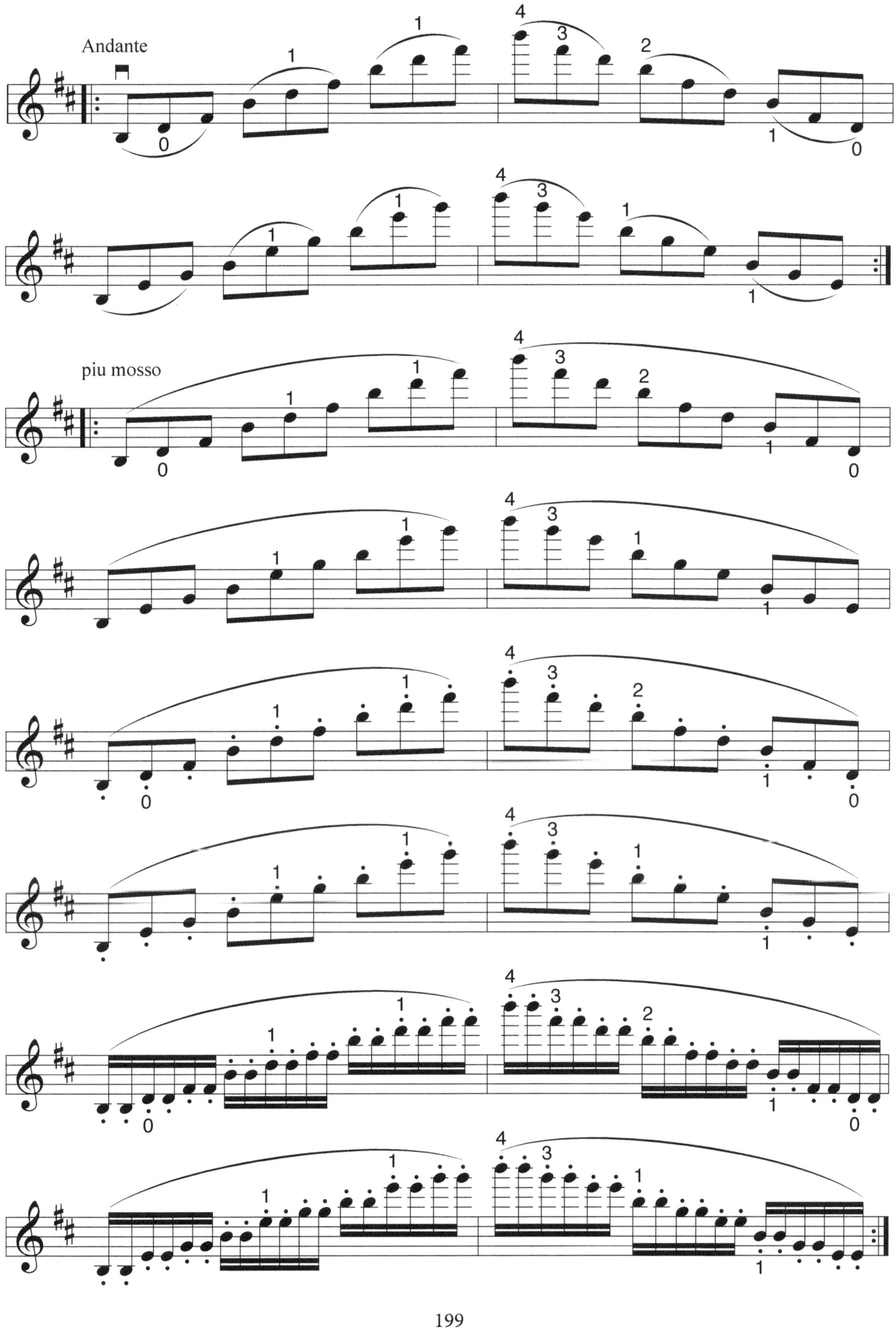
Andante
piu mosso

*tempo increases with each successive exercise

*tempo increases with each successive exercise

*tempo increases with each successive exercise

*tempo increases with each successive exercise

*tempo increases with each successive exercise

g minor

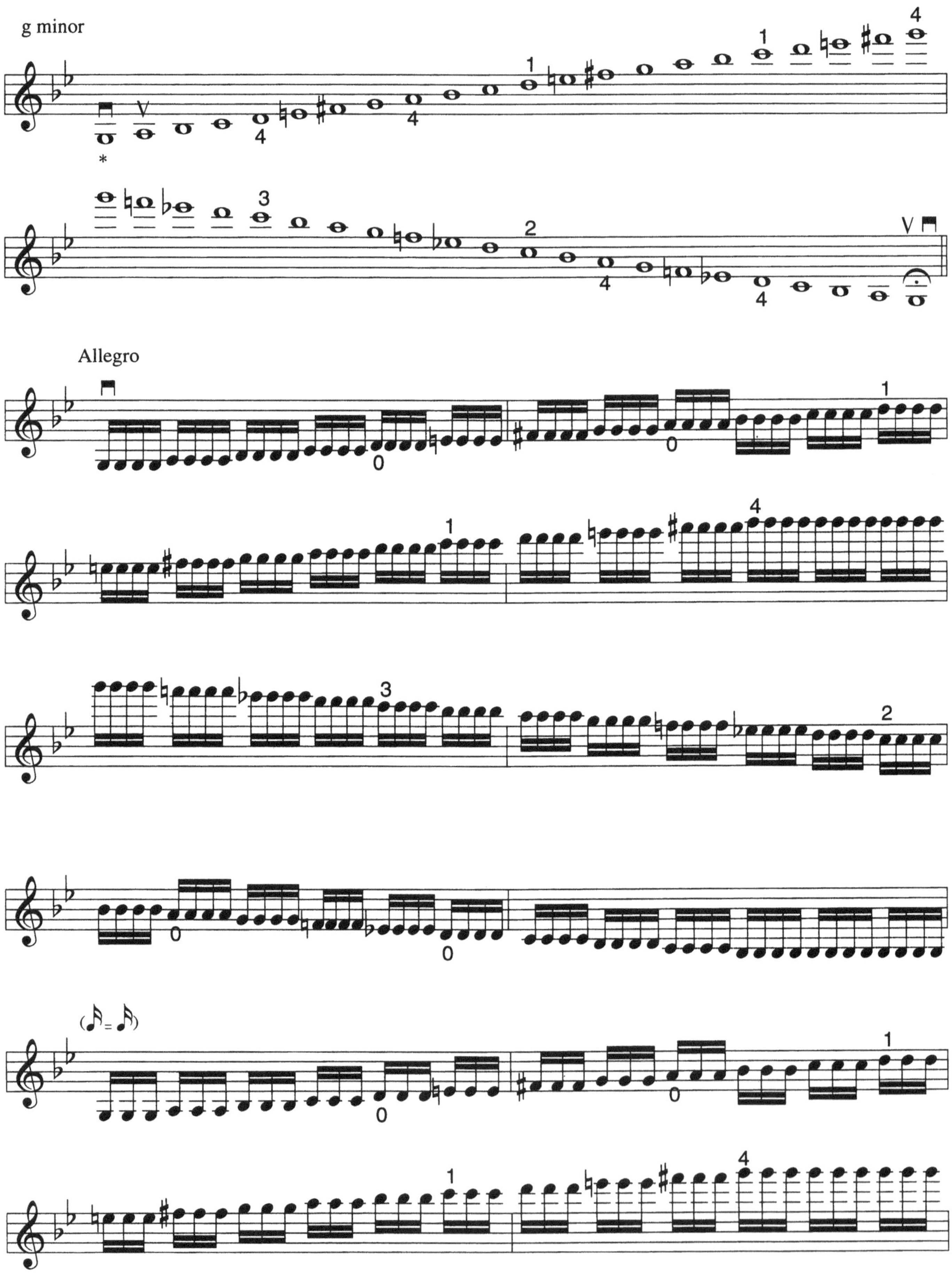

*each note as long as possible (10-20 seconds)

4 times detache/ 4 times spciccato

*tempo increases with each successive exercise

*tempo increases with each successive exercise

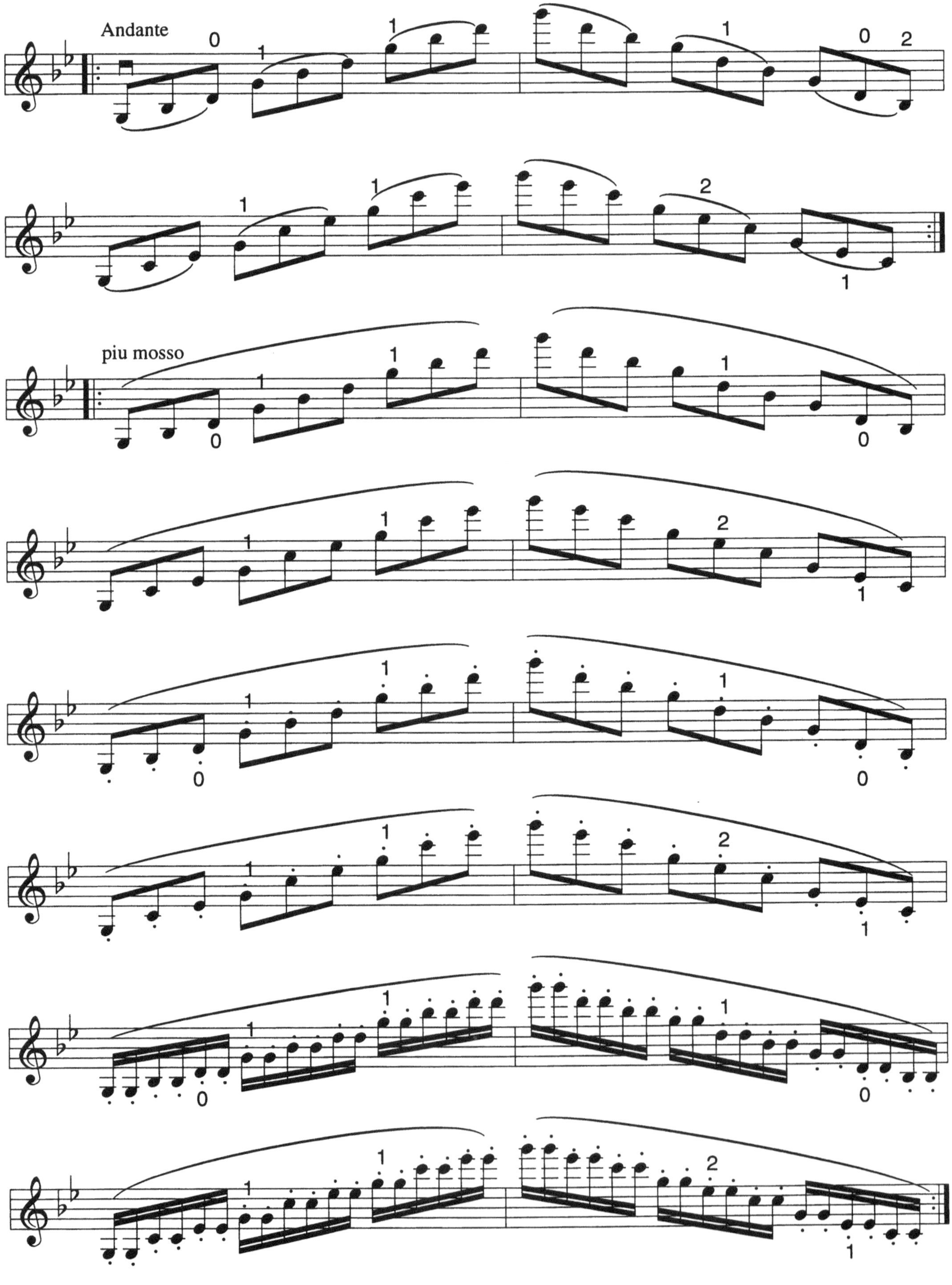
Andante
piu mosso

Four-octave arpeggios

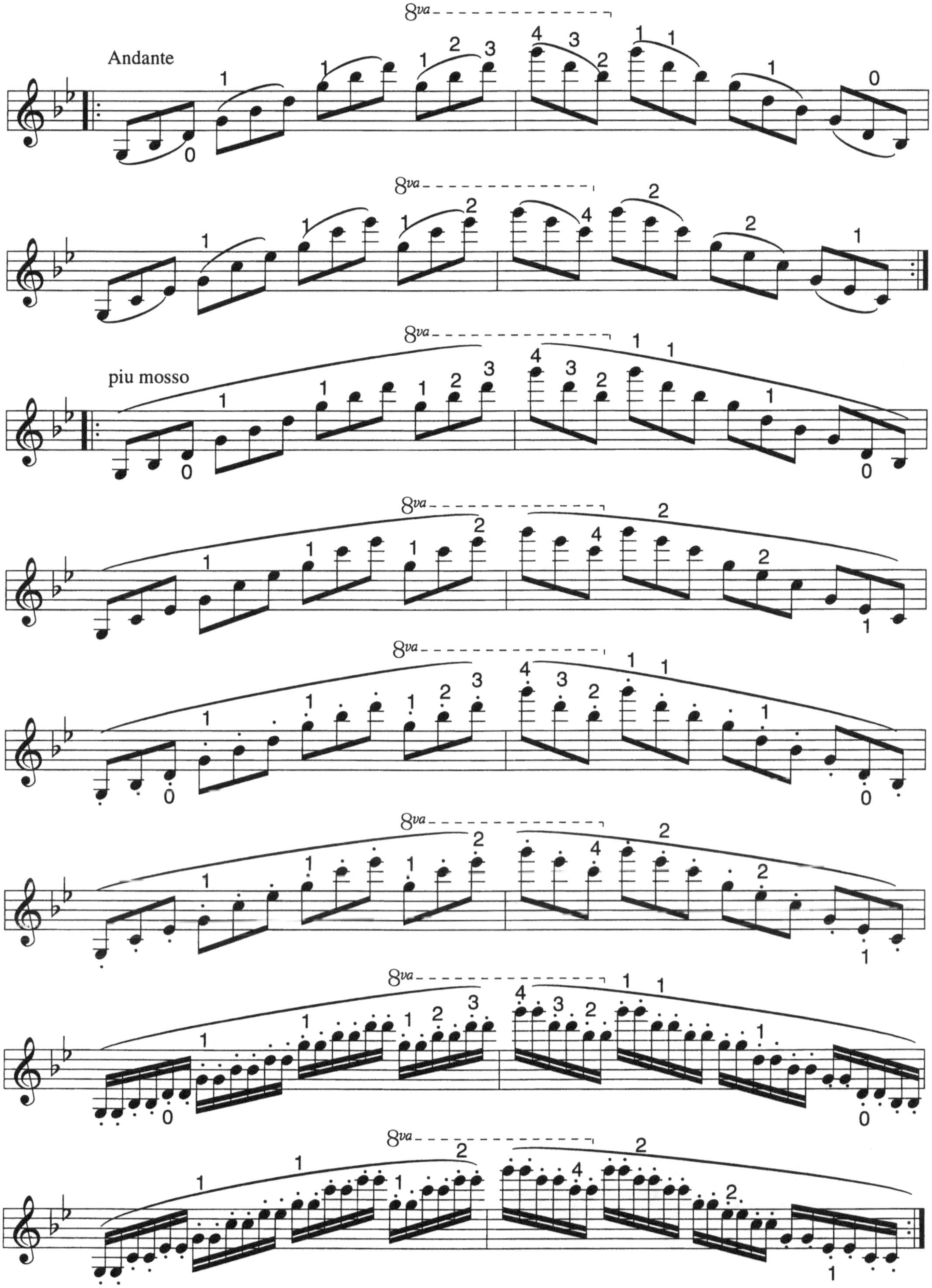

*tempo increases with each successive exercise

Three-octave scales in thirds

Andante

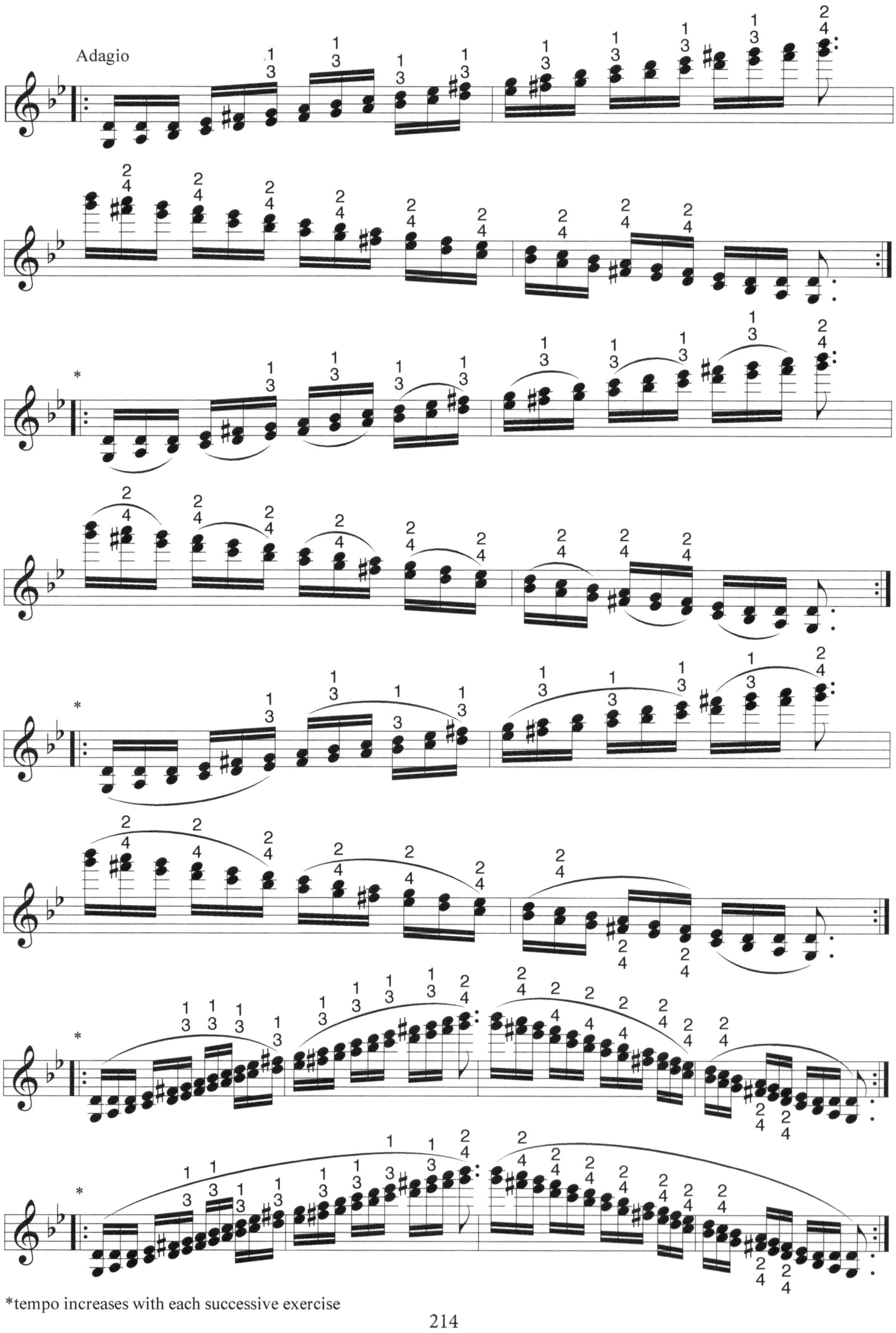

*tempo increases with each successive exercise

Andante

Adagio

*tempo increases with each successive exercise

*tempo increases with each successive exercise

*tempo increases with each successive exercise

*tempo increases with each successive exercise

f-sharp minor

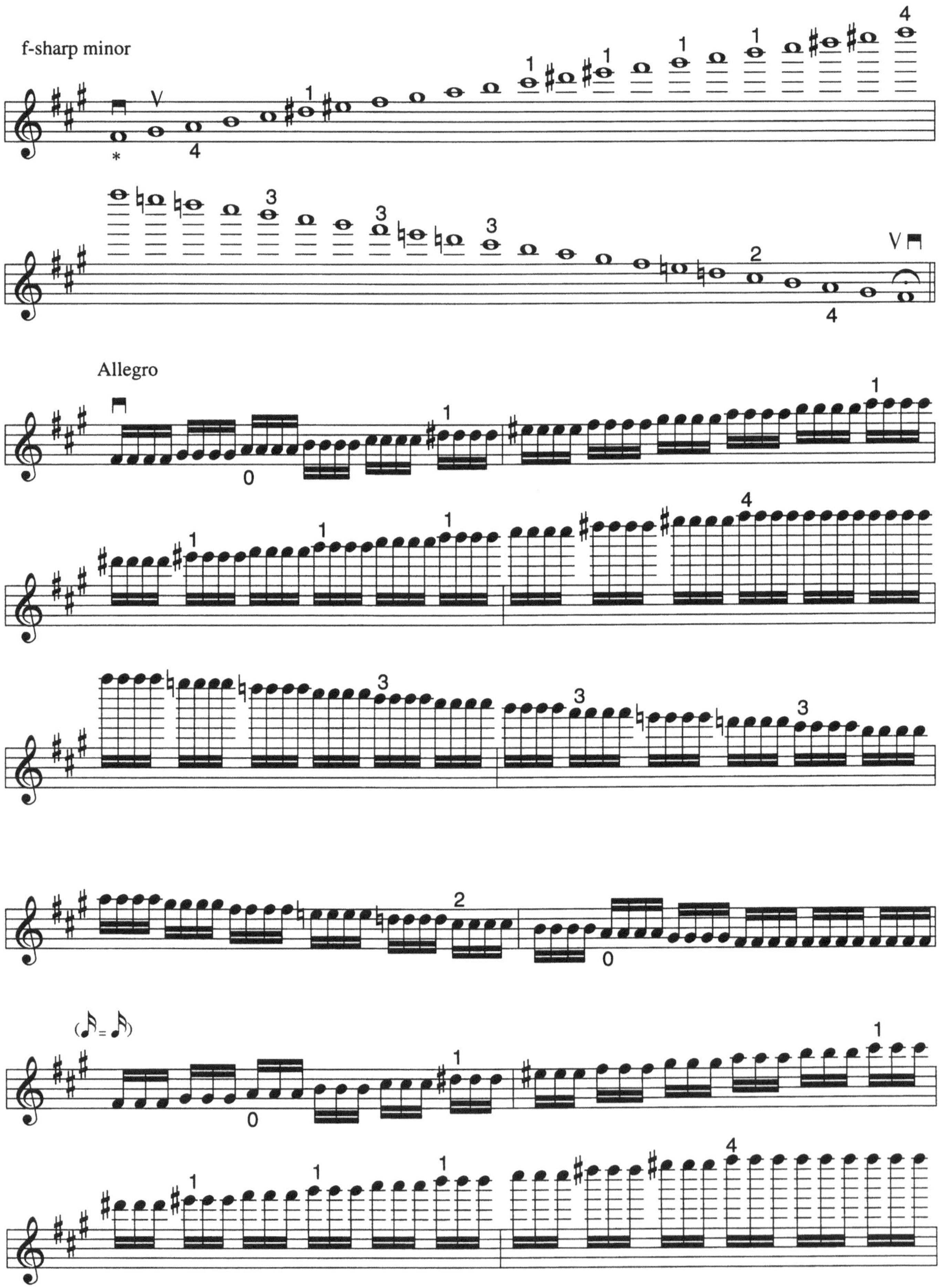

*each note as long as possible (10-20 seconds)

4 times detache/ 4 times spiccato

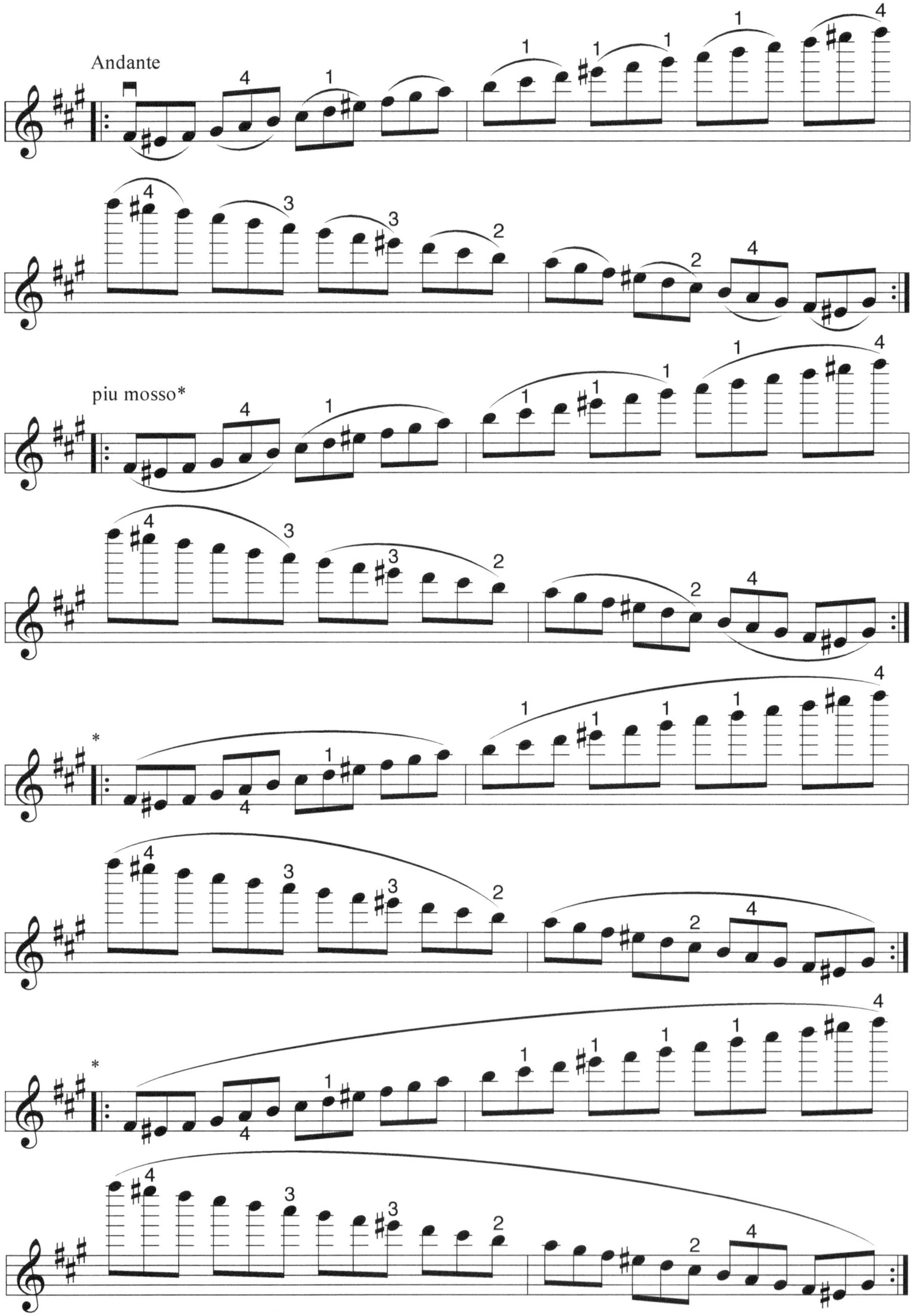

*tempo increases with each successive exercise

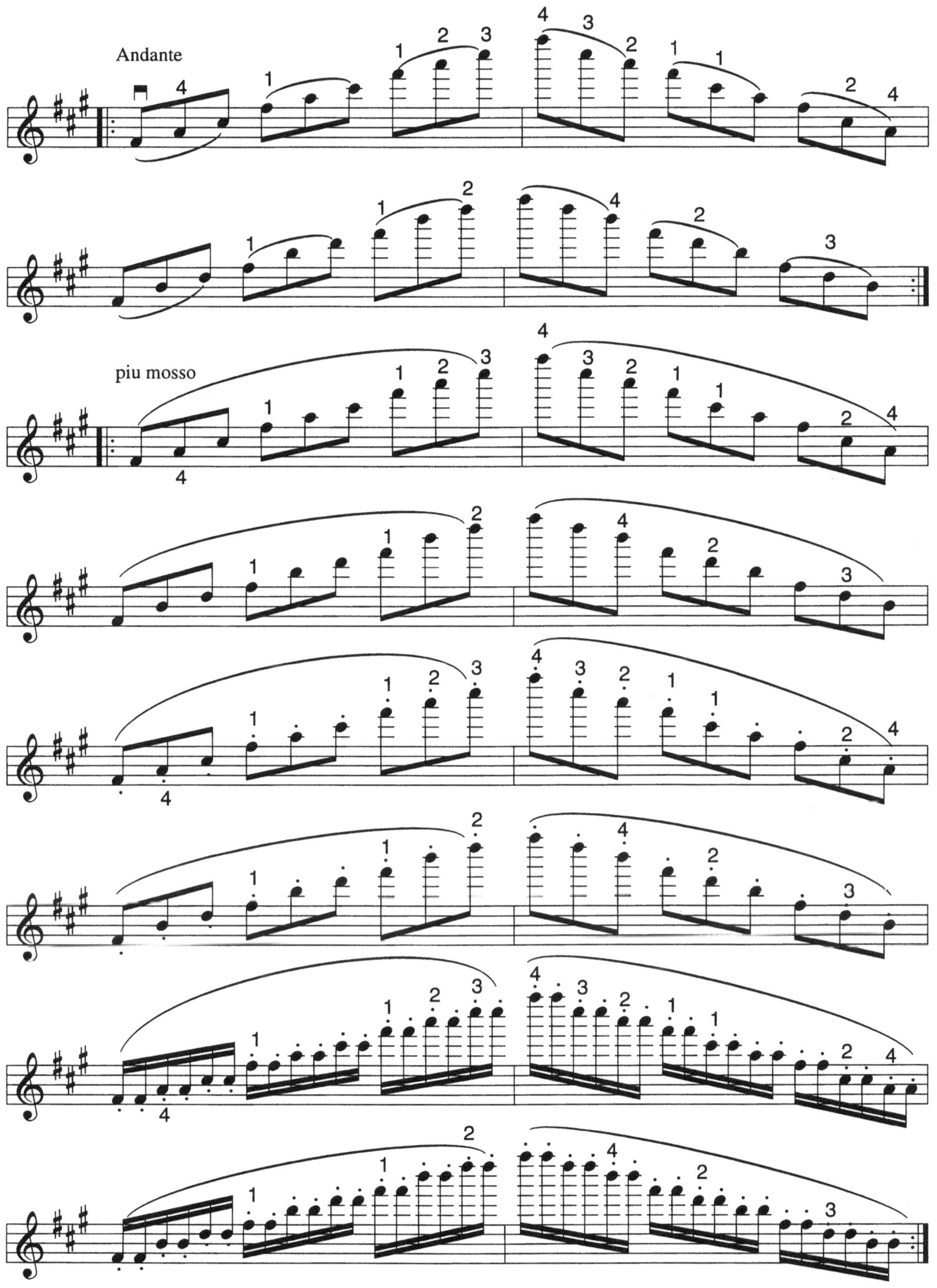
Andante
piu mosso

*tempo increases with each successive exercise

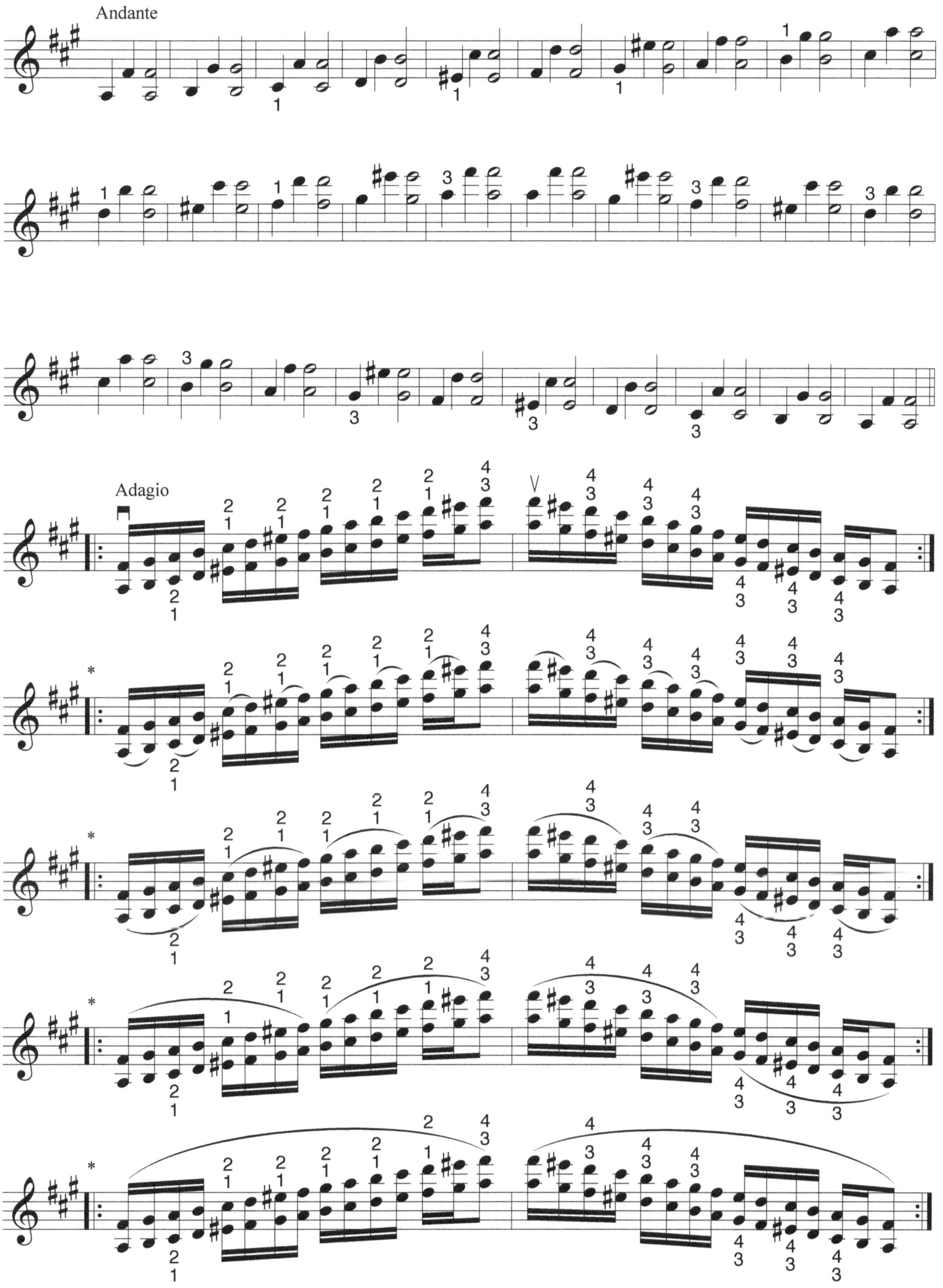

*tempo increases with each successive exercise

*tempo increases with each successive exercise

*tempo increases with each successive exercise

*tempo increases with each successive exercise

c minor

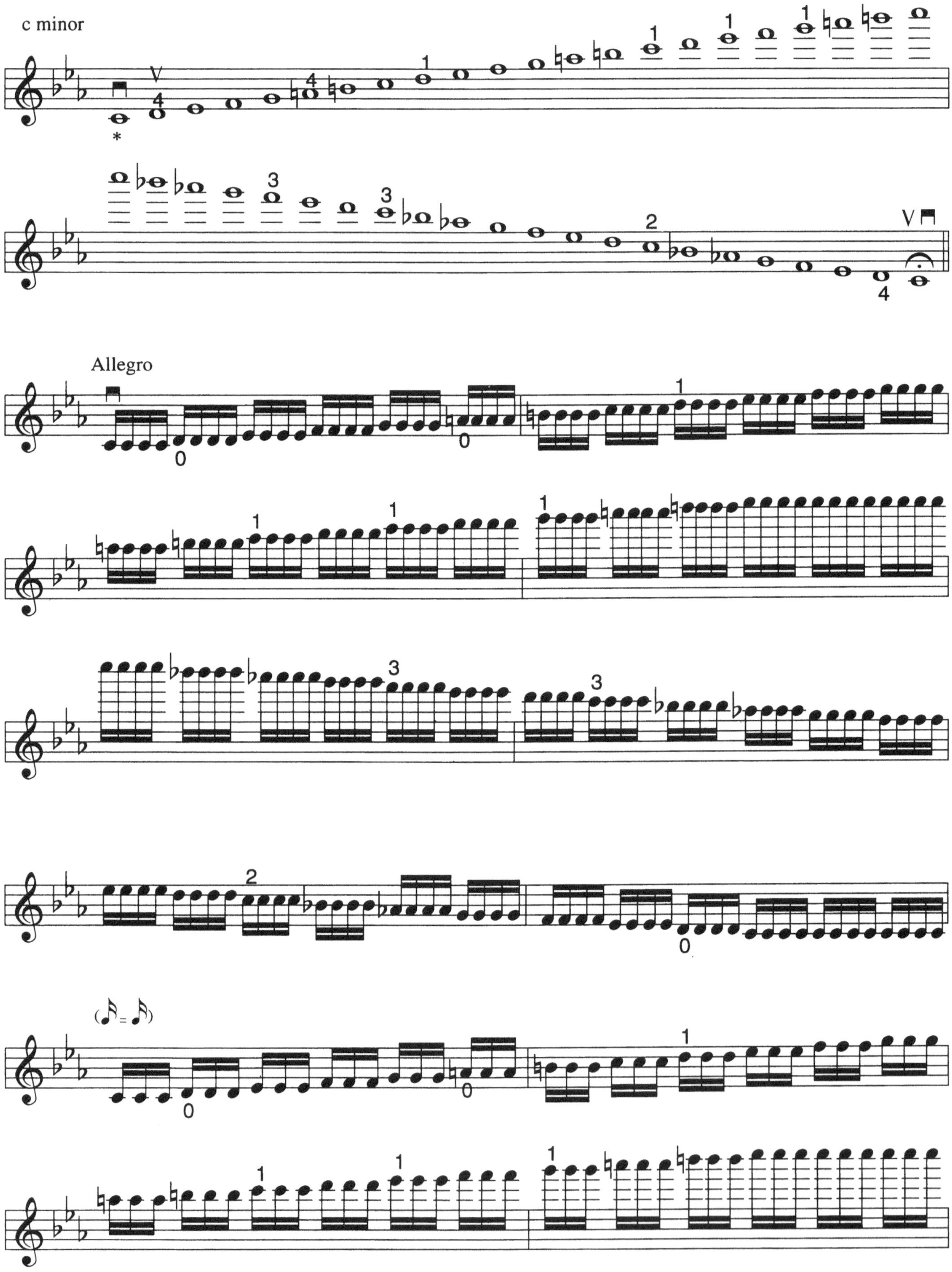

*each note as long as possible (10-20 seconds)

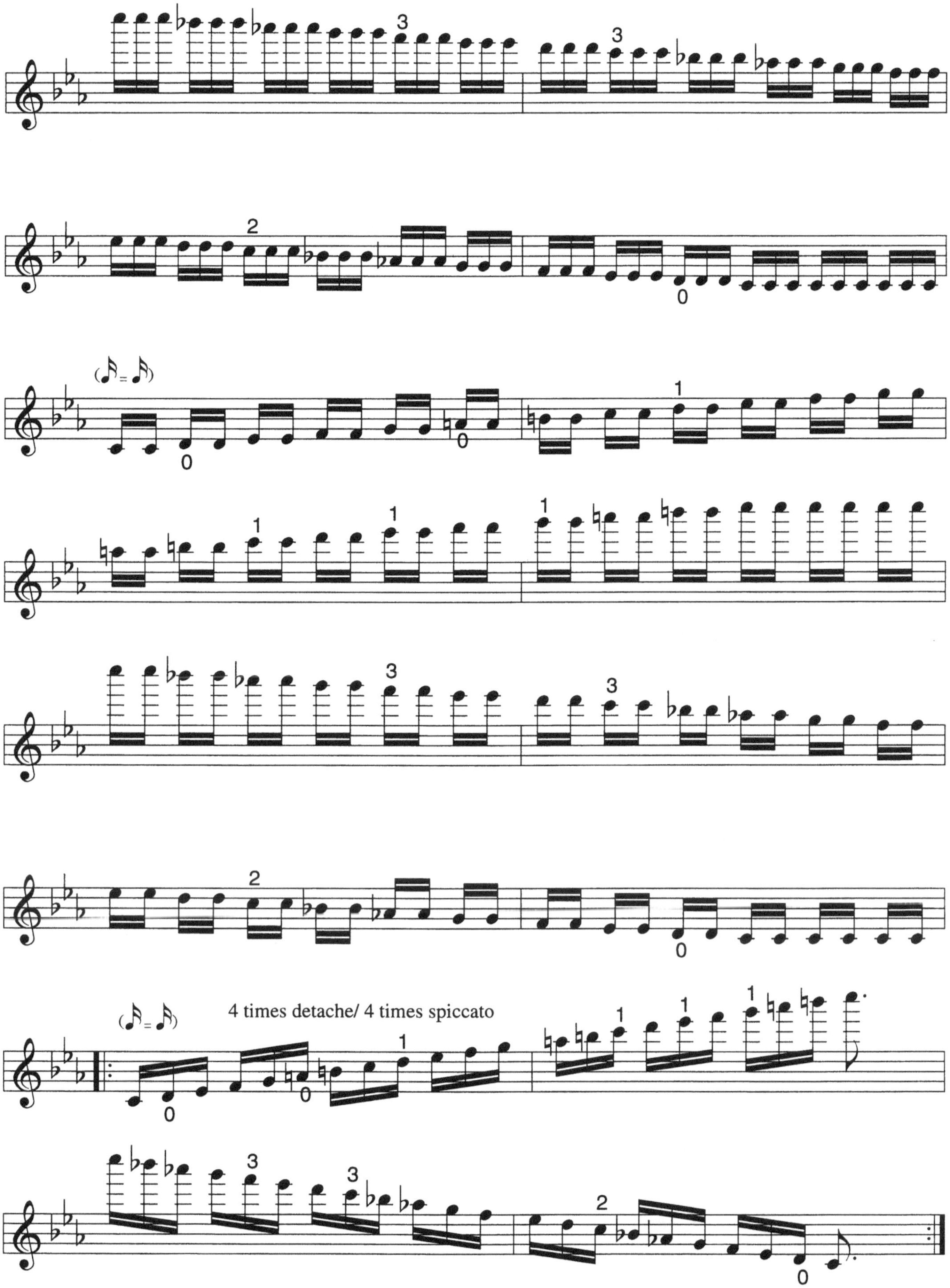
4 times detache/ 4 times spiccato

*tempo increases with each successive exercise

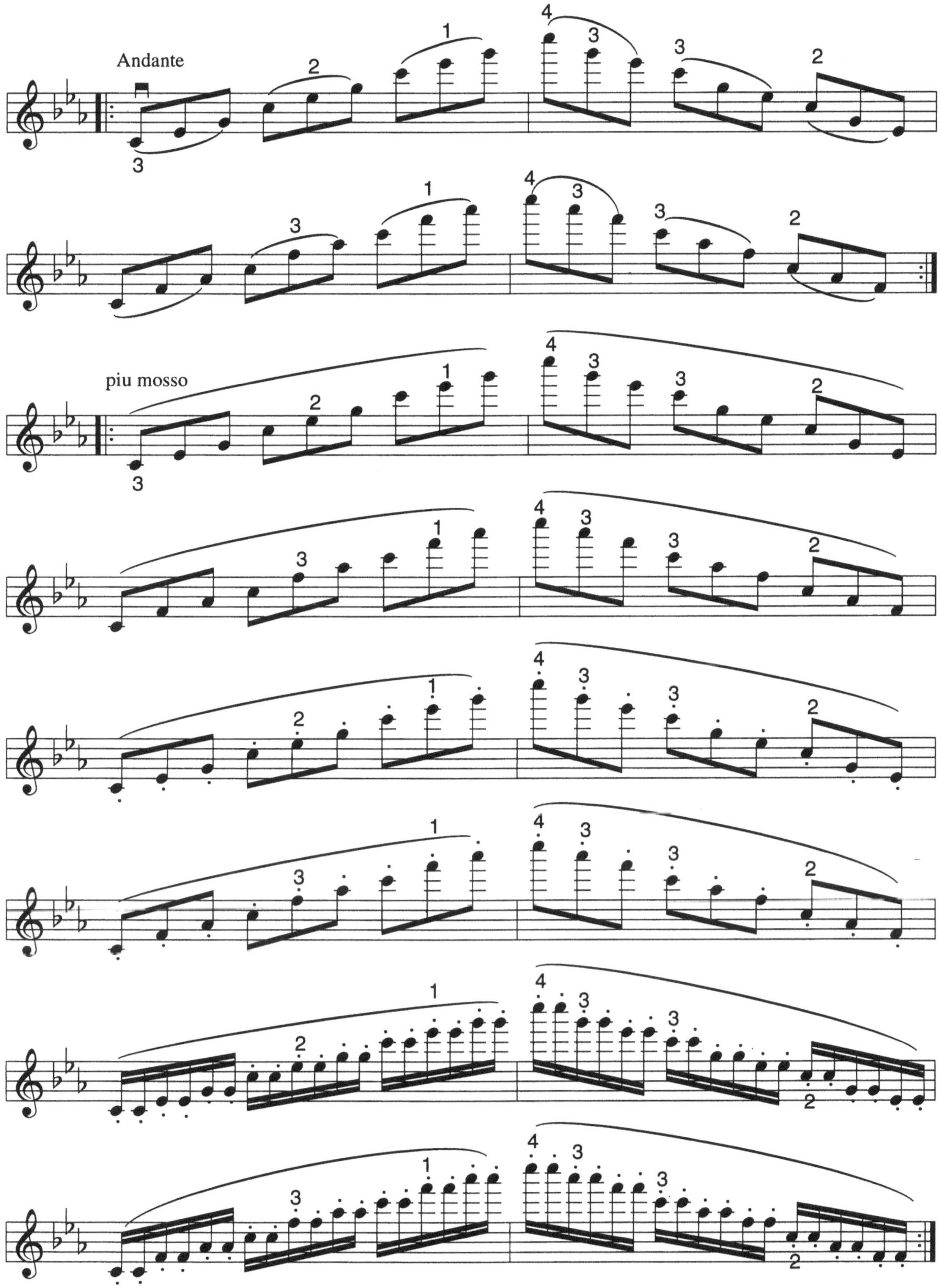
Andante
piu mosso

*tempo increases with each successive exercise

*tempo increases with each successive exercise

*tempo increases with each successive exercise

*tempo increases with each successive exercise

*tempo increases with each successive exercise

c-sharp minor

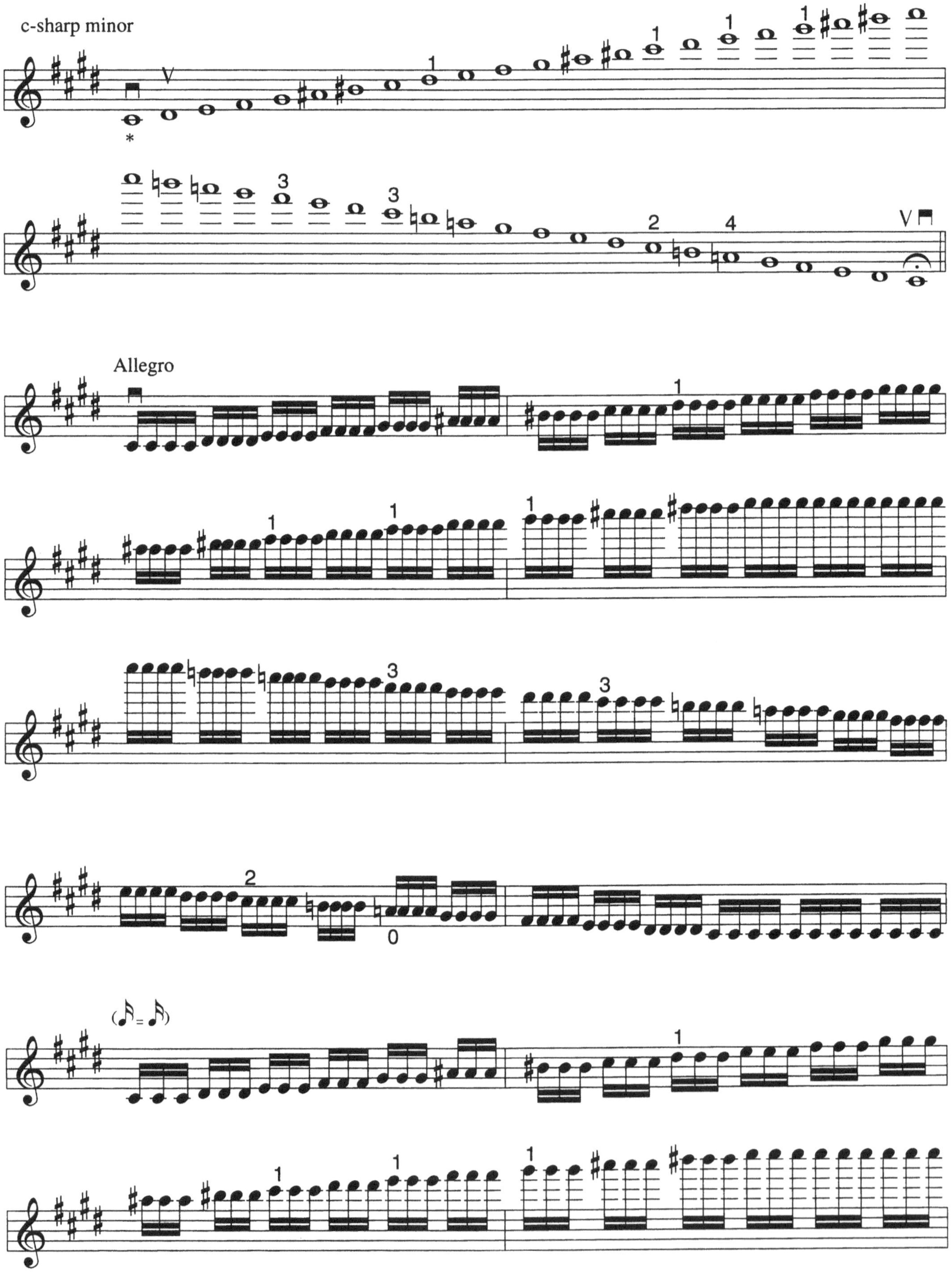

*each note as long as possible (10-20 seconds)

4 times detache/ 4 times spiccato

*tempo increases with each successive exercise

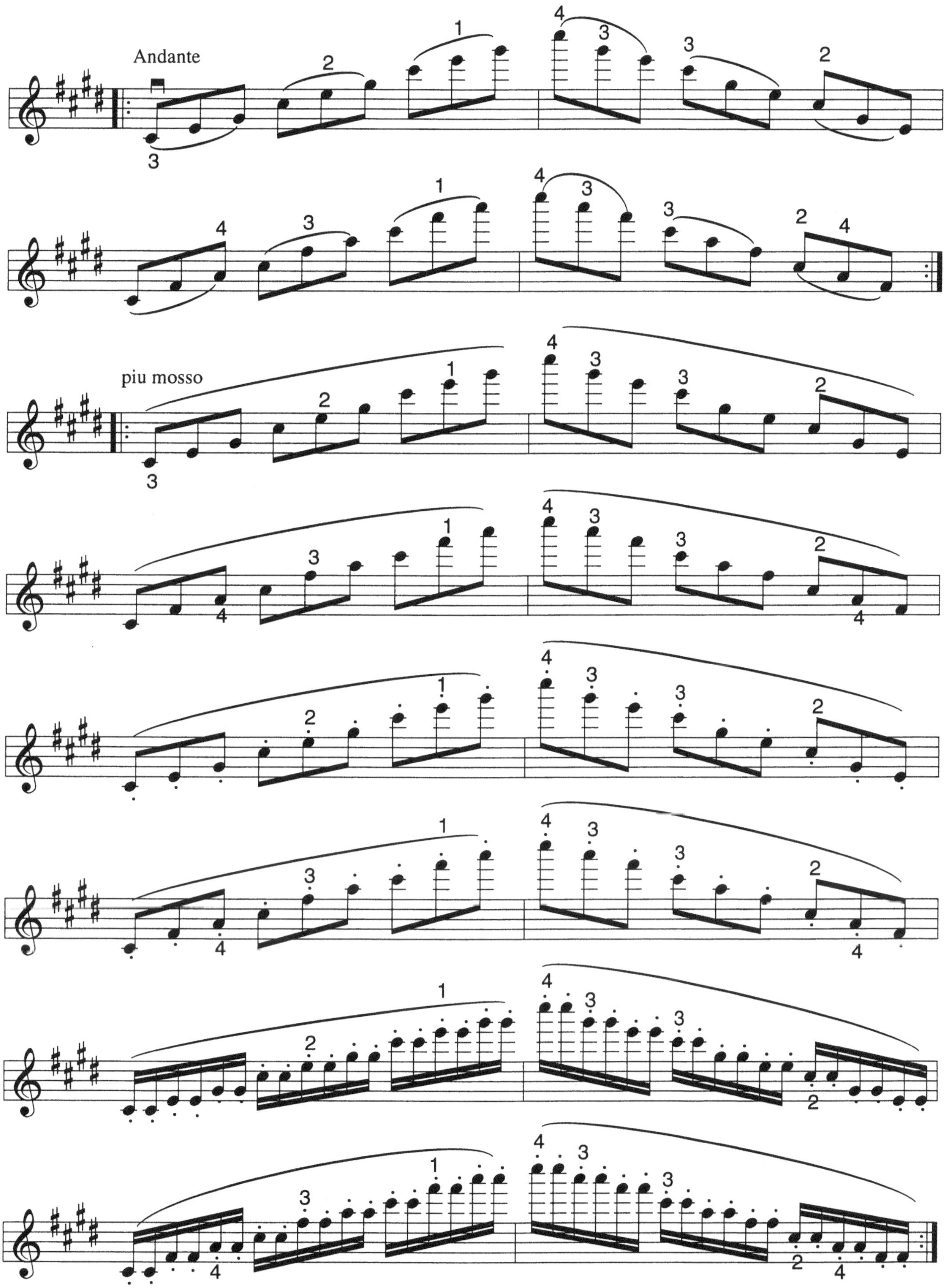
Andante
piu mosso

*tempo increases with each successive exercise

*tempo increases with each successive exercise

*tempo increases with each successive exercise

*tempo increases with each successive exercise

*tempo increases with each successive exercise

f minor

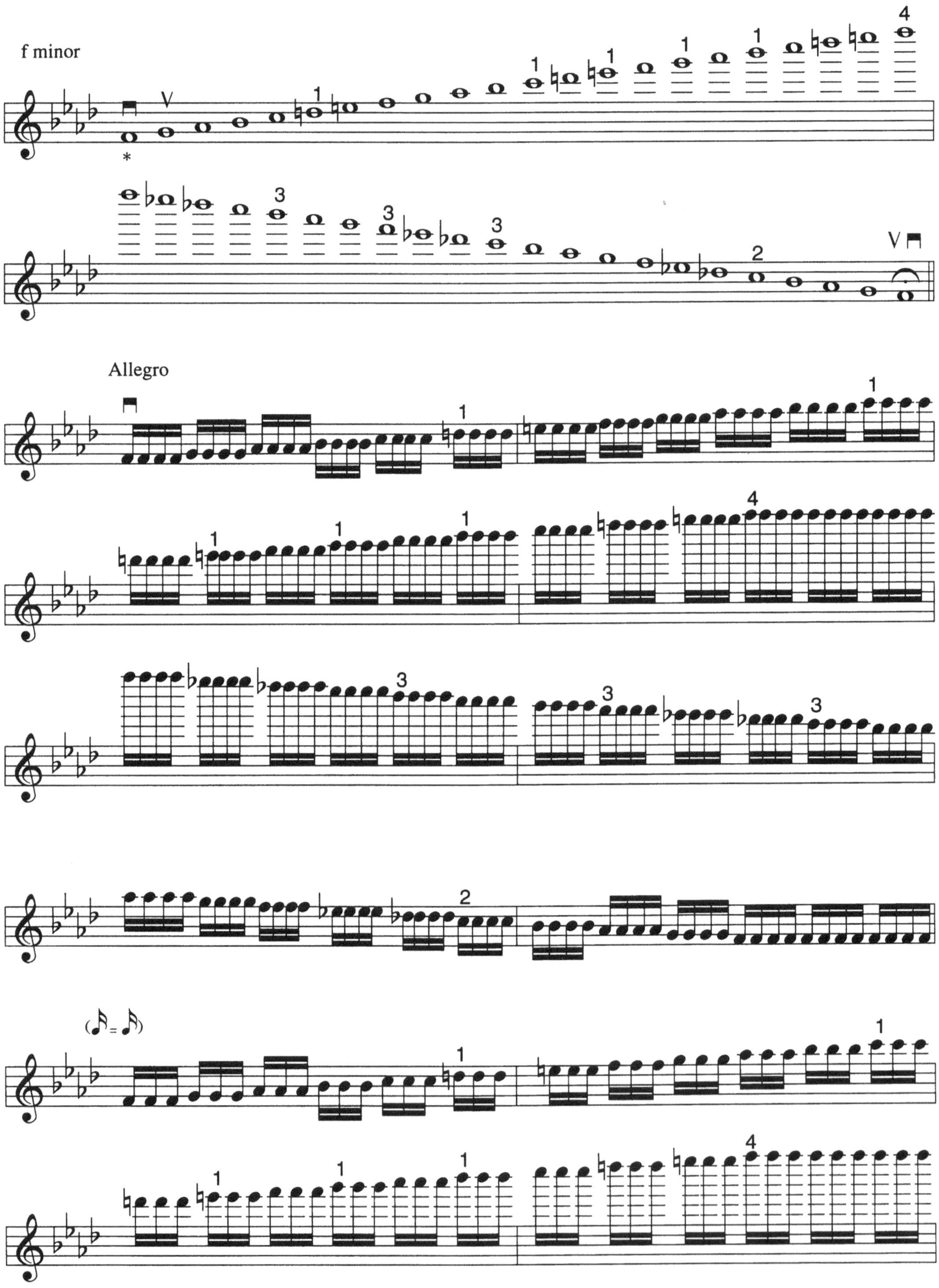

*each note as long as possible (10-20 seconds)

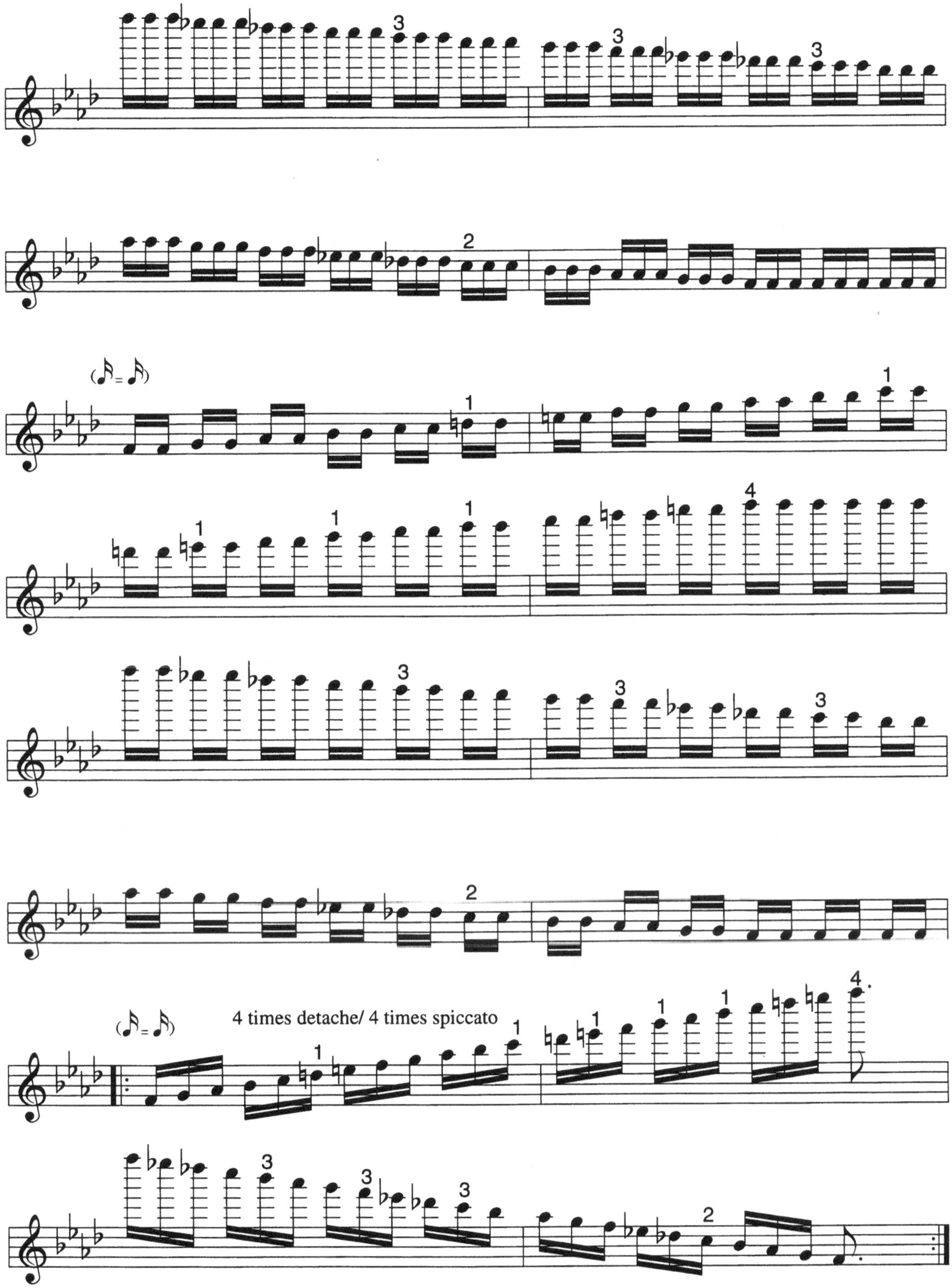
4 times detache/ 4 times spiccato

*tempo increases with each successive exercise

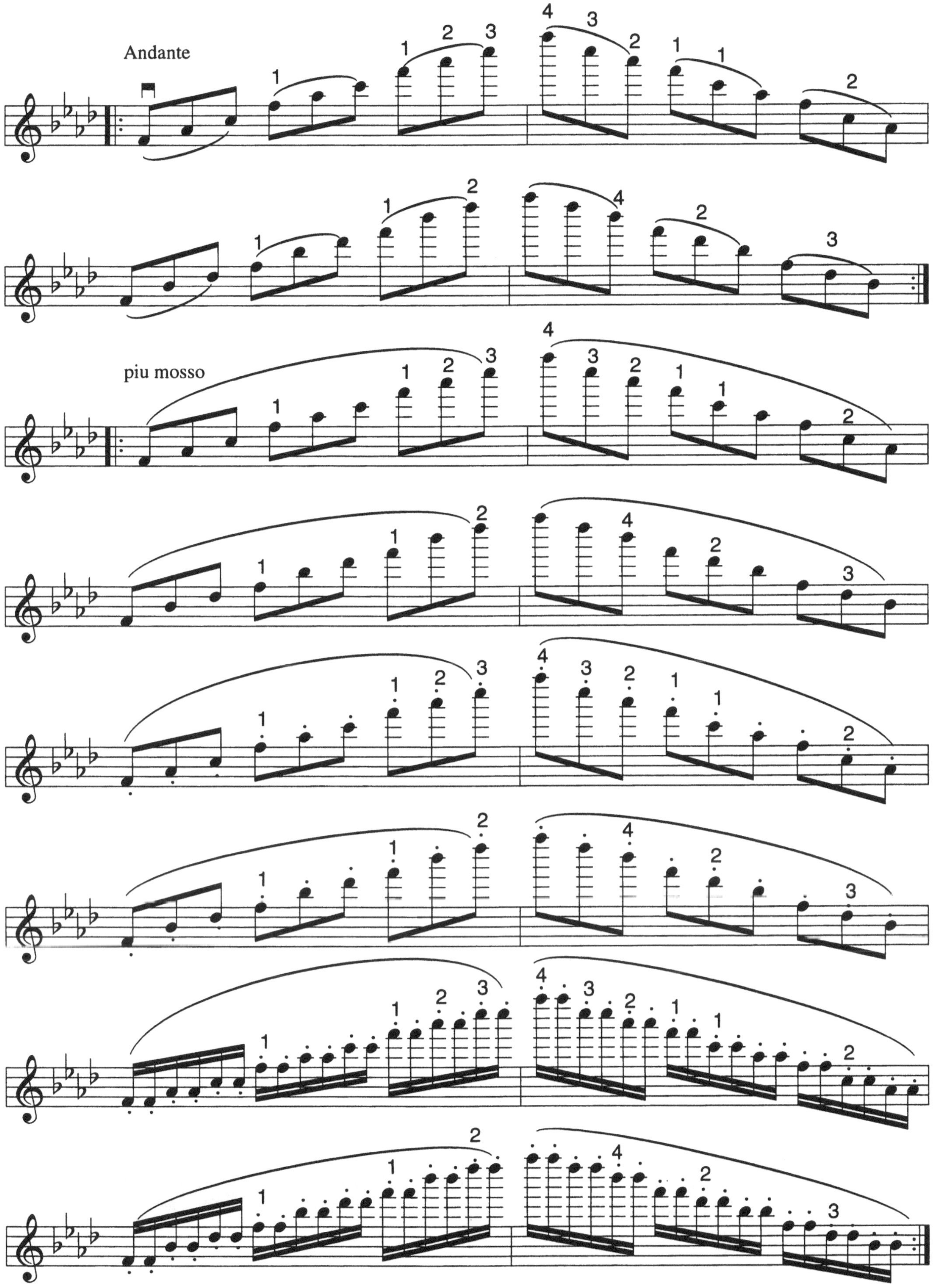
Andante
piu mosso

*tempo increases with each successive exercise

*tempo increases with each successive exercise

*tempo increases with each successive exercise

*tempo increases with each successive exercise

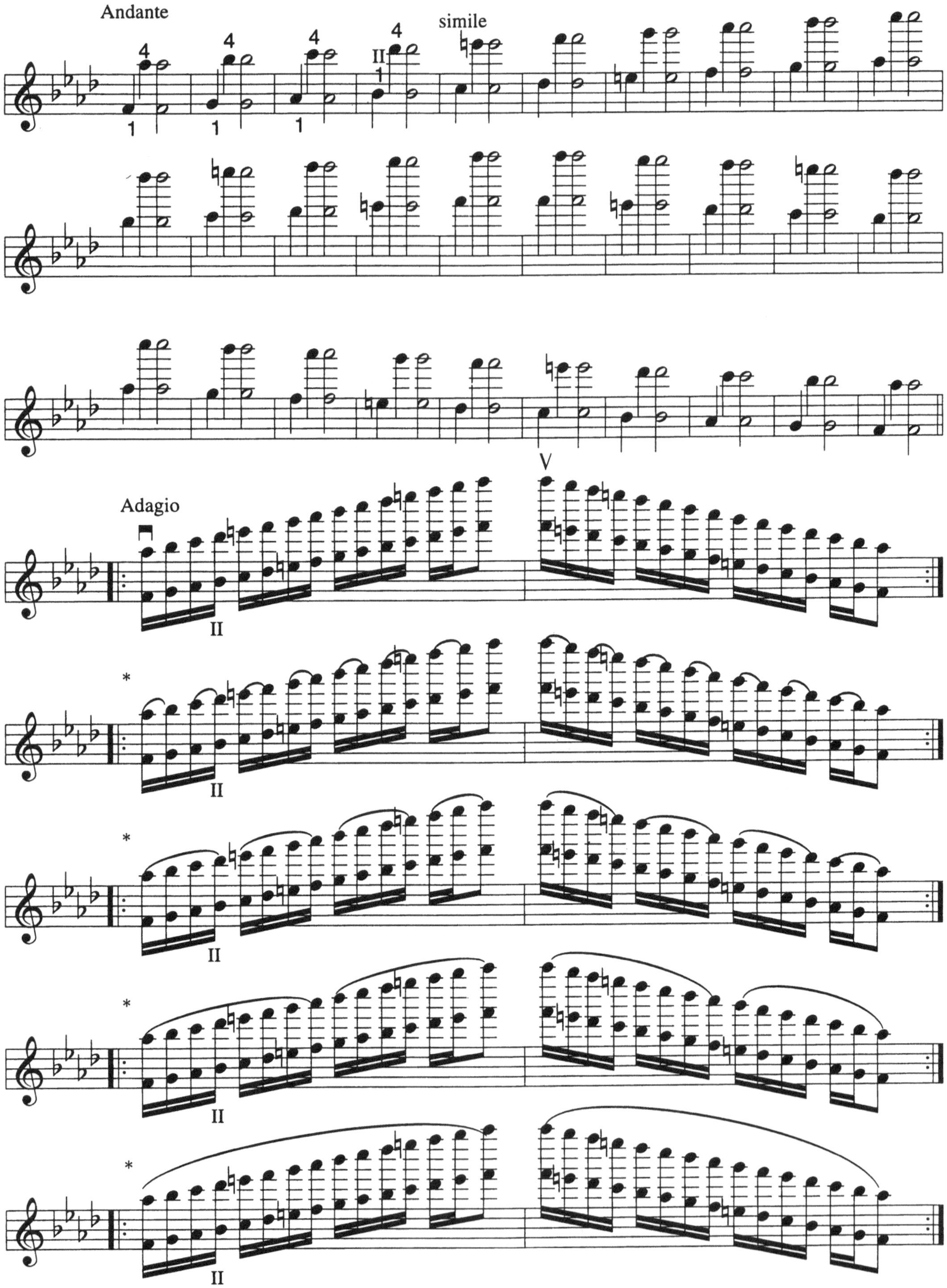

*tempo increases with each successive exercise

g-sharp minor

g-sharp minor

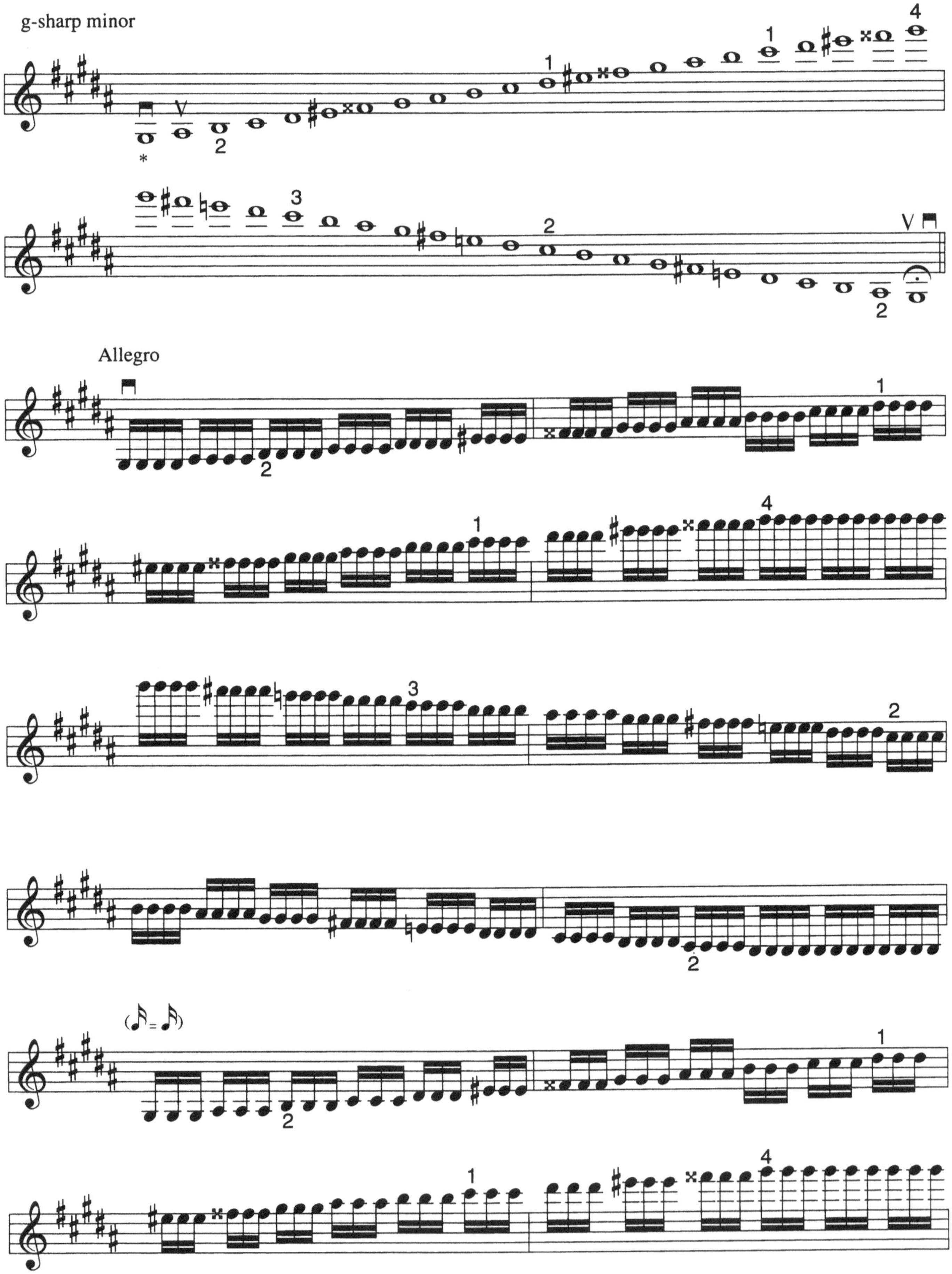

*each note as long as possible (10-20 seconds)

4 times detache/ 4 times spiccato

*tempo increases with each successive exercise

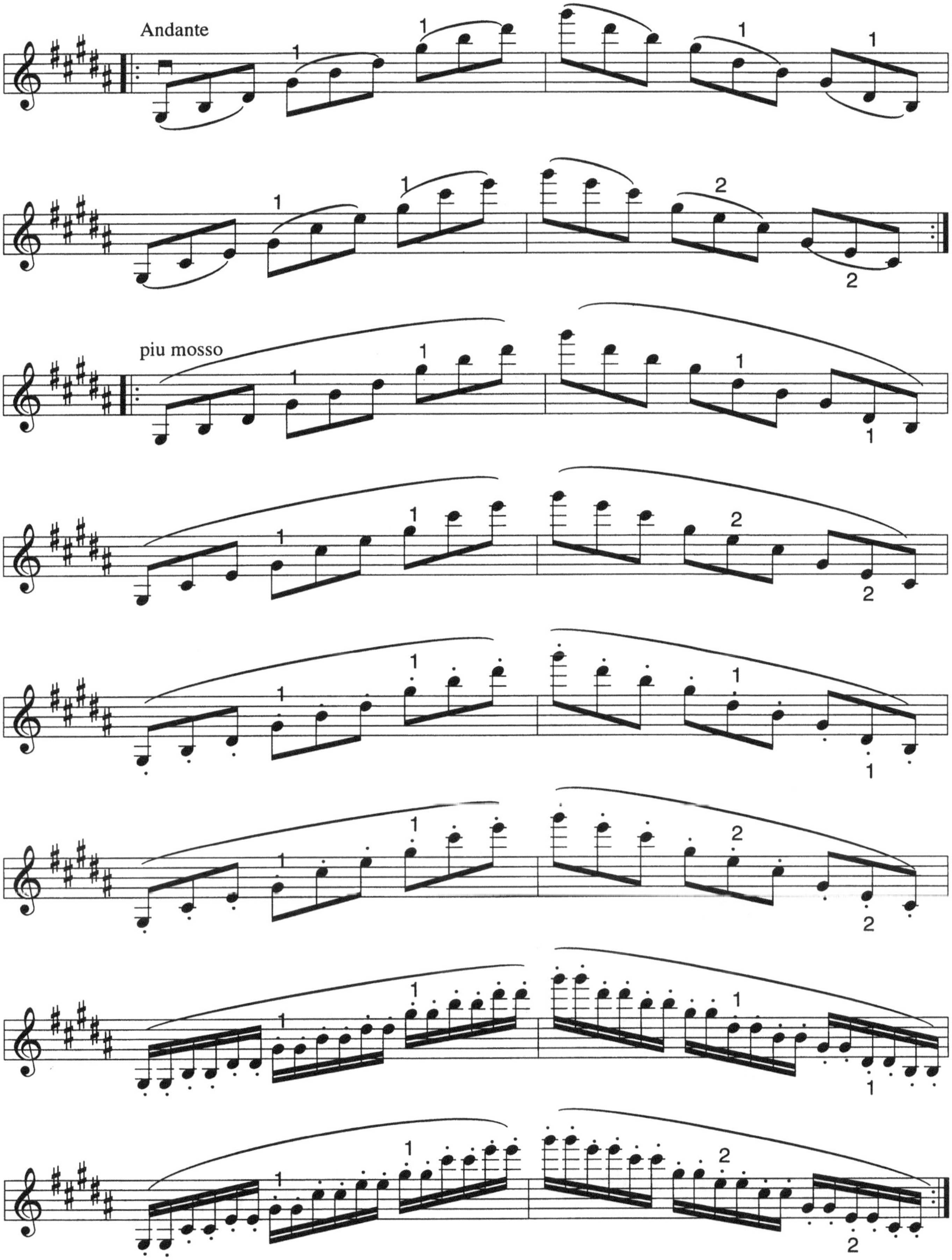
Andante
piu mosso

*tempo increases with each successive exercise

*tempo increases with each successive exercise

*tempo increases with each successive exercise

*tempo increases with each successive exercise

*tempo increases with each successive exercise

b-flat minor

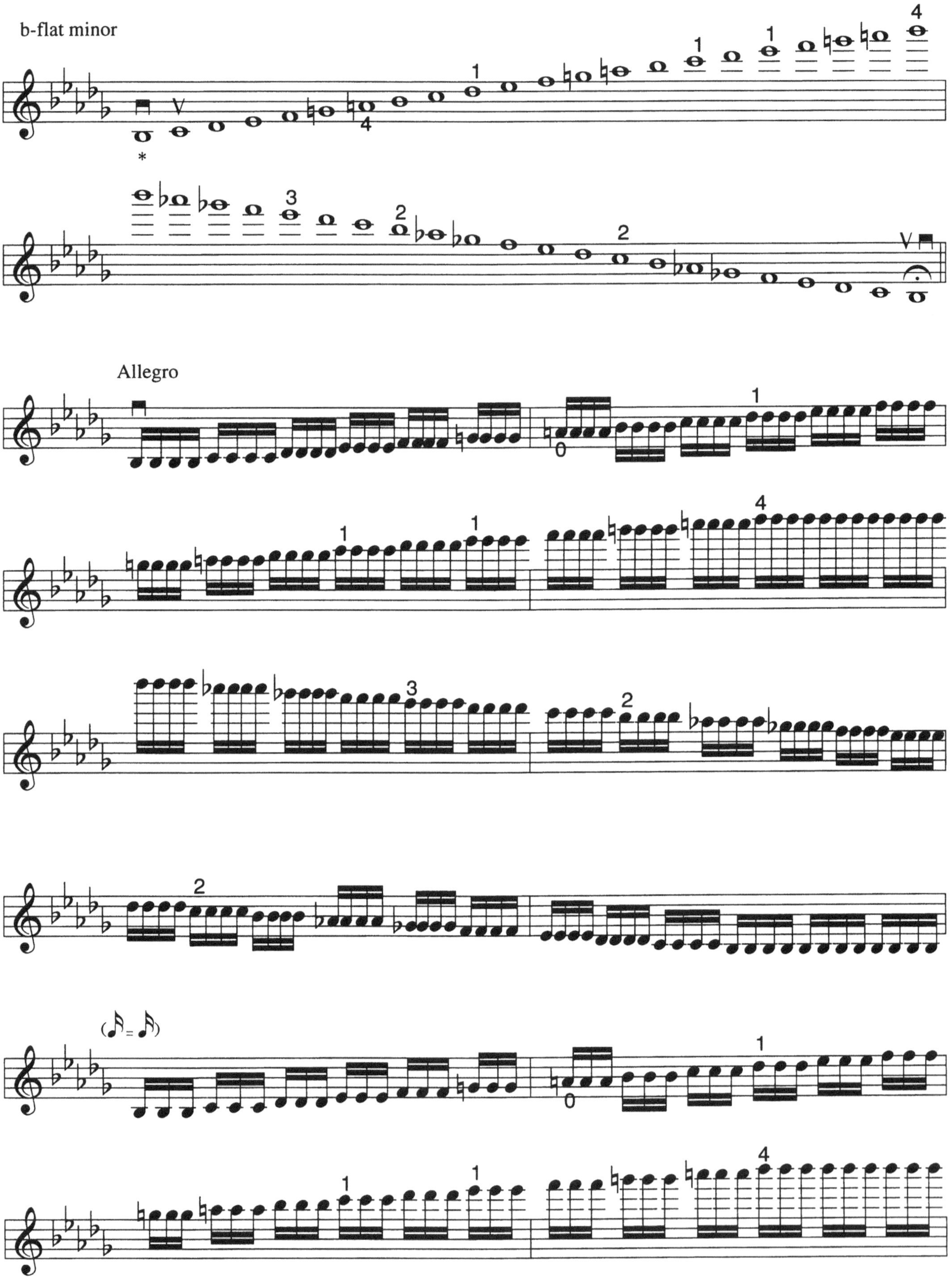

*each note as long as possible (10-20 seconds)

4 times detache/ 4 times spiccato

*tempo increases with each successive exercise

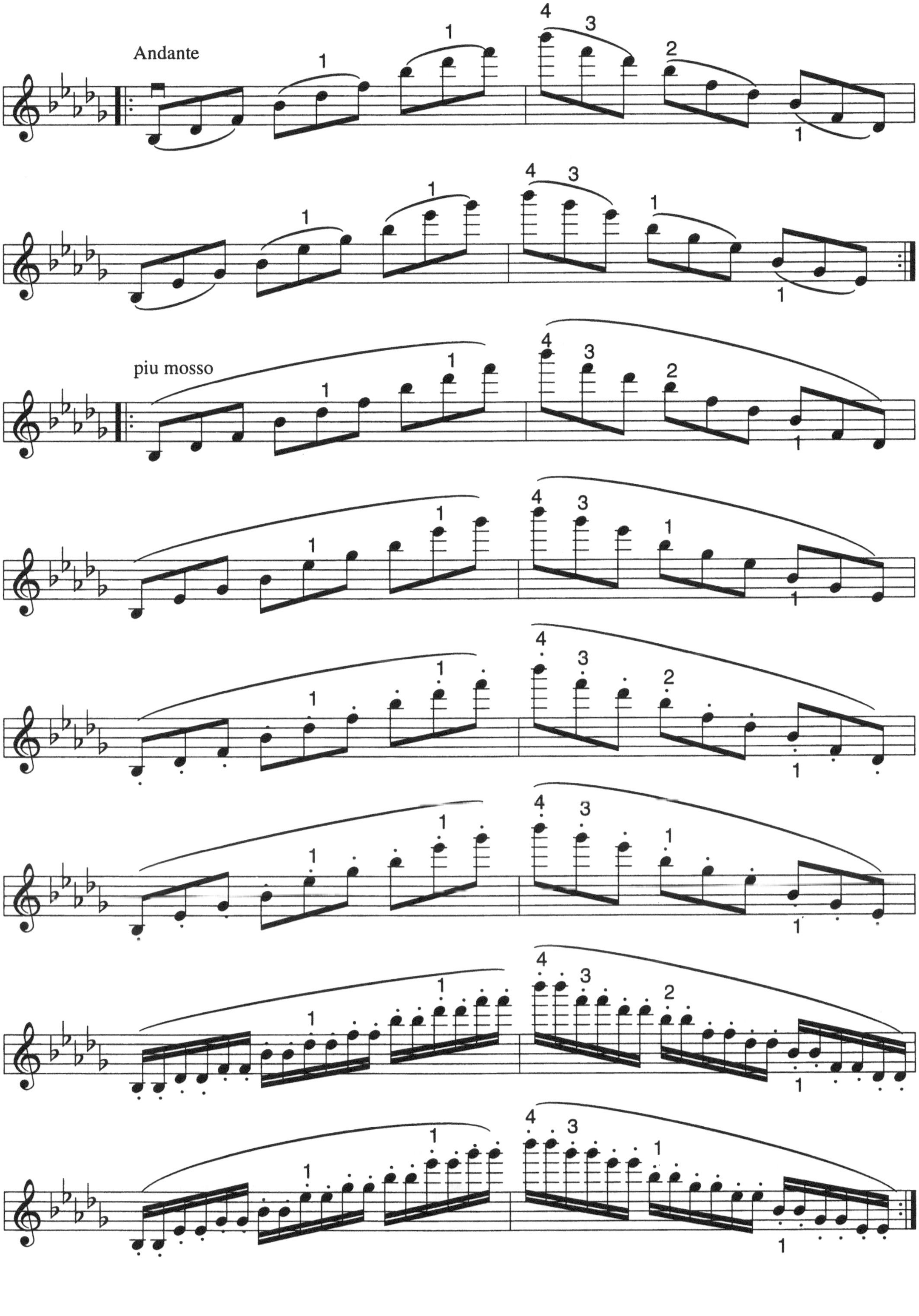
Andante
piu mosso

*tempo increases with each successive exercise

Andante

Adagio

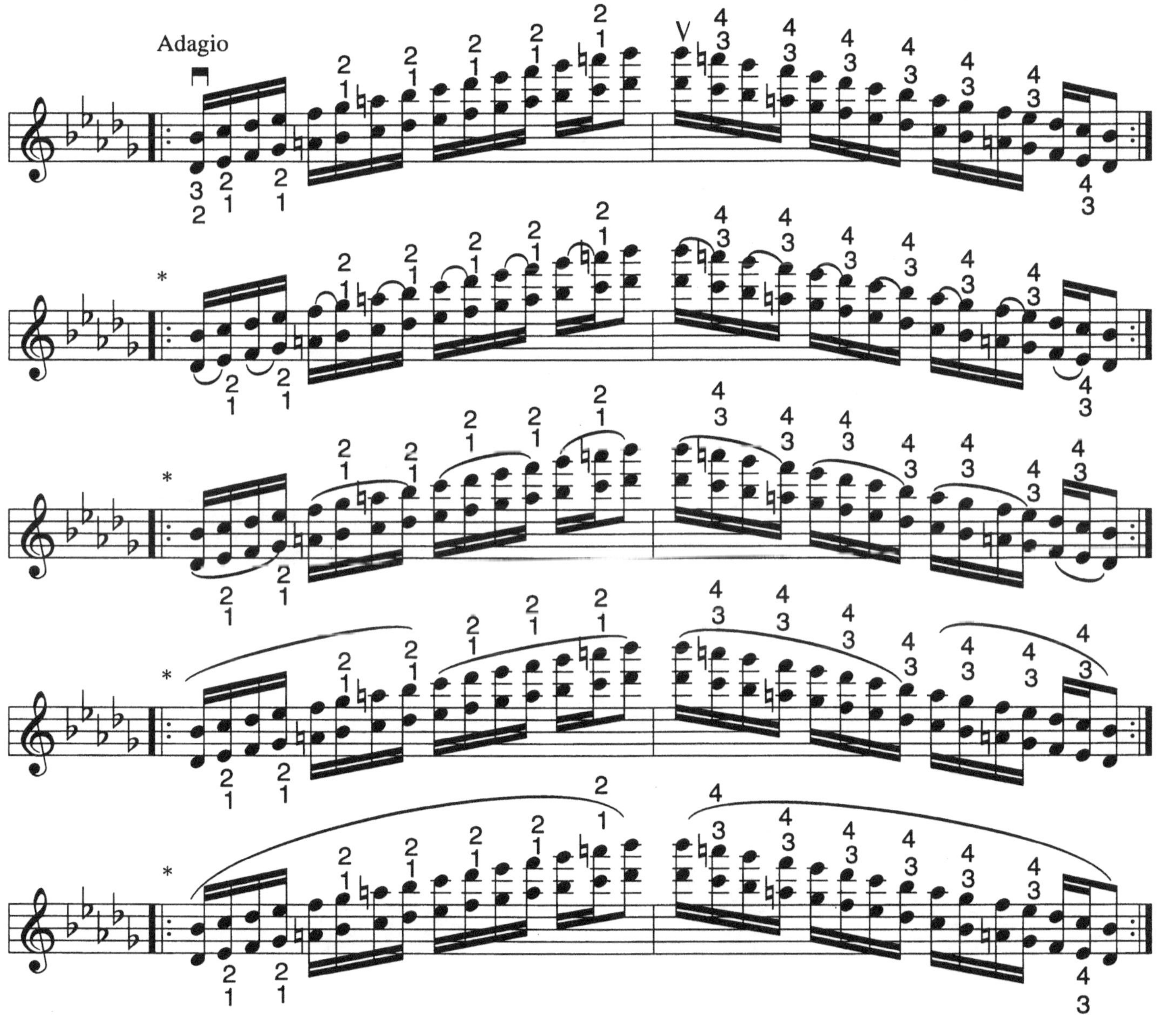

*tempo increases with each successive exercise

*tempo increases with each successive exercise

*tempo increases with each successive exercise

*tempo increases with each successive exercise

d-sharp minor

d-sharp minor

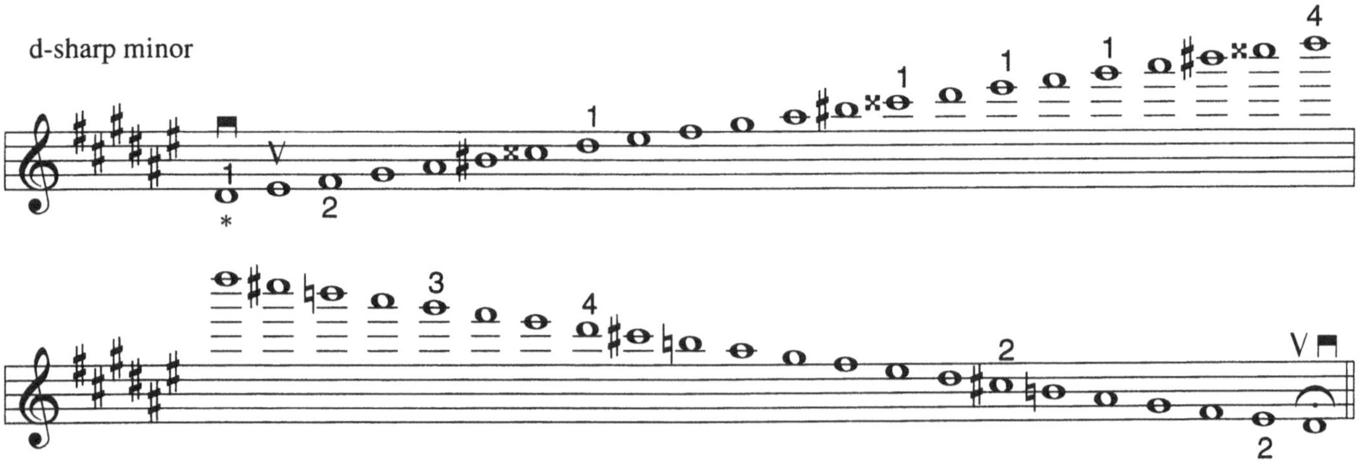

Allegro

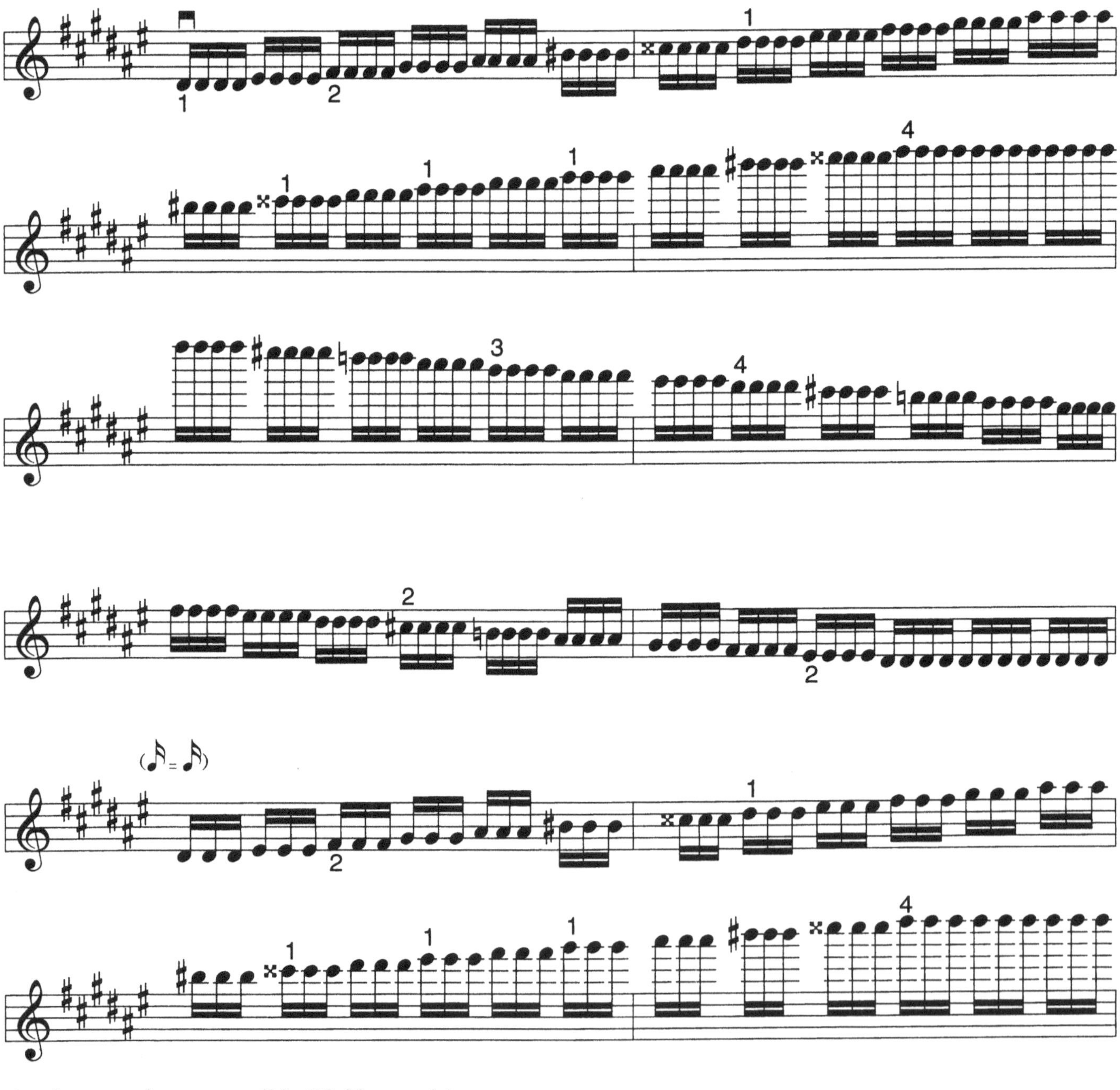

*each note as long as possible (10-20 seconds)

4 times detache/ 4 times spiccato

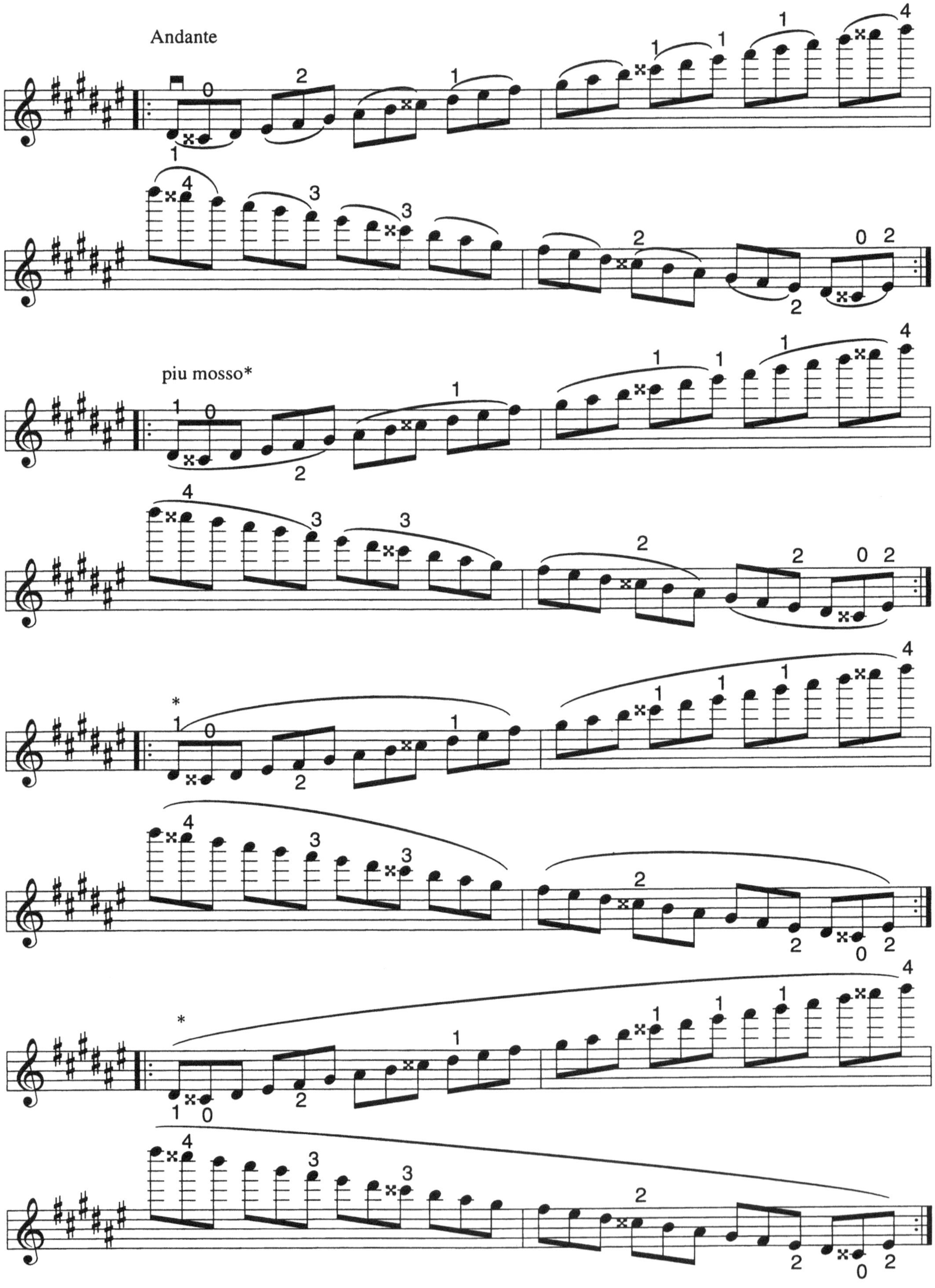

*tempo increases with each successive exercise

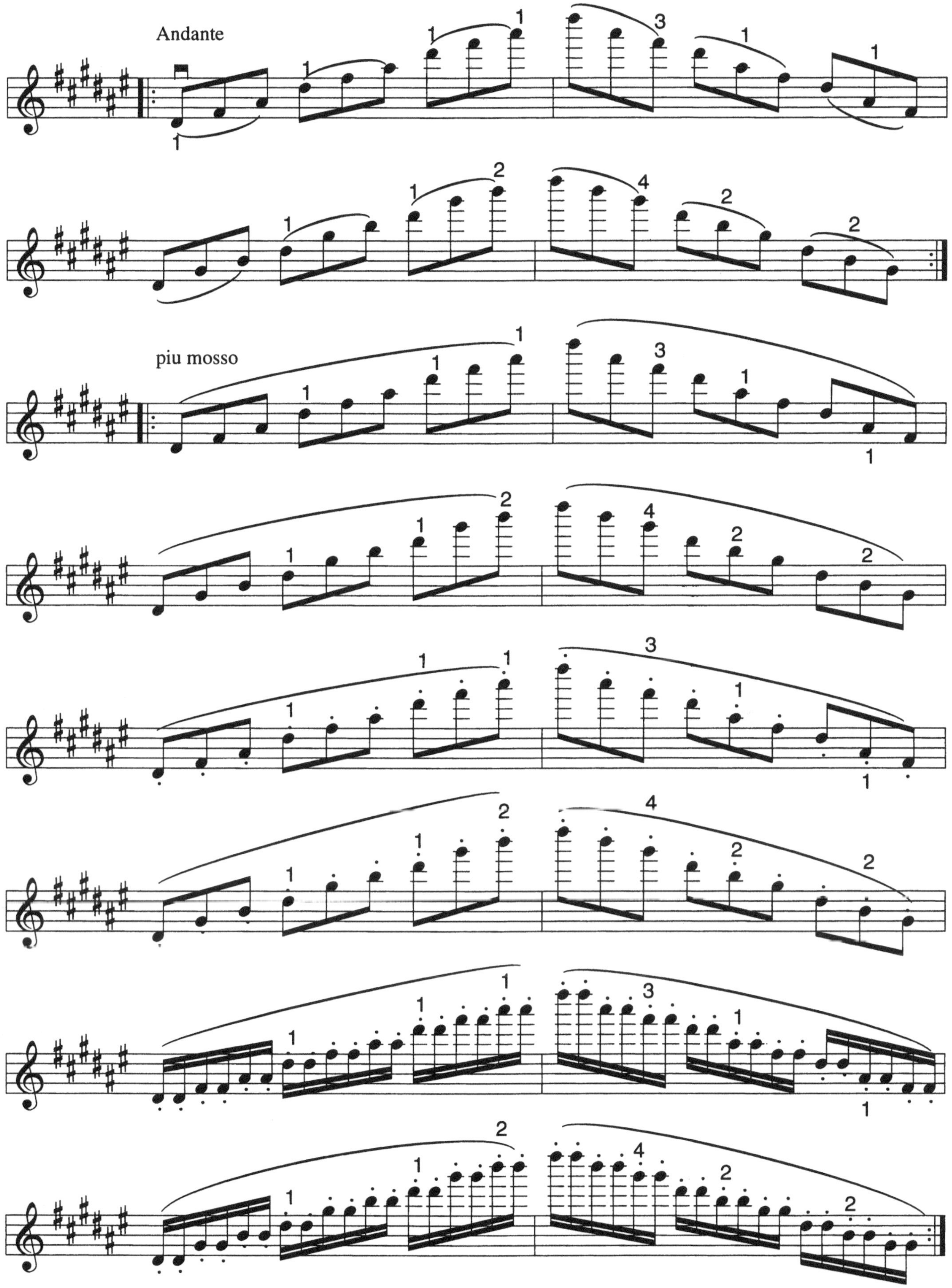
Andante
piu mosso

*tempo increases with each successive exercise

*tempo increases with each successive exercise

*tempo increases with each successive exercise

*tempo increases with each successive exercise

*tempo increases with each successive exercise

e-flat minor

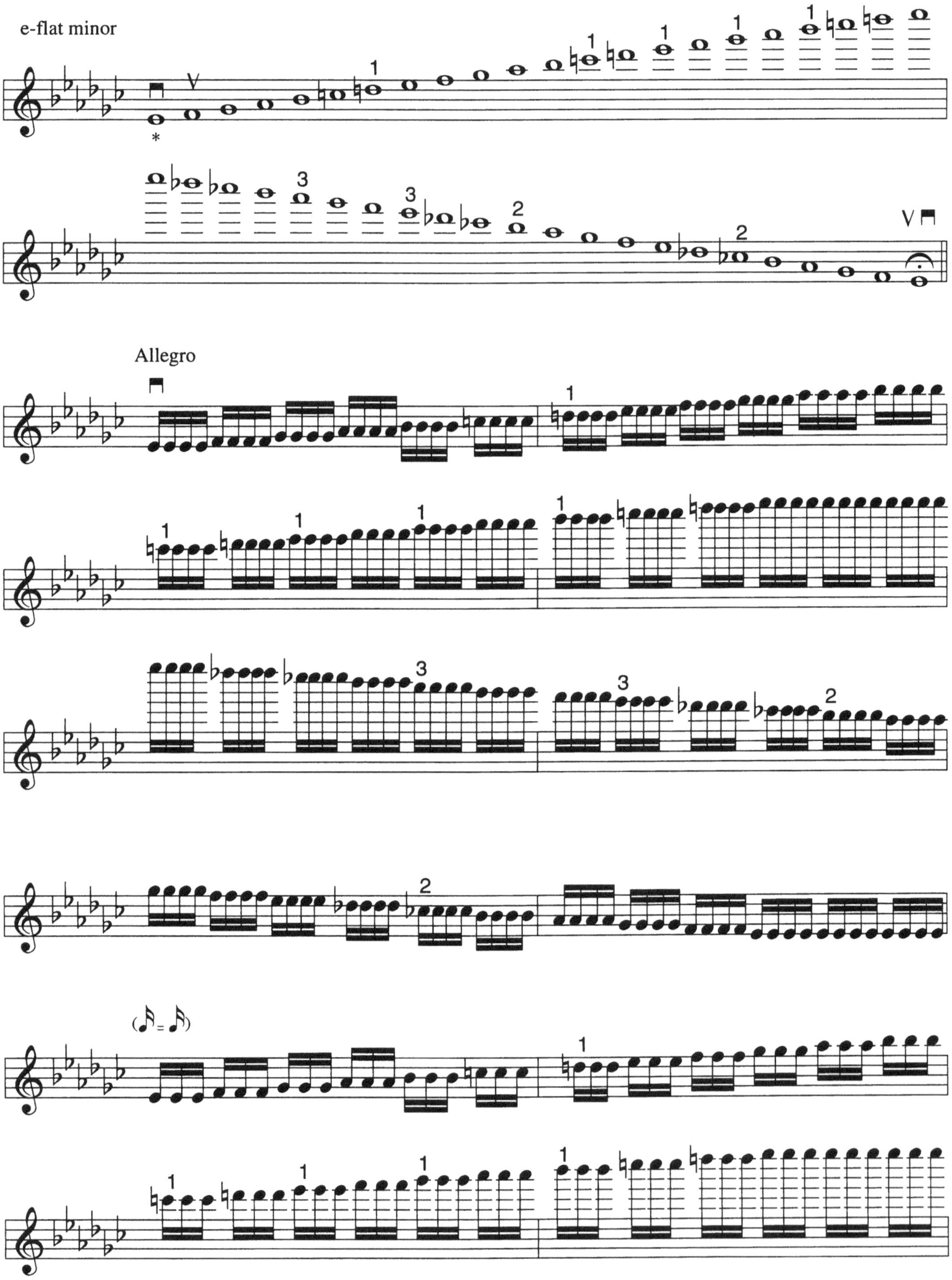

*each note as long as possible (10-20 seconds)

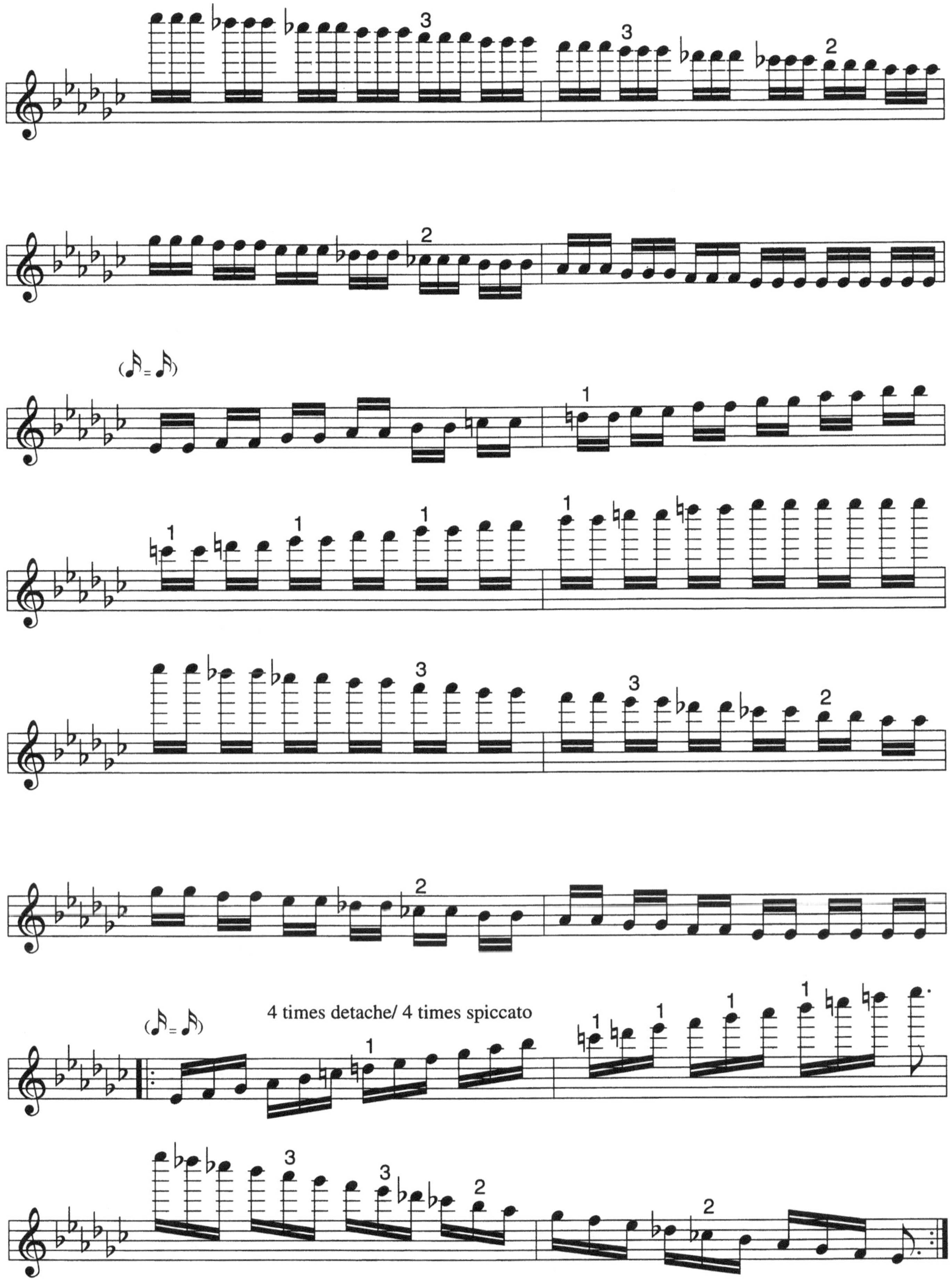
4 times detache/ 4 times spiccato

*tempo increases with each successive exercise

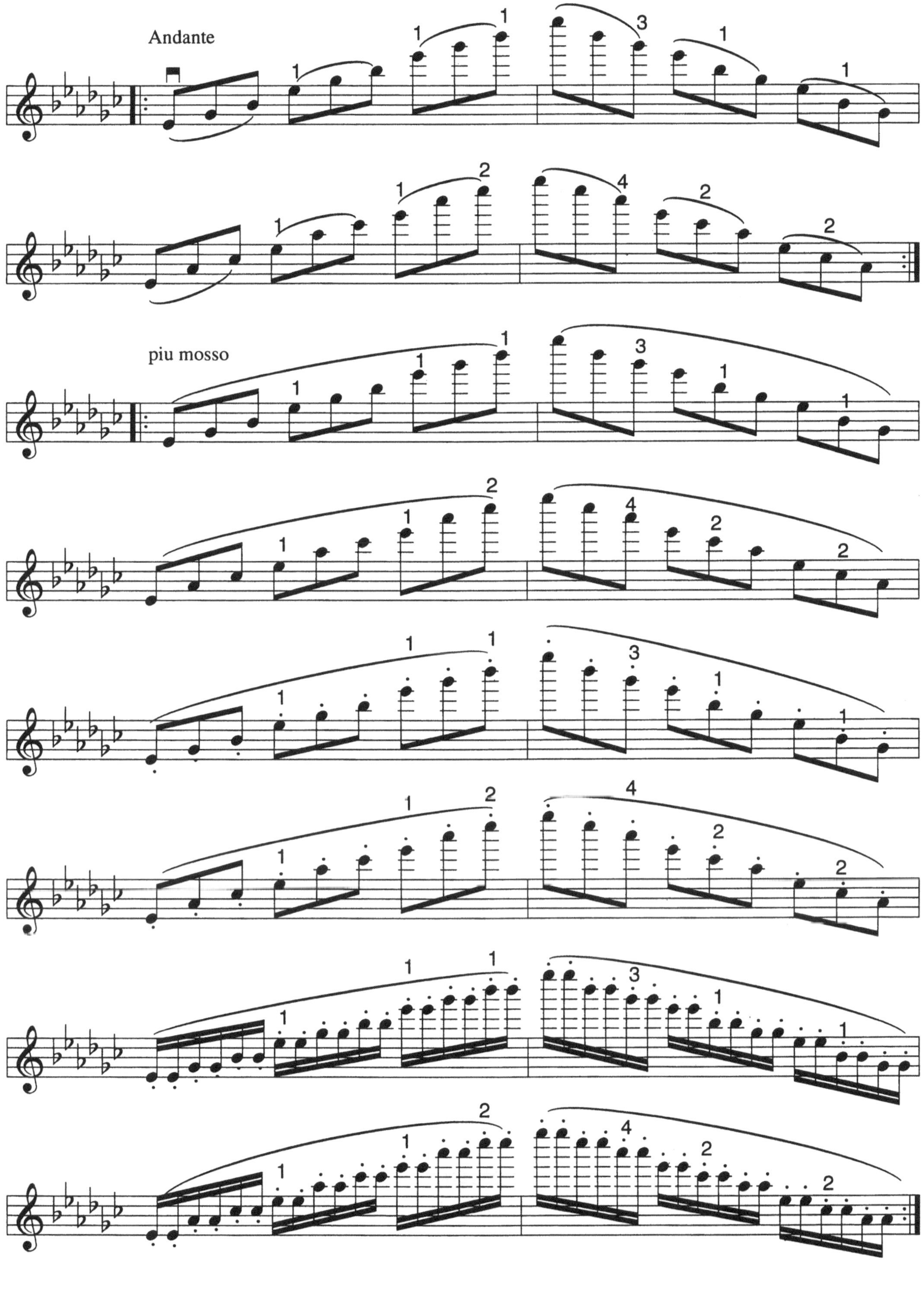
Andante
piu mosso

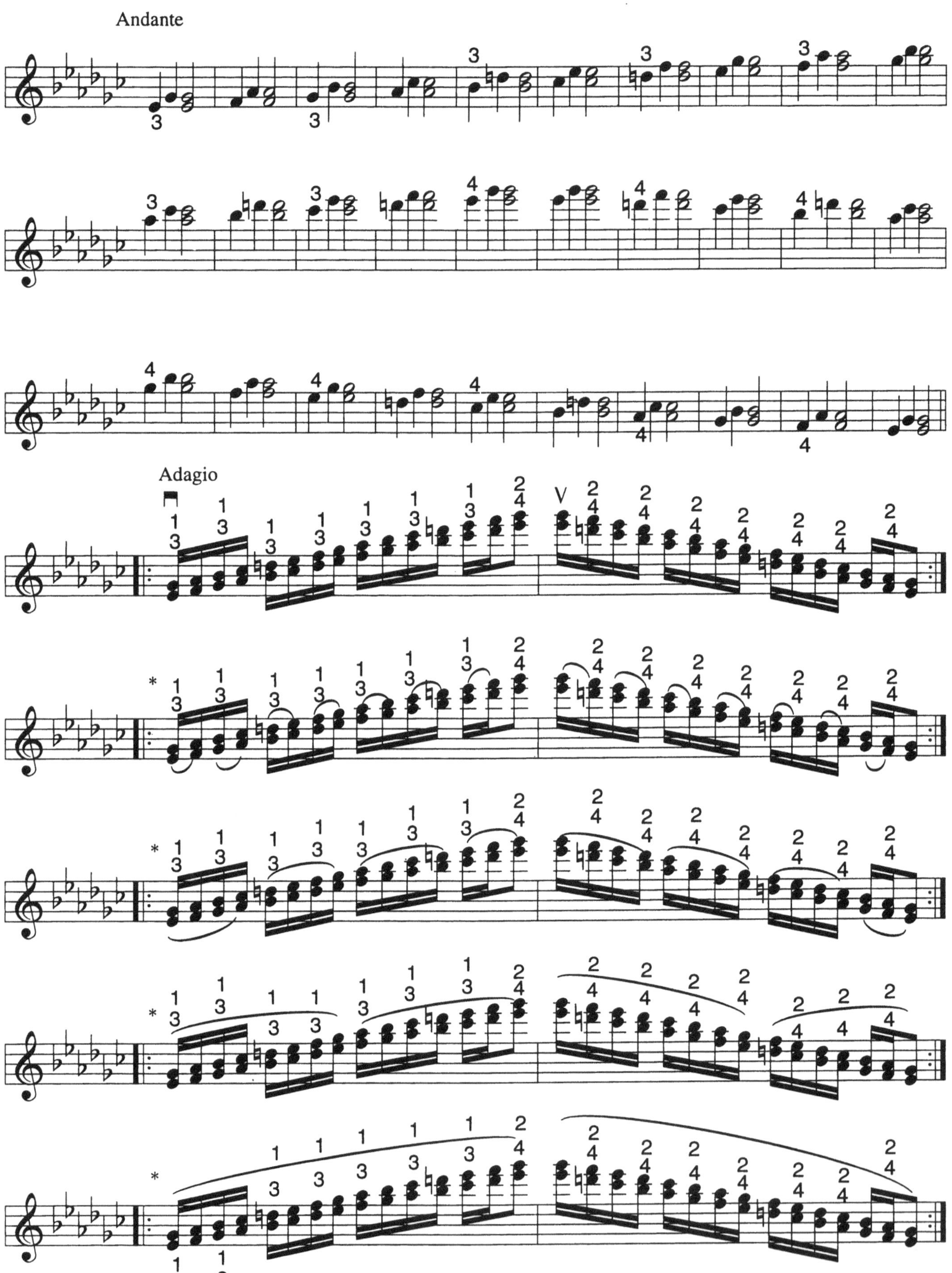

*tempo increases with each successive exercise

*tempo increases with each successive exercise

*tempo increases with each successive exercise

*tempo increases with each successive exercise

*tempo increases with each successive exercise

a-sharp minor

a-sharp minor

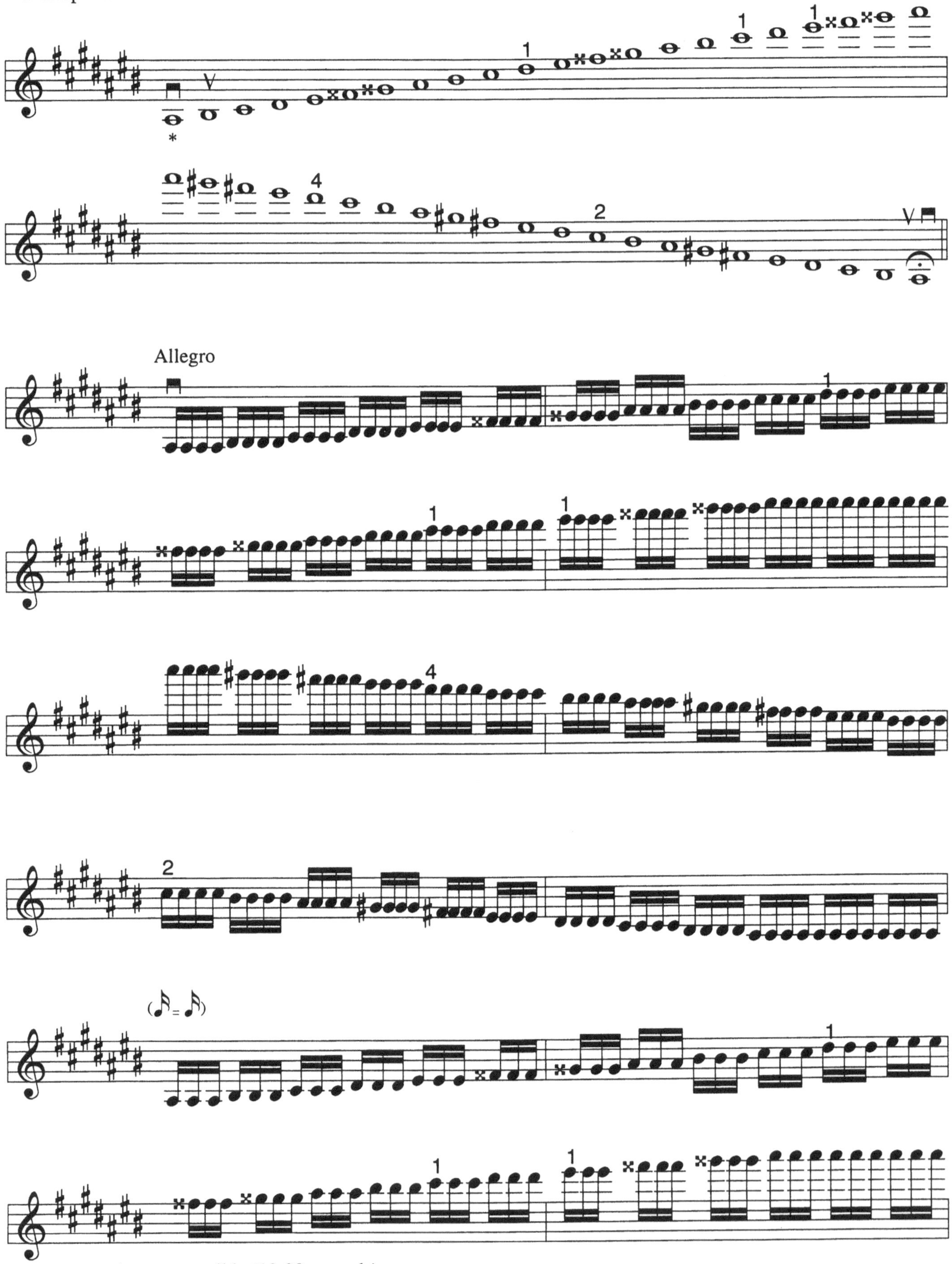

*each note as long as possible (10-20 seconds)

4 times detache/ 4 times spiccato

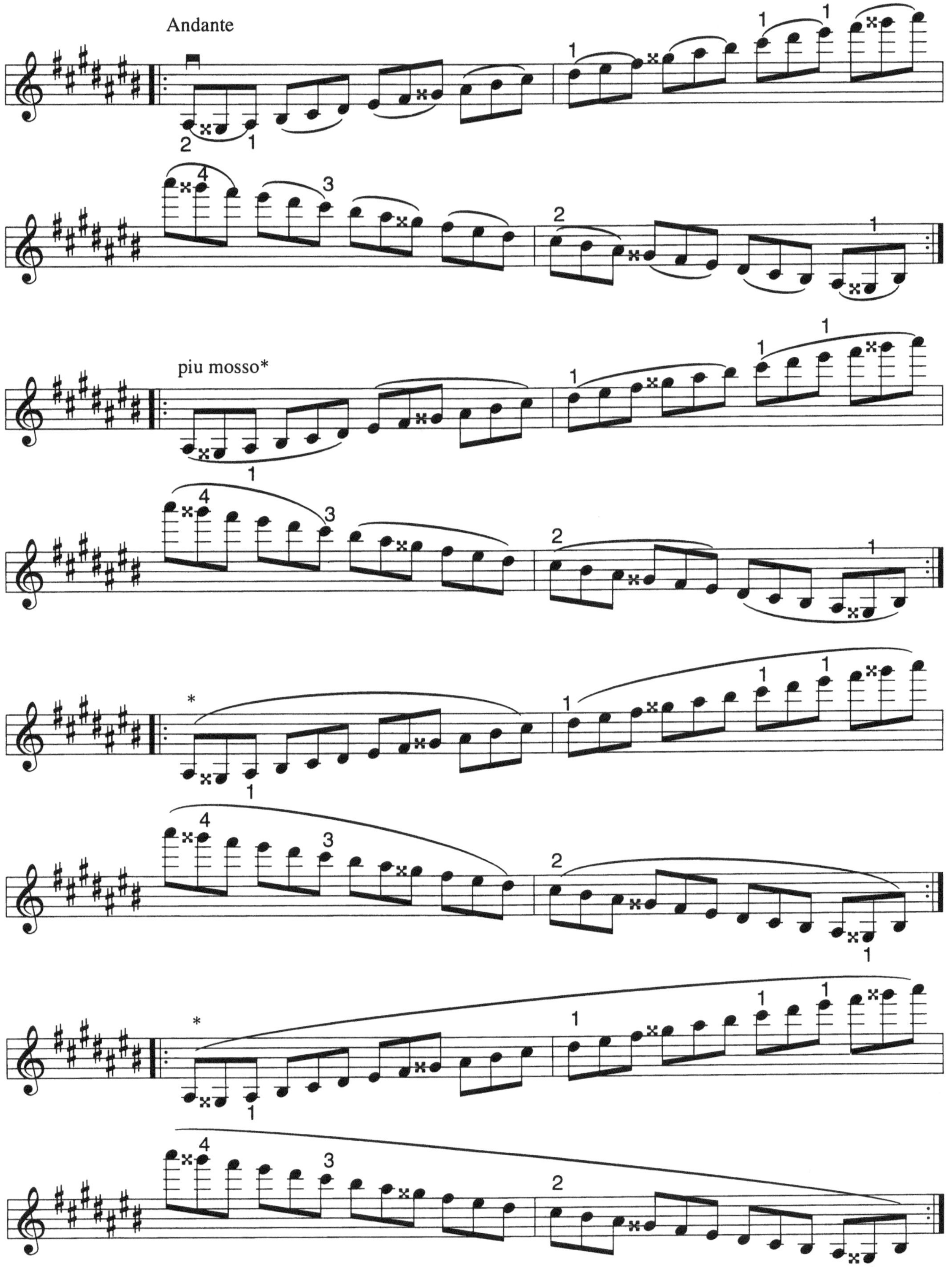

*tempo increases with each successive exercise

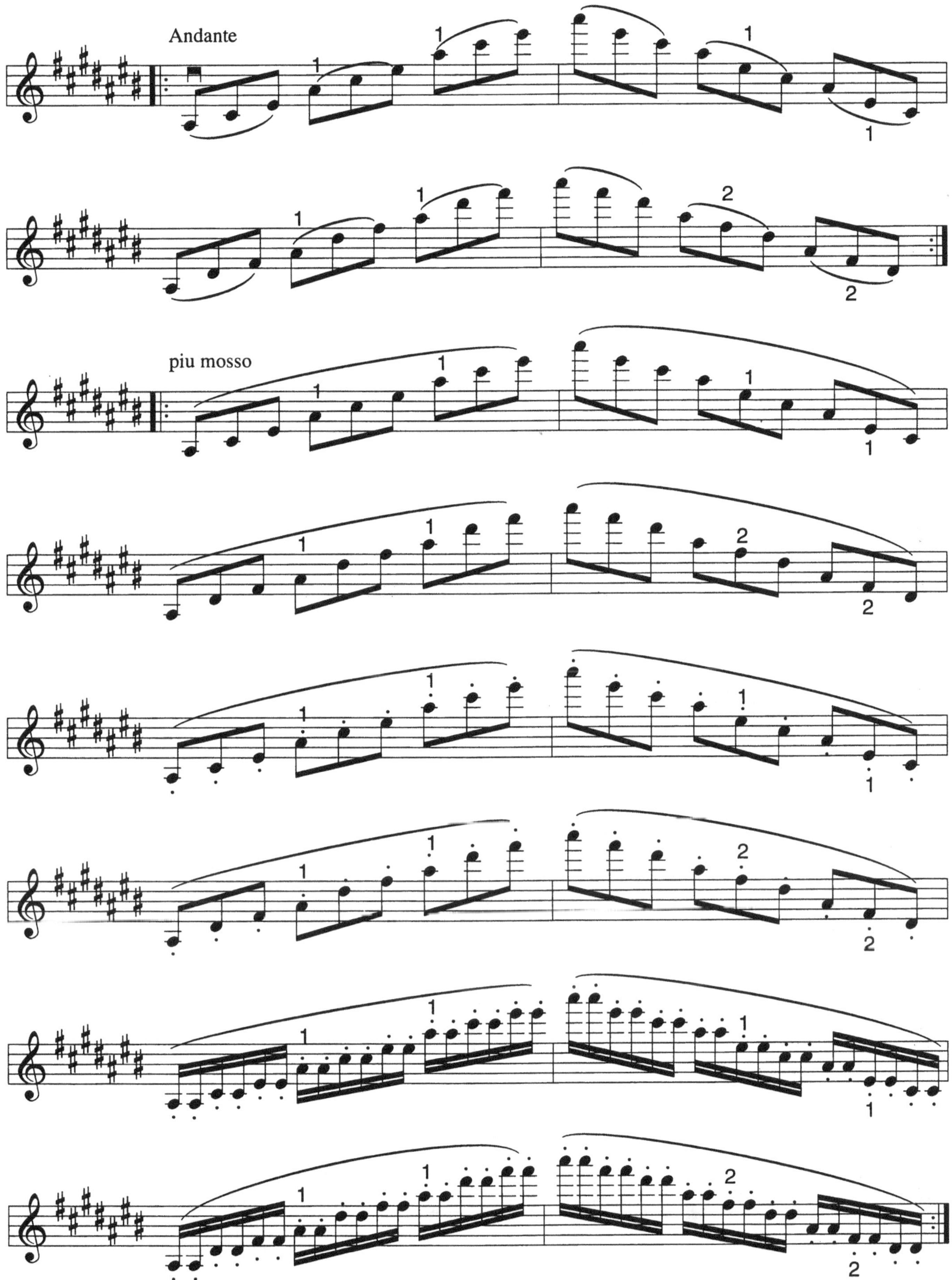
Andante
piu mosso

*tempo increases with each successive exercise

*tempo increases with each successive exercise

*tempo increases with each successive exercise

*tempo increases with each successive exercise

*tempo increases with each successive exercise

a-flat minor

a-flat minor

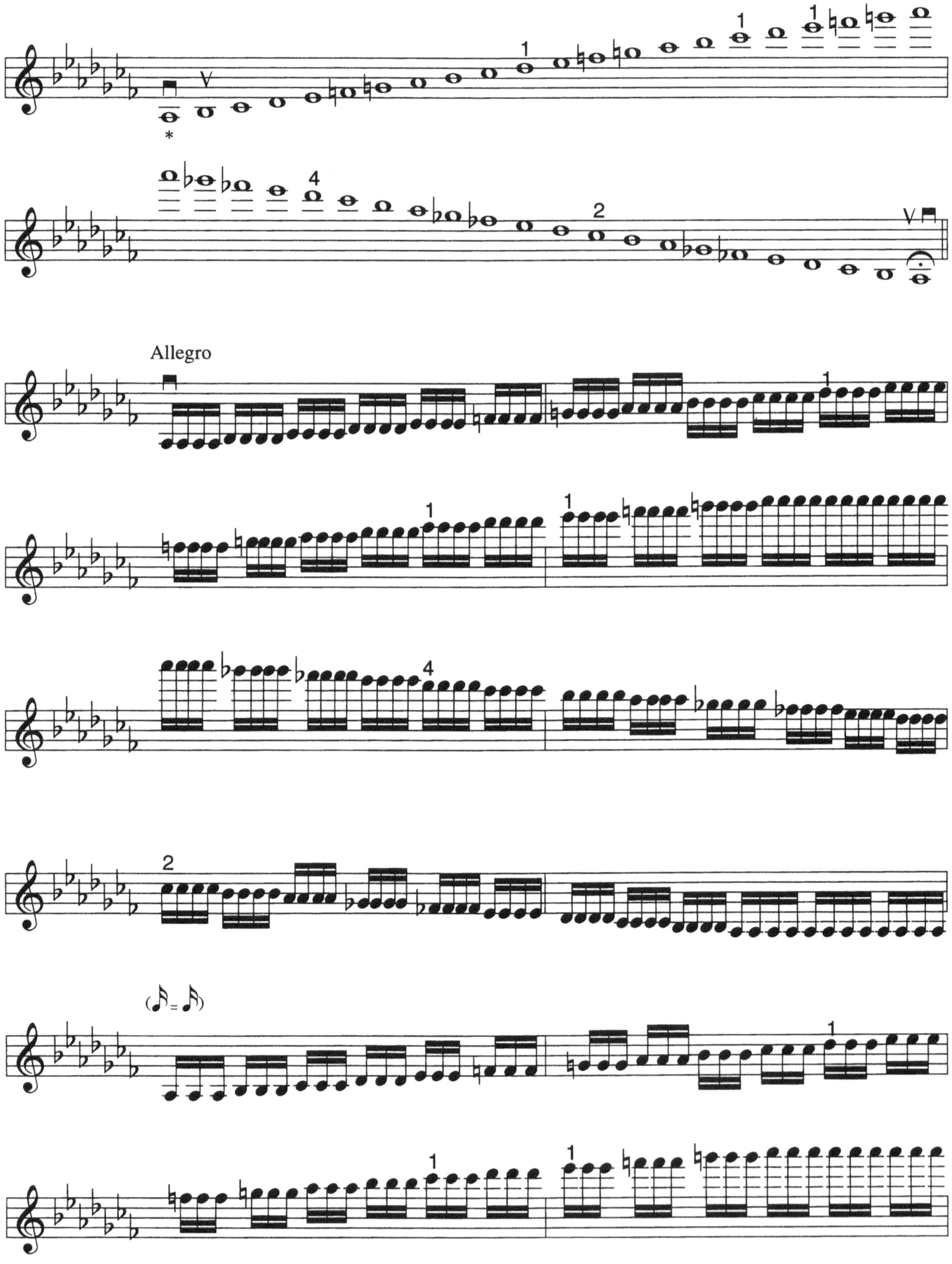

*each note as long as possible (10-20 seconds)

4 times detache/ 4 times spiccato

*tempo increases with each successive exercise

Four-octave scales

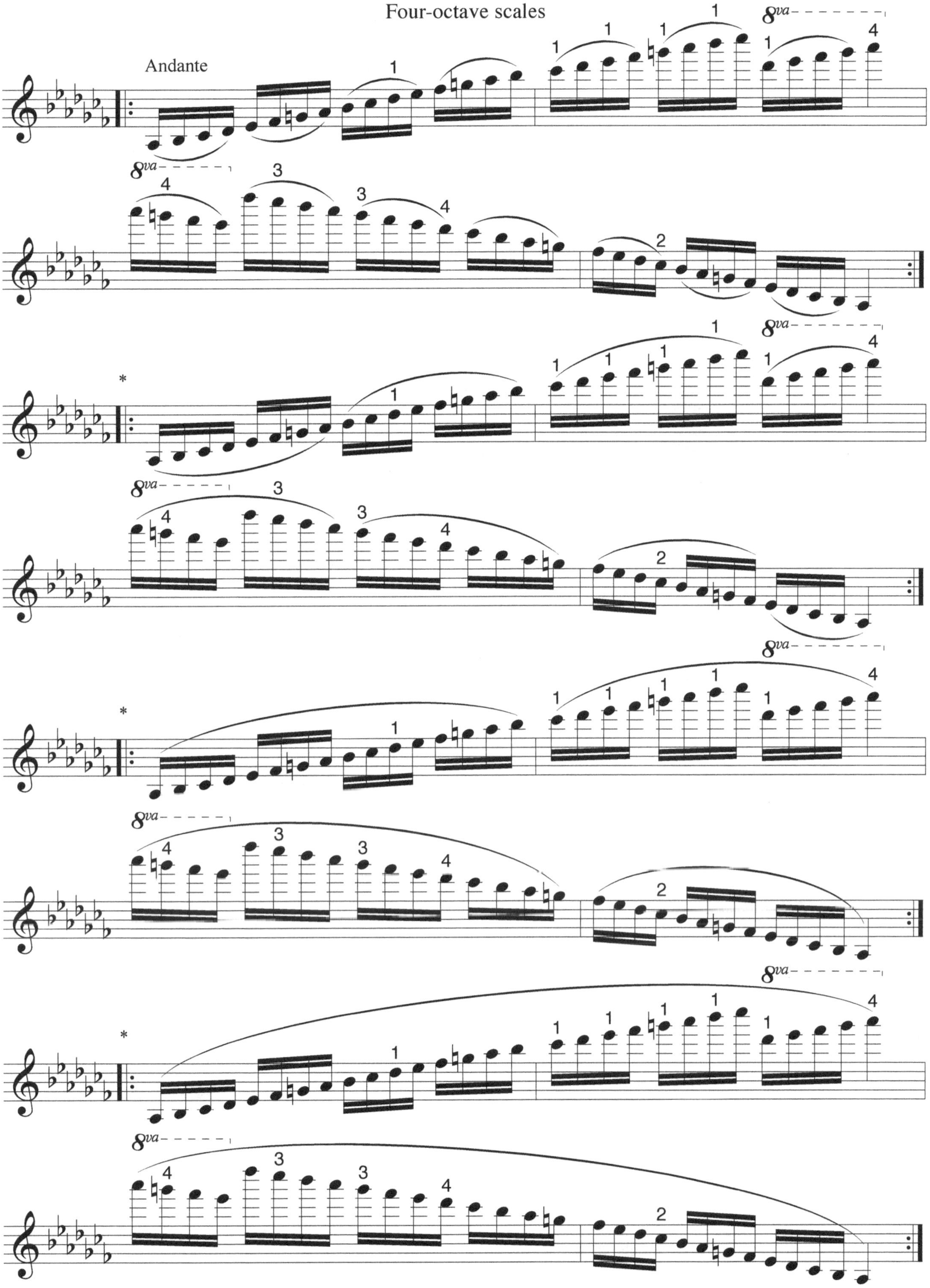

*tempo increases with each successive exercise

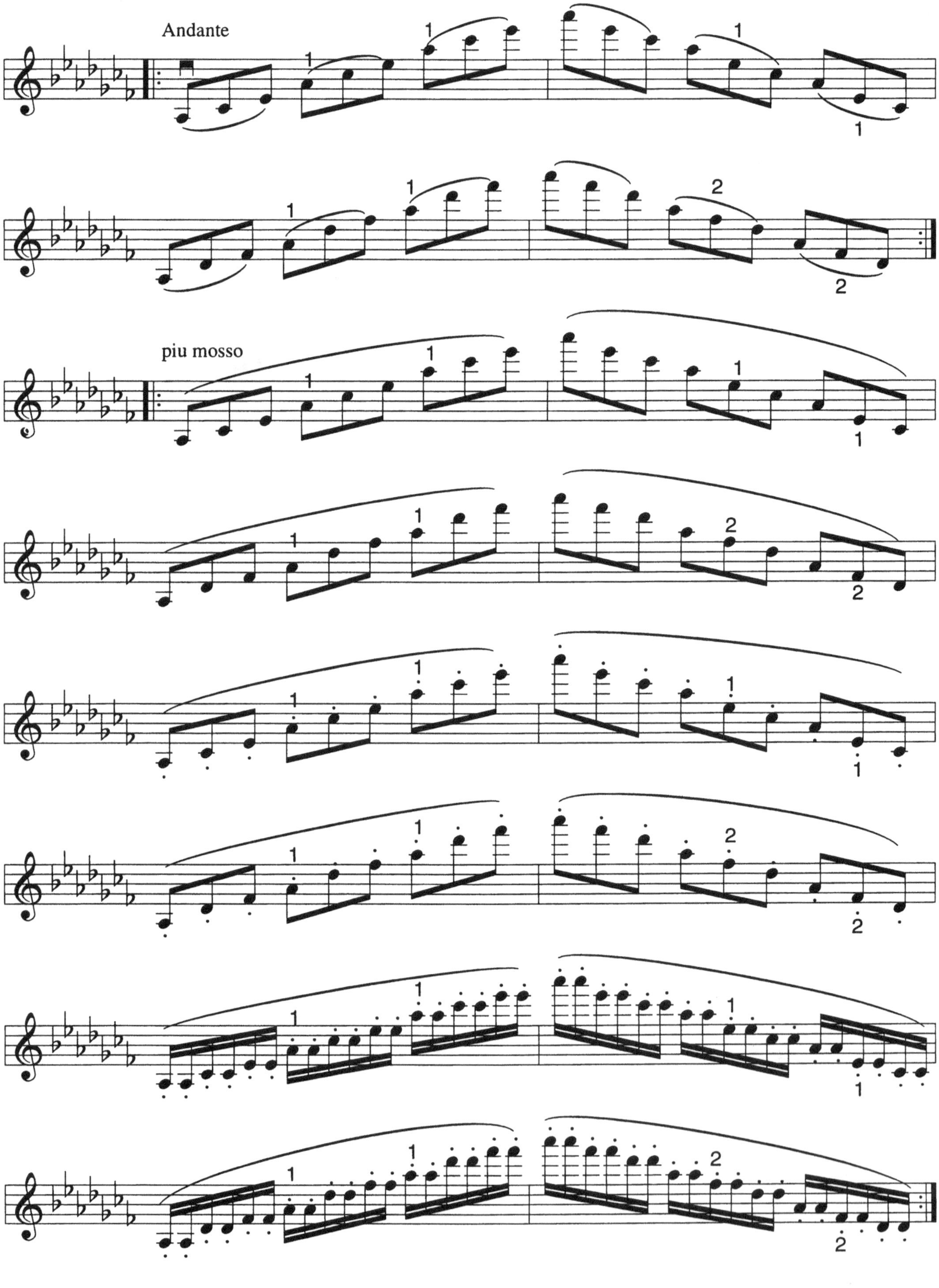
Andante
piu mosso

Four-octave arpeggios

*tempo increases with each successive exercise

*tempo increases with each successive exercise

*tempo increases with each successive exercise

*tempo increases with each successive exercise

*tempo increases with each successive exercise

Chromatic Scales

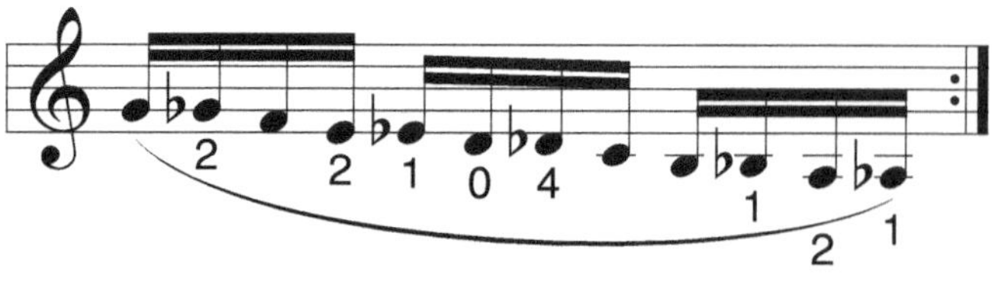

Practice both with and without slurs.

Other Mel Bay Violin Books

Bach: Three Sonatas and Three Partitas for Solo Violin (Golan)
Cabaret Violin Treasures (Harbar)
Complete Book of Violin Concertos (Isaac)
Complete Book of Violin Solos (Isaac)
Great Fiddling Tunes - Early Music Gems (Duncan)
Johann Paul von Westhoff/Six Suites for Solo Violin (ed. by Dr. Sarah Jones-Hayes)
Solo Pieces for the Intermediate Violinist (Duncan)
Solo Pieces for the Advanced Violinist (Duncan)
Advanced Violin Scale Studies (Fine)
Complete Violin Scale Dictionary (Isaac)
Daily Scale Exercises for the Violinist (Chang)
Forty Studies for Violin (Chang)
Past the Print (Waller)
Plugging In: A Guide to Gear and New Techniques for the 21st Century Violinist (Deninzon)
Practice for Performance for Violin (DeForest)
Progressive Scale Studies for Violin (Bauer)
Sensible Scales Plus! (Waller)
Speed-Reading for Violin (Bauer)
The Violin/Fiddle Manual and Encyclopedia of Techniques: How to Do Anything on the Instrument (Willis)
Violin Wall Chart (Norgaard)
Warm-Ups for the Violinist (Wheeler)
American Fiddle Tunes for Solo & Ensemble: Violins 1 & 2 (Duncan)
Beautiful Melodies from Around the World (Cooper)
Celtic Fiddle Tunes for Solo & Ensemble: Violins 1 & 2 (Duncan)
Christmas Music Arranged for Violin Duet (Staidle)
Come Fiddle with Me Volume 1 (Hay)
Come Fiddle with Me Volume 2 (Hay)
Eastern European Music for Violin Duet (Harbar)
Fiddling Classics for Solo & Ensemble: Violins 1 & 2 (Duncan)
J. S. Bach: Duets for Two Violins (Spencer/Engle)
Jazz Duets: Violin Edition (Biondi)
Music from Around the World for Solo & Ensemble: Violins 1 & 2 (Miller)
Ragtimes for Two Violins (Brydern)
Scottish Airs and Dances for Violin Solo or Duet (Witt)
Scottish Melodies for Violin Solo or Duet (Witt)
Violin Duet Classics Made Playable (Harbar)
Wedding Music for String Quartet (Staidle)
Wedding Music for Two Violins (Staidle)
Winter-Violin & Cello (Parks & Groschang)

WWW.MELBAY.COM